Sir William Garrow

His Life, Times and Fight for Justice

John Hostettler

and

Richard Braby

Sir William Garrow
His Life, Times and Fight f[

John Hostettler and Richard Brab

Published 2010 by
Waterside Press Ltd.
Sherfield Gables
Sherfield on Loddon
Hook
Hampshire
United Kingdon RG27 0JG

Telephone +44(0)1256 882250 Low cost UK landline calls 0845 2300 733
E-mail enquiries@watersidepress.co.uk
Online catalogue www.WatersidePress.co.uk

ISBN 9781904380 559 (Hardback)

UK distributor Gardners Books
1 Whittle Drive, Eastbourne, East Sussex, BN23 6QH.
Tel: +44 (0)1323 521777; sales@gardners.com; www.gardners.com

North American distributor International Specialised Book Services (ISBS)
920 NE 58th Ave, Suite 300, Portland, Oregon, 97213-3786, USA
Tel: 1 800 944 6190 Fax 1 503 280 8832; orders@isbs.com; www.isbs.com

Printed by CPI Antony Rowe, Chippenham

e-book *Sir William Garrow* is available as an ebook (e-book ISBN 9781906534820) and also to subscribers of Myilibrary and Dawsonera.

Sir William Garrow

His Life, Times and Fight for Justice

John Hostettler

and

Richard Braby

≋ WATERSIDE PRESS

About the authors

John Hostettler was a practicing solicitor in London for thirty-five years as well as undertaking political and civil liberties cases in Nigeria, Germany and Aden. He sat on the bench as a magistrate for a number of years and has also been a chairman of tribunals. He played a leading role in securing the abolition of flogging in British colonial prisons and served on a Home Office Committee to revise the rules governing electoral law in Britain. He holds several university degrees (BA, LL.B. (Hons) MA, LL.M, PhD (London)) and two doctorates (PhD (Sussex)). His earlier books embrace several biographical and historical works, including about the lives of Thomas Wakley, Sir James Fitzjames Stephen, Thomas Erskine, Sir Edward Carson, Sir Edward Coke, Lord Halsbury and Sir Matthew Hale. His books for Waterside Press include *The Criminal Jury Old and New: Jury Power from Early Times to the Present Day*; *Fighting for Justice: The History and Origins of Adversary Trial*; *Hanging in the Balance: A History of the Abolition of Capital Punishment in Britain* (with Dr Brian P. Block); and, most recently, *A History of Criminal Justice in England and Wales*.

Richard Braby is a direct descendent of Sir William Garrow and as an avocation is a family story teller. He collects and preserves the stories of his family's ancestors. Now retired, his career was conducting educational research during the emergence of the personal computer. His work concerned how to use computer technology and simulation techniques in the design and delivery of adult education focused on learning job skills. Much of this career was with an interdisciplinary study group for the United States Navy's Chief of Naval Education and Training, and centred on applying the results of laboratory research to the critical issues raised by the director of Navy training. Dr. Braby is an author of over 50 technical publications, and was a long time member of the Human Factors Society. He is a graduate of Columbia University, New York City (MA. and Ed.D.) where he specialized in the design of instructional materials.

Geoffrey Robertson QC began his career at the Old Bailey defending in such notable trials as that of *Oz* magazine, Peter Hain, John Stonehouse, the ABC Official Secrets case, *Gay News* blasphemy trial and the Matrix Churchill 'Iraqgate' trial, as well as in IRA and other terrorist cases. He developed a *pro bono* practice defending at the Privy Council men condemned to death in Commonwealth courts. He is founder and head of Doughty Street Chambers, a Recorder, a bencher of the Middle Temple and served as the First President of the UN Special Court for Sierra Leone and is currently a member of the UN Justice Council. His books include *The Justice Game* – a memoir of some of his notable trials – and *The Tyrranicide Brief* – an account of how Cromwell's lawyers brought the King to justice.

Contents

Preface

This first biography of Sir William Garrow has two objectives. One, to introduce the reader to the life of a remarkable man in the context of his time and family. And, secondly, to present him as the criminal lawyer who led the way in altering the whole relationship between the state and the individual by his role in the revolutionary introduction of adversary trial.

This is not the first writing about William Garrow. Recently, scholars of the development of the common law have documented in great detail the changes that were taking place in the 1780s and 1790s and rediscovered the part he played in the Old Bailey with his aggressive defence of clients creating a new phenomenon in the criminal trial. After being essentially forgotten following the 1840s, Garrow's role in the emergence of the adversary criminal trial has recently been documented, debated and analysed by those investigators who continue to push back the frontiers of our understanding of the origins of the present type of criminal trial. But these scholars concentrate their interest on just ten years of Garrow's career, the first ten years. Now that Garrow has become a much discussed figure in the development of the criminal trial, it is time to present more of the life of this extraordinary man, more than the often quoted brief remarks summarizing his life before and after the fateful first ten years of his career at the Old Bailey.

The rediscovery of William Garrow was led by John Beattie who published "Garrow for the Defence" in the February 1991 issue of *History Today*.[1] This article captured the interest of many concerning the part this "brilliant young defence lawyer played in altering the course of justice." This was followed by Beattie's "Scales of Justice: Defence Counsel and the English Criminal Law in the Eighteenth and Nineteenth Centuries" in the October 1991 issue of *Law and History Review*, which documented in great detail the new courtroom style pursued by Garrow.[2] Then, in 2000, David Lemmings published *Professors of the Law, Barristers and English Legal Culture in the Eighteenth Century* which gave a detailed account of Garrow's work.[3] In turn this was followed by Allyson May's *The Bar and the Old Bailey, 1750-1850*.[4] May did her doctoral study under John Beattie and greatly extended the analysis of Garrow's participation in the court scene in the Old Bailey, which she presented first in her dissertation and then in her book. During this same period John H. Langbein published his *The Origins of Adversary Criminal Trial* in which he devoted a good

---

1. J. M. Beattie (1991) "Garrow for the Defence." *History Today*. History Today Ltd.
2. J. M. Beattie (1991) "Scales of Justice: Defence Counsel and the English Criminal Trial in the Eighteenth and Nineteenth Centuries." 9(2) *Law and History Review*. University of Illinois Press.
3. David Lemmings. (2002) *Professors of the Law. Barristers and English Legal Culture in the Eighteenth Century*. Oxford, Oxford University Press.
4. Allyson May. (2003) *The Bar and the Old Bailey, 1750-1850*, Chapel Hill, The University of North Carolina Press.

deal of space to the Old Bailey, including Garrow's participation and impact on the way that criminal trials were being conducted.[5] In 2006 John Hostettler published *Fighting for Justice: The History and Origins of Adversary Trial* in which he documents the role of Garrow in this courtroom drama, and relates it to an evolving culture of human rights.[6]

Today any discussion of the rise of the adversary style of criminal trial must address the issue of Garrow's role in its evolution. However, little outside of his being a barrister for ten years in the Old Bailey has been presented. There are the few observations about his father's Scottish background and his lack of a classical education, but if Garrow is to be celebrated as a significant character in the history of the evolution of the common law, it is time for a more detailed account of his life to be given. This book is such an effort.

Richard Braby is a direct descendant of William Garrow who has spent many years researching the story of Garrow and his family, which he brings to life in what follows. His many contacts with the living members of the extended Garrow family and his access to both published and unpublished family records makes it possible to present Garrow in a family context, that would not be possible without this network of people interested in the family stories of this remarkable man and his extended family.

John Hostettler is a lawyer who has made a special study of the eighteenth century procedural transformation in England that he and a few others are claiming was to produce, "the very first sighting of a recognisable human rights culture in western, if not global, civilization."[7] The origins of adversary trial have only recently been discovered and this exposure has also brought into the light the amazing role played by the hitherto almost unknown Garrow. Hostettler's book, *Fighting for Justice; The History and Origins of Adversary Trial,* gives the legal background to the present book and the world-wide significance of adversary trial but it is Braby's family research that has uncovered so much about the personal and family life of our subject.

Garrow was admitted by Lincoln's Inn on 27 November 1778 and was called to the Bar on the same date five years later. He made his name at the Old Bailey where he raised cross-examination to an art and won numerous trials for which he became justly celebrated. Later, he became in turn a Member of Parliament, Solicitor-General, Attorney-General and finally a judge. He had become a barrister at a time when counsel were beginning to break down the ancient common law rule that men, women and children charged with capital felony could not be represented by counsel. Even as the law was slowly being changed counsel were still not allowed to address the jury on the prisoner's behalf. Bounty hunters were common and

---

5.   J.H.Langbein. (2003) *The Origins of Adversary Criminal Trial* Oxford, Oxford University Press..

6.   John Hostettler. (2006) *Fighting for Justice: The History and Origins of Adversary Trial.* Winchester, Waterside Press.

7.   Richard Vogler. (2005) *A World View of Criminal Justice.* Aldershot, Ashgate Publishing Company. p. 131.

would often accuse innocent people of crimes in order to obtain blood money that, in the absence of an effective police force, was paid by the government for successful prosecutions. Garrow, by means of powerful and aggressive cross-examination of such prosecution witnesses, generally persuaded juries to acquit his clients, and played an historic role in bringing to birth adversary trial whereby the lawyers took over the courtroom.

As part of this process, rules of criminal evidence were established to protect the rights of prisoners based upon the principle that they were innocent until proved guilty. These rules, alongside adversary trial, helped secure the modern doctrine of human rights whereby citizens are able to take a stand against the power of the state and vested interests. Subsequently, along with trial by jury, adversary trial was given constitutional recognition in the United States *Bill of Rights* and spread to all countries influenced by the common law.

This English model of criminal justice was also adopted in the French Revolution until reversed by Napoleon in 1808 when he reintroduced the secret, authoritarian inquisitorial system based upon torture. Today, most of the countries in Europe, Asia and South America that have used the inquisitorial system are now proceeding to embrace adversary trial which was England's gift to the world.

Such was the political and legal significance of Garrow. His personal life and his family are equally fascinating. Indeed it is the purpose of this book to put Garrow into a family context, to put flesh on a man who up to now is viewed almost entirely as a young aggressive barrister in the crude circumstances of the Assize court of London dealing with the typical crimes of the time such as murder, larceny, robbery and other crimes common to the streets of the capital and the highways leading into the city.

Garrow grew up in The Priory in Monken Hadley near the Great North Road leading into London, in the home of a schoolmaster. His father, an ordained minister and headmaster of his own school, lived in a nine acre estate that was thought to have been part of an ancient abbey. His uncle, a wealthy physician in the neighbouring town of Barnet, was an important part of the family. His brothers would become wealthy merchants in India and give the extended family a rich mixing of Indian blood with the English, some remaining in India and others returning to England. His sister married a wealthy landowner. His son would graduate from Charterhouse, and then complete his studies at Christ Church College, Oxford University, for the degree of Doctor of Divinity, and serve as Chaplain-in-Ordinary to the Prince of Wales and Rector of the parish in East Barnet. His published writings add to the family story. William Garrow's daughter married the son of John Coakley Lettsom, a famous Quaker physician, and the two fathers became good friends. The turbulent business dealings of the younger Lettsom is the basis of an interesting family story. The next generation of Garrow's, all known and cared for in their childhood by William Garrow, include authors from the Trollope family, diplomats, ministers, and military leaders well positioned in English history. At the end, Garrow died in his Pegwell Villa on the cliffs at the coast near Ramsgate in Kent on 24 September 1840 aged 80. His significance and influence are profound and are long overdue for wider recognition than they have received hitherto. It is to be hoped that this book will assist in that process.

Oil painting of William Garrow by Harlow, 1815.
**Reproduced by kind permssion of
the Treasurer and Benchers of Lincoln's Inn.**

Foreword

Geoffrey Robertson QC

It is a pleasure to welcome this study of the life of William Garrow, the first great cross-examiner at the English Bar. He can truly be said to have revolutionised the practice of criminal law, not by any seminal writing or legislation, but through the extraordinary force of his character and conduct in the first ten years of his practice, during which he defended over 1,000 clients (trials were very short in those days). In 1783, when he burst upon the Old Bailey stage, defendants had no rights other than to a counsel who could merely ask polite questions of prosecution witnesses. No speeches were allowed, there were few rules of evidence and absolutely no prosecution disclosure even of the depositions taken in the magistrates' court. It was Garrow's genius to change all that and to inject for the first time an element of "equality of arms" into what eventually became a true adversary process. That he appeared at a time when the English Penal Code was at its most barbaric, with several hundred minor felonies carrying the death penalty, made his achievement all the more necessary and all the more dramatic – as the BBC has recently discovered with its re-enactments of some of his cases.

But talk to criminal counsel of my generation and it is Darrow, not Garrow, to whom they have turned for inspiration. Why has this great advocate been ignored for so long? Partly because of the lamentable bias of legal history education, which has disdained State trials and trialists in favour of teaching the tedious history of contract and land law, partly because of the inability of historians to comprehend the dynamics of forensic practice and how this impacts on the rules of the trial process. There has also been the prejudice exemplified by the sniffy comment of one celebrated Law Lord: "The Old Bailey is hardly the SW3 of the profession". (This prejudice is still evident in the reluctance to appoint criminal lawyers to the higher courts.)

There is also, importantly I think, the fact that Garrow, after his incandescent first decade at the defence Bar, "went over to the dark side", became a reactionary Tory and conducted some of Pitt's paranoid prosecutions against radicals. They were defended by his friend and rival Lord Erskine, who became in consequence the man more celebrated. But our recent conversion to human rights brings Garrow – who did so much to kindle them at the coal face of legal history – back into focus.

Garrow's early career needs to be set in the context of a late eighteenth century society where, as Oliver Goldsmith reminds us,

> *Each wanton judge new penal statutes draw,*
> *Laws grind the poor and rich men rule the law.*

It was a London that comes down to us now in the painting of Hogarth, and in the poetry of William Blake who had the moral vision to see the tears of the chimney sweeps and to hear the curses of the city harlots, and to feel the cruelty done to children in the Poor House. Electorates were all gerrymandered, power was in the hand of corrupt politicians and court favourites, and there were 50,000 prostitutes living among the million people in London, not to mention such colourful characters as mudlarks, scuffle hunters, bludgeon men, Morocco men, flash coachmen, grubbers, bear baiters and strolling minstrels. Wealth, of course, was all inherited: you were born into a certain rank and station in life and you were expected to stay in it. Hence the old nursery rhyme "Tinker, tailor, soldier, sailor, rich man, poor man, beggar man, thief". Their lives were costume dramas in which the costumes were handed out at birth. So when born in poverty you stayed in poverty, making ends meet by snapping up the gentry's unconsidered trifles.

Why was Garrow such a different class of counsel? Unlike his better connected rivals, this young barrister of humble birth was prepared to mix with and to understand the *demi-monde* of coiners and counterfeiters, thieves and thief-takers. He was prepared to take the unheard-of step of meeting his clients in plague-infested prisons to take their instructions. Criminal trials still resembled the ill-conducted public meeting from which they had originally developed and he immediately saw the potential of humour, even robust humour - to get the jury on side and to laugh a case (or at least a witness) out of court. He became renowned for his sarcasm during cross examination, but the transcripts reveal that this "lowest form of wit" could readily turn into deadly irony at the expense of the prosecuting societies and the well-rewarded thief-takers, whose zeal and greed produced many miscarriages of justice. Denied a peroration, he turned his questions into mini-speeches, to the enlightenment of the jury and the enragement of prosecutors. He was certainly no "trickster", as Langbein mistakenly labelled him, but rather an advocate who came into court equipped with savage wit, a fearless capacity to object to unfair evidence, and clever tactics. He crashed through the barriers of class, overcame judicial hostility and popular jury prejudice, and his courage soon inspired other barristers to adopt similar strategies. In due course, it was this pressure from the Bar that won increased latitude for the defence and made trials more fair, as counsel insisted upon evidential rules (such as the rule against hearsay), equal rights for defence barristers and the transformation of the role of the judge from that of active inquisitor and jury-director to that of a more neutral umpire.

Not that all or even most of his cases ended with acquittals. He was not defending honest radicals but dishonest rascals, whose necks were at stake. He played for sympathy verdicts in cases where the law required that all who stole more than 40 shillings worth of goods must go to the gallows. It was the jury, however, which valued the stolen property, and Garrow's skill was to deflate the estimates of indignant owners and to engage the jury's sense of mercy. Success meant trans-portation instead of hanging, and slowly the prisons filled with the human debris of Georgian England whose sentences had been commuted by the mercy of their juries. Transportation to Botany Bay began in 1787 and it is remarkable how many of these convicts were recorded as having stolen goods that were worth precisely 39 shillings. The founders of Australia were the beneficiaries of the jury's bargain with the barbarity of the law, negotiated by Garrow and his barrister contemporaries.

Garrow's other notable achievement was to end bounty hunting as a means of law enforcement: his savage cross examination of men who had a financial incentive to send innocent accused to the gallows hastened the decline of "thief-taking" for substantial reward. Although no intellectual, his innate sense of fairness combined with his querulous nature to produce impromptu objections to evidence that, once upheld, became precedents for developing rules - about how to treat the testimony of accomplices, for example, and for the exclusion of hearsay. For all the reac-tionary views that Garrow espoused in later life, he never waivered in his hatred of slave owners or of torture. The former he refused to defend, no matter how much they offered him and the latter he memorably condemned when prosecuting the Governor of Trinidad who had resorted to Spanish practices.

He ought to have remembered that in England torture is unknown, not because the subject has never been discussed but because it is so abhorrent to all our feelings, to our regard for personal liberty and the fair administration of justice, that it never has been and never can be tolerated here. (See *Chapter 7, The Picton trials*).

Why, at age 33, did this shooting star of the Bar decide to set himself in the Tory firmament? He accepted a silk gown and briefs in Pitt's sedition prosecutions of members of the London Corresponding Society and other early democrats accused of being Jaccobin revolutionaries. Perhaps his own humble birth led him to crave a respectability that could not come from saving the necks of lowlife at the Old Bailey, or perhaps his bravado in the commoners' cause was a means to get himself noticed and started, and disguised his true conservative instincts. At any event, he threw over his Whig friends (he had become a favourite of Charles James Fox) and ascended the greased pole of right-wing politics. Soon he had a knighthood and became an MP for a rotten borough, and pursued an undistinguished Parliamentary career during which he opposed all of Romilly's necessary legal reforms, including the abolition of hanging, drawing and quartering. As a law officer he conducted oppressive prosecutions for treason and sedition and blasphemous libel and ended his legal life with some years of run-of-the-mill service on the Bench. It can be said that he prosecuted with a modicum of fairness, but it was a Faustian bargain: Pitt offered him status and elevation for no better reason than to remove his talents from the defence of reformers, republicans, and the courageous booksellers who dared to stock Tom Paine's *The Rights of Man*. Instead, it was Erskine who was carried in triumphant from the Old Bailey after his speeches had secured their acquittals. Henceforth, Garrow was on the wrong side of history.

But that does not make his early achievements any less relevant for the development of the key role of the advocate in the adversary process. It will sometimes be necessary for modern barristers to emulate his bravado and ingenuity. I took up practice in the Old Bailey in the 1970s at just such a time when the "Vaudeville routine" of police verbals was in its hey-day, and Scotland Yard's thief taking would invariably begin with a confession (e.g. "It's a fair cop, guv") allegedly recorded in police notebooks. Ferocious judges would intimidate counsel who defended aggressively by describing them as "loud speakers for a maladjusted set", whilst those barristers who accepted briefs for bomb trials had their career cards marked by the Lord Chancellor and were described as "members of the alternative Bar". Miscarriages of justice were rife and Lord Denning, refused to contemplate "the appalling vista" if *The Birmingham Six* had been wrongly convicted. It took another generation of barristers to use Garrow's tactics by exposing police malpractice and hastening reforms such as the recording of all police interviews and the establishment of the Criminal Cases Review Commission.

So it is because we may need Garrow's youthful steel again that this account of his life, his times and his fight for justice, by John Hostettler and Richard Braby, is particularly welcome. It deserves to be read alongside John's important account of *Thomas Erskine and Trial by Jury* as a tribute to the men who made defence advocacy what it is today: a vital tool for the exposure of dishonesty, arrogance and injustice. Hiliare Belloc famously defined a jury as "twelve persons summoned at random to decide which party has the better lawyer", but cynicism about the advocate's role overlooks the reason why the right to cross-examine witnesses is central to the fair trial guarantee in the European Convention On Human Rights. Against the Goliath of State power, the voice of the advocate serves as David's slingshot, because the law of forensic battle now allows it to present the possibility of innocence. That great safeguard for all in peril in the courts we owe not only to Thomas Erskine and Henry Brougham who appeared for those politically persecuted, but to the youthful William Garrow who, in a thousand cases, raised his voice with wit and ingenuity on behalf of poor criminals.

Geoffrey Robertson – Doughty Street Chambers 2009

CHAPTER 1

Family Background

SCOTTISH ORIGINS

According to the genealogist E. C. Pilkington, the Garrow family is thought to have originally lived on a farm on the Aberdeenshire coast, called Kirkton of Slainson, and to be descended from the Garriochs of Kinstari, an ancient Scottish royal line.[1] In that area, from 1695 to 1699 there was a famine and in 1700 a cattle disease. People deserted their farms and died of hunger in the streets. This period was known as "King William III's Years" and the hunger was initiated by a mini ice-age when the snow never melted in the Grampians, the region around Aberdeen, and the crops never ripened. The Grant Clan on Speyside (where our Garrow story starts) must have lost most of their farming population, and so they advertised improved farms and buildings for experienced families. Possibly a small circle of Garrow families accepted tenancies and guarantees from the Grant estates. The Garrows of our Sir William Garrow story became the Garrows of Allachy on the hills above Aberlour.

The grandparents of Sir William Garrow were William Garrow and his wife Jean Moir. According to published historical notes on the family, they lived on a farm called the Mains of Allachy.[2] And according to family tradition, and records of the time, they lived for a number of years at a farm called Knockside. While the exact location of the Mains of Allachy remains unknown, it is apparent that these farms would have been next to each other on the hillside just south of the river Spey at Aberlour in Banffshire, Scotland. The farms were located in that part of Scotland, about fifty miles northwest of the city of Aberdeen, where the River Spey runs east before turning north to empty into the North Sea.

We do not know the birth dates of William and Jean, but we do know they were married on 8 November 1713, and were buried at Aberlour beneath a stone with an inscription bearing the date 4 May 1742. During their married lives (1713-1742), they raised a large family. Five daughters were born, Elizabeth (Elspet) (bapt. 1717), Isobel (bapt. 1719), Jean (bapt. 1725), Janet (bapt. 1728) and Margaret (bapt. 1734), their baptisms and marriages recorded in the parish records. There were four sons, David (bapt. 1715), William (bapt. 1722), Robert (bapt. 1730) and Joseph (bapt. 1735), whose baptisms are also in the parish records. These records indicate

---

1. E.C. Pilkington. (about 1995) *A History of the Elwin Family in Australia.* p. 76.
2. F. C. Cass. (1880) *The Parish of Monken Hadley.* Westminster. Nichols & Sons, p. 182. Frederick Charles Cass was Rector of Monken Hadley.

that most of the children were baptized at Allachie or Aberlour, while the last two births (Margaret and Joseph) were listed for Knockside.

The remains of a cottage at Knockside.

It must have been clear to William, the father, that his sons had no chance of cadetships in the East India Company, as these were reserved for Grant relatives. So with the assistance of the local schoolmaster and the Grants of Aberdeen, David and William became graduates of Aberdeen University, which would have given them a start in a number of professions, and his youngest son, Joseph, would make his own way with a career in the British Navy.

David, the father of Sir William Garrow, graduated with a Master of Arts from Aberdeen University on 1 April 1736. He was ordained in the Church of England and shortly thereafter created a school for young gentlemen in Monken Hadley, Middlesex, just north of London. His lifelong career as a school master will be described in the next chapter.

David's younger brother, William, graduated with a Master of Arts from Aberdeen University on 1 April 1741, and studied medicine at Elgin, not far from his home. The record shows that he "walked the wards at Dr. Gray's hospital in Elgin." He called himself "Doctor of Physick" and his career was that of a prosperous apothecary, surgeon and physician in Barnet, Hertfordshire, near Monken Hadley. One observer of the day noted that he would prescribe and then mix his own medicines, which gave him "a general monopoly about Barnet." He remained unmarried. Pilkington noted that in his will he left much of his fortune (£30,000) to his nephew Sir William Garrow. And in Sir William Garrow's own will, he asked to be buried "as near the remains of my late Uncle Doctor William Garrow as conveniently without parade or unnecessary expense" - a request that was ignored by Sir William's survivors.

Joseph joined the Royal Navy as a Volunteer, was commissioned a Lieutenant on 19 June 1761 and rose to command the "Garland", a twenty-eight gun man-of-war built in 1779. He died in 1796, and presumably remained unmarried.

HISTORICAL PERSPECTIVE

Some observations about Scotland during the early 1700s may help put the life of these generations of Garrows in perspective. They may also explain why the two Garrow sons left there for England. We know that about the year 1747, David and William settled respectively in Monken Hadley and Barnet, north of London.

Two years before this date, Bonnie Prince Charles (the Young Pretender) landed in Scotland (3 August 1745) to lead a Jacobite uprising in his attempt to return the throne of Scotland and England to the House of Stuart. He led an army of Scottish clansmen as far south into England as Manchester and Derby. Historians speculate that perhaps they could have gone all the way to London and accomplished their goal, but the expected uprising of people with Jacobite sympathies was not taking place. Few were joining their cause and Bonnie Prince Charlie's army commanders chose to retreat to Scotland where the clansmen were massacred at Culloden by the Government troops.[3]

The clans that had taken part in the rebellion were dispossessed, and their land sold cheaply to rival neighbours. The clan system was smashed and the clan way of life was systematically destroyed by King George's troops who swarmed over the countryside throughout the summer of 1746, being given a free hand to destroy the "savages" they came across. The Clan Gordon fighters from Aberdeen and Banff were strongly represented in the Jacobite ranks in this rebellion and Clan Hay centred in this area had been a historic supporter of Jacobite causes. It must have been chaos in the countryside around Aberlour in 1746.

These events can be understood only with some understanding of the religious tensions of the period. Bonnie Prince Charles was Roman Catholic and wanted to return a Catholic to the throne of England and Scotland. The two nations were Protestant, and except for the Jacobite minority, wanted to remain that way. However the Protestant church in Scotland was split into two major groups. In the 1690 new constitution of Scotland, responding to the religious revolution that had swept the land, Presbyterianism had replaced Episcopalism (i.e., Church of England) as the Church of Scotland. However, the revolution was not complete. People in some areas, including Aberdeen, expressed allegiance to the older ways. Ferguson describes the situation in 1745:

> ... again prospects were dashed by episcopalian support for the Young Pretender in 1745 ... The penal laws were tightened and some of the clergy and laity (of the episcopalian church) were transported. Fresh disabilities were impaired to keep Scottish episcopalians out of parliament and places of public trust ... Many of the nobles and gentry gave up episcopacy, finding congenial enough ministrations in an established church ... And in the nature of things it could scarcely have been otherwise. (The presbyterians had fought to free the church and its finances

---

3. Culloden is in the vicinity of Aberlour. There are no stories linking the Garrows to the massacre there.

from control by the state, i.e., politicians, but now had fallen into the same pattern when they gained political power.) ... episcopalians after the Revolution displayed all the obstinacy and heroism of the presbyterians of the Restoration period ... They fought much the same fight, refusing to allow the church to become the mere plaything of politicians.[4]

It would appear that the Garrows were inclined to an Episcopalian point of view. This would help explain why David and William Garrow moved to the London area, David as an ordained minister of the Church of England and William as a medical doctor.

Today the Scottish community where William and Jean Garrow had their farm is called Charlestown of Aberlour. The current detailed map shows the hillside south of the River Spey. On this small hillside area, specific sites are named the "Wood of Allachie," "Daugh of Allachie," "Knock of Allachie," "Burnside of Allachie" and "Knockside." While the "Mains of Allachie" is not specifically noted, this area is Sir William Garrow's ancestral home.

THE REVEREND DAVID GARROW

We can assume that Sir William Garrow's father, David Garrow, was born at the Mains of Allachy and baptized in the parish church in Aberlour on 4 August 1715. In his later teens, he would have spent time at Knockside. He would have attended school in Aberlour where the schoolmaster from 1720 to 1725 was a Patrick Gordon, who had studied at King's College, Aberdeen. His early education gave David the grounding needed for attending college. He was graduated from Aberdeen University with a Master of Arts in 1736.

After taking orders in the Church of England, he may have travelled to South Carolina as a missionary. This is suggested by an entry in the Calendar of Treasury Books and Papers indicating the Reverend David Garrow received £20 from the Money Book on 28 August 1745 "being passage money as a Minister to South Carolina."[5] If indeed he served as a minister there, he returned to England in time to take a lease on a large sixteenth century property at Monken Hadley called The Priory on 12 March 1747, and start his school or academy for young gentlemen. It was soon after this, on 5 June 1748, that he married Sarah Lowndes, a spinster from Camberwell, Surrey, at St. Stephen, Walbrook, London. With these two decisions he commenced building both his family and school. Then, during June 1760, David formally purchased The Priory. [6]

---

4. W. Ferguson. (1968) *Scotland: 1689 to the Present*. Edinburgh & London, Oliver & Boyd, p. 129.
5. Unpublished paper, "The Garrow Family" by J.D. Remnant. The Genealogy Library, Independence, Missouri.
6. F. C. Cass. *The Parish of Monken Hadley, Op. cit.* p. 183.

The Rev. David Garrow, age 76, after George
Romney in mezzotinto, by C.H. Hodges, 1787.
By permission of the National Portrait Gallery London

CHILDREN

David and Sarah were to have ten children; William, Edward, Eleanora, Jane, John
Rose, William, Joseph, William, David and Anne. Three of their sons died while
very young, and the two youngest who survived childhood, died early in their lives.
It is interesting to note that three of their children were named William, the first
two dying as infants. The third child named William survived and became the Sir
William Garrow of this story. The children that survived to adulthood were:

Edward (1751-1820) He made a fortune in India with the East India Company,
returned to England where he became High Sheriff of Hertfordshire, and inherited
The Priory from his father.

Eleanora (1752-1805) She remained a spinster residing at home at The Priory, cared for her parents and continued to live at The Priory until her death aged fifty-one.

Jane (1754-1841) She travelled to India, presumably to visit her brothers in the East India Company. Upon her return to England in the 1780s she married William Monk, a gentleman farmer, and had a large family.

Joseph(1757-1792) He served in the East India Company where he became Secretary to the Commander-in-Chief, Madras, and a person of considerable means. He had a natural son, Joseph, by Sultan, said to be a high caste Brahmin, and died in India in 1792.

William (1760-1840) He became the lawyer who made a name for himself as a barrister at the Old Bailey, then a prosecutor for the government, Member of Parliament, Attorney-General, Baron of the Exchequer, and the subject of this story.

A more detailed account of the lives of William Garrow's siblings and extended family appears in *Chapter 14*.

The Priory on Dury Road in Monken Hadley.

BOARDING SCHOOL

David Garrow's school was a boarding academy and well-suited to families with businesses in London opting to live in the high and healthy neighbourhood away from the smoke of the city, yet conveniently near the Great North Road into London.

The school at The Priory, which stood in grounds of about nine acres, did not neglect the social graces, in contrast with the local Grammar School of Queen Elizabeth which offered a classical education, The Priory aimed at preparing students for commercial careers, such as in the East India Company.

David's own sons were educated in his school and gained noteworthy careers in trade and government. It was located on Dury Road not far from St. Mary the Virgin Church at Monken Hadley, and was demolished during 1961 due to its dilapidated condition. A drawing of the house was made just prior to its demolition and shows a building in the style historians sometimes describe as "modern Gothic". Many local residents were upset when demolition was proposed, because the property was considered to be part of a particularly interesting corner of town. However, as a derelict property it would have been too expensive to save.

We know something of the curriculum by reading the school prospectus as found in a book by Mr. Cass, now in the Barnet Museum. It reads as follows:

Conditions
of the
Boarding School
at
Hadley, near Barnet, Middlesex,
The Revd. David Garrow, Master.

	£	s	d
Entrance Board, Washing and Lodging	5	5	0
(English, Writing and Arithmetic, Greek, Latin and French.) per Annum	25	0	0
Geography and the Use of the Globes	2	2	0
Merchants Accounts	2	2	0
Algebra and Geometry	2	0	0
Dancing per Quarter		10	6
Entrance to ditto		10	0

Breakings-up only at Christmas and Whitsuntide

The Reverend David Garrow died on 19 March 1805. He was buried on March 27 in the Monken Hadley churchyard, where there are monumental inscriptions to him, his wife and other family members. His obituary appeared in the *Gentleman's Magazine* of April 1805 and is an interesting record of his life. It states:

> At Hadley, co. Middlesex, aged 89, the Rev. David Garrow, who had kept a flourishing school there many years ... He was brother of William Garrow, M.D. of Barnet, who died 1795, and father of Mr. G. the very eminent counsellor (and now M.P. for Gatton in Surrey), and of Edward G. esq. of Totteridge, many years in the East Indies, and last year sheriff of Hertfordshire; and of two daughters, one of whom, after her return from India, married Mr. Monk, a gentleman-farmer at Cheshunt, and the other was living single with her venerable parent.[7]
>
> The house at Monken Hadley, where the Rev. Mr. Garrow lived and died, is supposed to have some relation to the abbey at Waltham, to which the manor and rectory belong. In some of the rooms there are Scripture histories carved over the chimney, and painted in the windows; but both these were of much later date.
>
> Mr. G (above) kept a school for boys (but not first at Hadley, or at least not in the same house). When his son the counsellor urged his father to give up the school, after repeating the request, the old gentleman declared that he was bent upon finishing the term of half a century in the employment, which he actually accomplished. Although he was reckoned a disciplinarian in his school, yet the boys loved him, and, when arrived at manhood, embraced every opportunity of visiting their old master, who expressed a pleasure in the expectation of seeing his former scholars (with the exception of few whom he had instructed). The large chamber in the house at Monken Hadley, where the greatest number slept, was, by his orders, always kept in the same state, to the day of his death, as when used by the boys.
>
> His affection for his wife, and regret for her death, led him to visit the room she died in every day; but he did not allow that room to be used or opened by any of his family. She conducted herself, in every respect, suitably to her station; and too much cannot be said in her praise, which will be read with pleasure by a grateful scholar.
>
> He felt his own gradual decay; and the loss of memory affected him so much that he avoided society, even that of his old neighbours, and, latterly, of his relatives, who were unremitting in their respectful attentions to the good old man who, when able to walk out in his village, generally used a long stick, presented to him by one of his family, which he called a Madagascar spear; and, as he wore his own hair, turned to silver locks, he reminded those who met him of one of the Patriarchs, as described in Holy Writ, particularly when, to his neighbour's address of salutation, he answered, with a benevolent as well as a cheerful countenance, "God bless you!"

In the codicil to his will, the Reverend David Garrow gave directions that nothing he had ever written should be published.

---

7. *The Gentleman's Magazine and Historical Chronicle.* (April 1805) London, p. 386.

CHAPTER 2

Education in Criminal Law

PUPIL BARRISTER

Until he was 15 years of age Garrow was entirely educated at his father's school at Hadley in Middlesex, mentioned above. Little is known about his education although in later life he was sometimes ungenerously described as "uneducated". There is nothing to show that we should take this seriously, being merely the superior approach of university graduates towards those educated privately.

By all accounts he knew the English language well, had a moderate acquaintance with Latin and became considerably proficient in French. At the age of 15, in 1775, Garrow was articled to Thomas Southouse, an attorney in Milk Street, Cheapside, it being one of the modes of legal education to place young men with attorneys and solicitors in order to teach them the practice of law and of the courts. They were chiefly engaged in copying precedents and drawing declarations and pleadings, thus relieving the attorney or solicitor from the burdensome part of his business. In this office he acquired practical knowledge of the profession.

The young Garrow showed so much ability and quickness that he was strongly recommended by Mr. Southouse to aim at the higher branch of the law, that of trial lawyer or barrister. Accordingly, at the termination of his articles, Garrow placed himself as a pupil under Mr. Crompton, then an eminent special pleader, whose practice was at this time the popular guide to the study of this branch of the law. According to Sir John Baker,

> By the end of the eighteenth century, the classical system of pupillage had replaced clerkship for intending members of the Bar ... The difference was that a pupil, instead of rendering clerical services, made a cash payment (usually one hundred guineas a year) for the privilege of `reading' for a year or two in the chambers of a member of the Bar ... to learn practice from the specialist practitioner's viewpoint.[1]

Every Bar student had to be a member of one of the four main Inns of Court in England and Garrow was admitted by Lincoln's Inn on 27 November 1778. He was called to the Bar on the same date five years later. By the time of his call he was twenty-three years of age, and was living with his future wife, Sarah.

Whilst a pupil barrister of Richard Crompton, Garrow industriously notated his copy of the 1677 edition of Euer's *Doctrina Placitandi* - a book in two volumes on

---

1. Sir John Baker. (2007) *Legal Education in London 1250-1850*. London, Selden Society. p. 19.

the Law of Pleading written in law French.[2] Hundreds of notes and comments in Garrow's own handwriting refer to relevant precedents from the works of Mr. Justice Yates and augmented by Mr. Justice Ashhurst and Mr. Justice Buller. His efforts won high praise from Mr. Justice Willis[3] and they show how extraordinarily industrious he was and, despite what Brougham said about his knowing little law, how he absorbed legal knowledge, even at that young age. The book is held in the Library of the Honourable Society of Lincoln's Inn to which it was presented by Montague Chambers QC in the nineteenth century.[4]

The record shows that Garrow took the study of criminal law seriously. In addition to his work under Mr. Crompton, he prepared himself in three other ways. First, in his own words, he frequently attended sessions of the Old Bailey, the criminal Assize of London and Middlesex, over a period of eight years prior to his call to the Bar.[5] Secondly, he formed a friendship with William Shelton, the clerk of arraigns at the Old Bailey, who was considered the most accomplished criminal lawyer of his day. In addition, determined to succeed, he trained himself in "the cut and thrust of argument and in public speaking" at the meetings of debating societies then flourishing in taverns and public rooms in London, where he first gained recognition.[6]

COACHMAKER'S HALL

In those days debating societies were the places where a young speaker could perfect his power of public speaking. This talent was vulgarly called "spouting" and in more polite society was known as the art of oratory. In these debating societies the speaker would confront not friends or fellow students who would fondly support him as one of their own, but a band of competitors gifted with various abilities, and generally well-informed audiences hoping to enjoy, at a modest price, the pleasure of witnessing a good display of intellectual struggle. Everyone in the hall would consider himself to be a competent critic, and would unceremoniously castigate the speaker for his faults.

The environment was severe, with interruptions, misrepresentations and derision that far overstepped the bounds of peaceful decorum. It was a common practice for the audience to employ "scraping", a noise made by their feet against the floor as a hint that they were tired of their speaker. But this was only the rough exercise

---

2. Subtitled "*Ou L'Art & Science De Bon Pleading*". (1677) London, R. & E. Atkins. 2 vols. Sampson Euer was a King's Serjeant.
3. Sir William Holdsworth. (1966) *A History of English Law.* London, Methuen & Co. Ltd. and Sweet & Maxwell. vol.v. p. 387. See also Sir John Baker. *Legal Education in London 1250-1850.* Op. cit. p. 20.
4. Guy Holborn, Librarian, Lincoln's Inn Library.
5. OBP Online. (www.oldbaileyonline.org) 12 January 1785. Ref: t17850112-12.
6. J.M. Beattie. (1991) "Scales of Justice: Defense Counsel and the English Criminal Trial in the Eighteenth and Nineteenth Centuries." *Law and History Review.* University of Illinois Press. p. 237.

by which the speaker could learn to turn these obstacles to profit, and to display his courage and vigour.

It was not easy at first, however, as is shown by a reprint in *The Times* of Saturday 7 November 1840[7] of a memoir of Garrow in the monthly *Law Magazine*. This claimed that when he went with friends to the Coachmaker's Hall in Foster Lane, Cheapside in order to learn the art of oratory his timidity was such that they had to force him from his seat and hold him while he delivered his maiden speech lest he should shrink back from the task he had undertaken. Although to those who knew him in later life this seemed incredible, it was, in fact, "perfectly in keeping with his reserved and retiring disposition."

Battling to overcome his shyness, he soon acquired a formidable reputation in the taverns as a speaker and was referred to in the press as "Counsellor Garrow, the famous orator of Coachmaker's Hall" which was where one of the largest of the debating clubs met.[8] As one contemporary writer stated in a record held in the London Guildhall, "He had scarcely passed his novitiate when he ran away with the palm of eloquence from all the frequenters of the club."[9] He is supposed to have been almost the death of a journeyman watchmaker "who had long rode the *high horse* in the society by vanquishing him in cool debate and dethroning him from his eminent position as champion."[10]

When Garrow chose to appear in a debate, the audience congratulated themselves on the certainty of an interesting discussion. It is recorded in *The Times* that when Mrs. Cornelya planned a new type of entertainment at Carlisle House in Soho Square including a debate as part of the event's amusement, her first care was to secure the assistance of Mr. Garrow.[11]

According to Edward Foss, he was a powerful debater, "and his speeches were so admired for their eloquence and ingenuity, that his presence was always welcomed."[12] Others also referred to Garrow as being in his profession, "as impudent as any of his brethren [but] in private is modest and reserved" and as having a, "peculiarly reserved and retiring disposition."[13] His shyness out of court was contrasted with his boldness in it, but after the death of his wife in 1808 he was credited with more self-assurance in society.[14]

---

7. See Appendix 3.
8. Beattie. "Scales of Justice". *Op.cit.* p. 263. Note 45.
9. *Public Characters.* (1799-1809) London, 10 vols. Frame 67.
10. *Ibid.*
11. *The Times.* (7 November 1840). *Memoir of Sir William Garrow.*
12. E. Foss. (1864) *The Judges of England; with Sketches of their Lives and Miscellaneous Notices Connected with the Courts at Westminster from the Time of the Conquest.* London, John Murray. vol. 9 p. 87.
13. J. Farington. (1796) *Diary.* (ed. K. Cave 1982) vol. ii. p. 614.
14. R.G. Thorne. (ed.) *The History of Parliament: The House of Commons 1790-1820.* London, Secker & Warburg. vol. iv. p. 6.

By these means Garrow prepared himself to speak in the courtrooms of the Old Bailey. As his critics, and even his friends, would point out, he never studied law as an academic scholar. He never became an authority on, or even comfortable within, certain areas of the law. What he did study, and become highly skilled at, was criminal law as practised in the Assize courts, such as the Old Bailey.

CHAPTER 3

Garrow and English Criminal Procedure

Although he was barely aware of it, Garrow's main achievement in life was momentous in helping to change the face of criminal procedure in England. He, with others who followed him, engendered a revolution in criminal law and to fully understand its significance it is first necessary to step back in time and consider the penal code in place before Garrow erupted upon the scene at the Old Bailey.

THE "NO-COUNSEL" RULE

Barristers have existed in England since the thirteenth century. Yet for five long centuries, by law prisoners on indictment for treason and felony were not permitted to have counsel appear for them, even though the sentence for these offences was death. It was in a case of rape[1] in the reign of Edward I (1273-1307) that the judges pronounced the rule and it was to remain law until the eighteenth century. The only exception was on a point of law, and then only at the direction of the court.[2] It was a serious blemish on the face of English justice (and in any event did not apply to trials for misdemeanours).

The reason for the rule lies in the fact that in English criminal law indictments for felony have always been taken in the name of the monarch and, in early times, it was considered *lèse majesté* for those indicted to be allowed counsel against the King or Queen. Hence, in this thirteenth century leading case the court told the prisoner that he could not have counsel "because the King is a party in this case, and sues *ex officio*, for which reason it is not proper that you should have counsel against the King"[3] This meant, of course, that lawyers could not speak out against the Crown in such trials and this may have been accepted by them since otherwise their careers and possibly their lives might well have been at risk.[4]

In consequence of the rule, every prisoner brought to trial for treason, murder, arson, rape, robbery, burglary, and most other forms of theft, had to defend himself in court without assistance. Indeed, says John H. Langbein, "when the surviving sources first allow us to see something of how criminal trials were actually conducted, we see the judges resolutely enforcing this prohibition on defence counsel, despite

---

1. Year Books 30 and 31. Edw.I. (Rolls Series) pp. 529-30.
2. For the exception on points of law cf. S.C.F. Milsom. (1981) *Historical Foundations of the Common Law.* 2nd edn. London, Butterworths. p. 413.
3. Year Books 30 and 31. *Op. cit.*
4. D. J. A. Cairns. (1998) *Advocacy and the Making of the Adversarial Criminal Trial.* Oxford, The Clarendon Press. p. 27.

persistent complaint from defendants."[5] Nonetheless, as Lord Chief Justice Jeffreys later told Thomas Rosewall on a charge of high treason in 1684, "[it] is a hard case that a man should have counsel to defend himself for a two-penny-trespass, and his witnesses examined on oath; but if he steal, commit murder or felony, nay, high treason, where life, estate, honour, and all are concerned, he shall neither have counsel, nor his witnesses examined upon oath."[6]

According to Langbein, "the main purpose of the trial was to give the accused the opportunity to speak in person to the charges and the evidence adduced against him," and he calls this style of proceeding the "accused speaks" trial.[7] There was no room, he says, for defence counsel to intermediate between the accused and the court. The logic of the rule was to pressure the accused to speak in his own defence. "Part of what motivated the rule", he continues, "was the fear (fully justified in hindsight) that defence counsel would interfere with the court's ability to have the accused serve as an informational source.[8] What hindsight really shows, however, is that often the accused, incarcerated in conditions of appalling squalor, frequently ill, illiterate, in awe of the trappings of the court, in fear of their lives and with no resources to prepare a defence, could not take advantage of Langbein's "accused speaks" style of trial and were frequently sentenced unheard.[9] Even if they could speak they were not permitted to give sworn evidence. In treason and felony trials, therefore, the defendant would have to attempt to make his own defence, often inadequately. Not surprisingly, to modern eyes the refusal of counsel is seen as barbaric.

Moreover, the rule did not apply to the prosecution and this left defendants at a severe disadvantage for centuries, particularly in trials for treason where the Crown was always represented. To make matters worse, accused persons were also not allowed to subpoena witnesses, nor, if they appeared voluntarily, could defence witnesses give evidence on oath. This placed them at a lower level than prosecution witnesses whose credibility was enhanced by testimonial evidence.[10] It is clear that prisoners suffered from serious handicaps in presenting a defence and were often saved from the gallows only by the mercy of juries or, in some cases, the judge. As an eminent English judge has put it, "[t]here is no intelligible sense in which the old form of trial was more apt than the modern criminal trial to elicit the truth. It was directed to establishing, by largely unjust means, the guilt of the accused as a prelude to brutal punishment or, occasionally, ostentatious clemency."[11]

---

5. J. H. Langbein. (2003) *The Origins of Adversary Criminal Trial.* Oxford, Oxford University Press. pp. 10-11.
6. 10 Howell's *State Trials.* p. 267.
7. J.H. Langbein. *The Origins of Adversary Criminal Trial. Op. cit.* p. 2.
8. *Ibid.*
9. See J.M. Beattie. (1986) *Crime and Courts in England 1660-1800.* Oxford, Clarendon Press. pp. 350-351.
10. G. Fisher (1997) 'The Jury's Rise as Lie Detector.' New Haven, 107 *Yale Law Journal.* p. 603.
11. Lord Justice Sedley. (25 September 2003) London Review of Books. p.15.

The First Breach in the Rule

The Whig politicians and grandees, in power after the Glorious Revolution empha-sized the growing importance of the individual in society and enshrined a number of fundamental rights in their Bill of Rights of 1689.[12] In an early manifestation of the modern concept of human rights, this provided, *inter alia,* for the free election of MPs; the right to trial by jury and the empanelling of jurors fairly; that excessive bail should not be required nor excessive fines be imposed; and that no cruel and unusual punishments be inflicted.

As part of the same process, the Whig leaders also introduced the radical Treason Trials Act of 1696,[13] a landmark statute which had an unexpected effect on the birth of adversary trial. Breaking with the centuries-long rule, it gave prisoners on trial for treason the right to have counsel act for them in all respects, including address the jury on the facts as well as on questions of law. As Beattie says, "It flowed from the Revolution of 1689 as a means of redressing a wrong the now-dominant Whig political class had suffered in the previous decade - the use of charges of treason to destroy political opponents."[14] It was also a response to lawyer-driven Crown prosecutions.

There were two official reasons put forward to justify the Act. First, that in treason trials two witnesses to an overt act were required. And secondly, and of greater significance, that the Crown always employed counsel to prosecute. These reasons did not exist in felony trials, however, where the wealthy and powerful were not involved, and similar legislation for such trials was believed to be unnecessary. Nevertheless, the conduct of felony trials itself was changing. With the incidence of crime appearing to increase, Associations for the Prosecution of Felons were formed in large numbers throughout the country to meet the growing demand for pros-ecuting counsel and to spread the cost of investigating crime and paying legal fees. At the same time the government sponsored a bounty system which encouraged reward-seeking thief-catchers. These, together with Crown witnesses induced to turn King's evidence and testify against their co-accused to save their own necks, were increasingly resulting in widespread perjury which could injure innocent defendants who were threatened with the scaffold even for trivial offences.

EARLY STEPS TOWARDS ADVERSARY TRIAL

With perjury endemic some judges came to believe that the scales were weighted too heavily against prisoners charged with capital offences in felony trials. As a conse-

---

12. 1 W. &. M. s. 2. c. 2.
13. 7 Will. 3. c. 3.
14. J.M. Beattie. `Scales of Justice: Defence Counsel and the English Criminal Trial in the Eighteenth and Nineteenth Centuries'. *Law and History Review.* University of Illinois Press. vol. 9 (2) p. 224.

quence, from the 1730s, and without legislation, a few of them sporadically allowed counsel to appear for defendants and cross-examine prosecutors and their witnesses. And, although it was a slow process, it allowed counsel, and not the judges, to establish adversariality.

However, even in such cases, barristers were still not permitted to examine their clients and were largely limited to cross-examination in order to retain the situation whereby the unsworn defendant himself told the jury his side of the story unembellished. What the judges did not envisage was that, in spite of this limitation, by skilled cross-examination the lawyers would capture the courtroom and reduce the previously active role of the judge and jury who respectively became solely umpire and fact finders.[15]

In this development a crucial role was played by William Garrow who appeared in over one thousand cases at the Old Bailey and established an aggressive and personal style of questioning prosecutors and their witnesses. As will be seen, this was vital in securing adversary trial and also helped lead to the introduction of rules of evidence, such as the presumption of innocence, the "best evidence" rule, the rule against accomplices' evidence and the hearsay rule, all of which gave new rights to prisoners. Beattie confirms that these evidential rights flowed from the involvement of defence lawyers. "It seems certain ..." he says, "that it was the insistent questioning by defense counsel that raised as matters of immediate urgency many of the issues whose resolution by the judges in their post-circuit meetings at Serjeants' Inn helped to form what amounted to a law of evidence in criminal trials."[16]

As a consequence of counsel being allowed a restricted appearance for prisoners, the adversarial system was slowly brought into existence in the course of the eighteenth and nineteenth centuries in what amounted to a "crucial formative period for English criminal justice."[17] Its origins, however, were for long unknown and even now are disputed by academic lawyers who cannot agree on how adversary trial arose.

Since Garrow, more than any other lawyer, was responsible for the extensive growth of adversarial criminal trials his role needs to be examined in detail. He is described by Beattie as tenacious, insistently and doggedly determined, and with a capacity for sarcasm.[18] He also came to know many prosecutors and their background, and they certainly knew and feared him, as was revealed when his wife's coach was held up by highwaymen.[19]

15. J. Hostettler. (1992) *The Politics of Criminal Law: Reform in the Nineteenth Century.* Chichester, Barry Rose Law Publishers. Chap. 4.
16. J.M. Beattie. `Scales of Justice.' Op. cit. p. 233.
17. P. Handler. (2005) Review of Allyson N. May's *The Bar and the Old Bailey, 1750-1850.* London, 26 *The Journal of Legal History.* p. 111.
18. J.M. Beattie. (February 1991) `Garrow for the Defence.' London, *History Today.* History Today Ltd. p. 51.
19. See post, pages 152-3.

Despite Langbein referring to the "trickster William Garrow", an examination of his cases shows the description to be unduly harsh. He always endeavoured to act with professional propriety in his advocacy and he and the urbane Thomas Erskine quite often acted together in trials. Indeed, Erskine said of him that, "he knows more of the real justice and policy of everything connected with the criminal law than any man I am acquainted with."[20] More than that, he may with justice be called the father of adversary trial.

The importance of the change to adversariality is brought out by Peter King when he writes that, "[c]ross-examination in particular developed as the century wore on into a means of commenting on the evidence, refuting or discrediting the prosecution case, and aggressively, even cruelly, battling for the accused."[21] The change was also described by John Wigmore as, "beyond any doubt the greatest legal engine ever invented for the discovery of truth."[22] And, for the purposes of this book, as Beattie says, "Garrow was the leading exemplar of aggressive advocacy in the 1780s" and extended it "by his willingness to do bruising battle with recalcitrant witnesses, to quarrel with judges, and by his sheer skill as an advocate."[23] Bringing into the light of day false evidence and malicious prosecutions did much to reveal the truth that Langbein claims adversary trial hides.[24]

An example of vigorous cross-examination by Garrow is found in the trial of *R. v. William Stevenson* who was charged with murder on 15 September 1784.[25] The case followed a disturbance in Clerkenwell Prison in the evening of 1 August 1784 and Garrow was briefed by the accused.[26] A number of women prisoners who had their beer allowance taken away broke open a gate, threw missiles and threatened to set the prison and the governor's house on fire. The prosecution alleged that some soldiers who happened to be in the prison were ordered to fire upon a number of the women. When they refused to fire the accused, who was a watchman, was alleged to have snatched a blunderbuss from one of the soldiers, levelled it at a pregnant prisoner named Sarah Scott and shot her dead.

One prosecution witness was prisoner Thomas Jones who described the scene and said he saw Stevenson fire the fatal shot. Garrow, defending Stevenson, cross-examined Jones:

---

20. A. Aspinall. (1963) (ed) *The Correspondence of George, Prince of Wales: 1770-1812.* London Cassell. vol. vii. p. 268.
21. P. King. (2000) *Crime, Justice, and Discretion in England, 1740-1820.* Oxford, Oxford University Press. p 228.
22. J. H. Wigmore. (1974 edn.) *Evidence in Trials at Common Law.* Chadbourn. vol.v. p. 32.
23. J. M. Beattie. `Scales of Justice: Defence Counsel and the English Criminal Trial in the eighteenth and nineteenth centuries.' *Op. cit..* p. 239.
24. J.H. Langbein. *The Origins of Adversary Criminal Trial. Op. cit.* p. 332.
25. OBP Online. (www.oldbaileyonline.org, 1 November 2004) 15 September 1784. Trial of William Stevenson. Ref: t17840915-66.
26. Another example of the speed with which prisoners were brought to trial.

Garrow: Mr. Jones, pray of what profession are you?

Jones: I am a watch-maker by trade.

Garrow: That is when you are out of gaol?

Jones: No, Sir.

Garrow: How then?

Jones: I get my livelihood as honestly as I can.

Garrow: That is exactly what I thought; honestly if you can, but if not?

Jones: Dishonestly you may suppose, but I do not say that.

Garrow: You was in for no harm?

Jones: No.

Garrow: What unrighteous set of men was it that sent you there for no harm?

Jones: My wife.

Garrow: Is it not the first unrighteous woman that has sent her husband there; by whose help did she send you there?

Jones: I cannot tell you, you must ask her that; I was sent from Hick's Hall, they would not let me speak there; here I am before an honourable Court, she could produce no marks.

Garrow: You half murdered her, and they convicted you?

Jones: The sentence was one month's imprisonment and two bail in ten pounds each, and myself in twenty pounds for my good behaviour for twelve months; I laid there eight weeks, I was in three prisons in three weeks time.

Garrow: Now I recommend to you to take care you do not get into Newgate?

Jones: I have escaped that.

Garrow: You have, have you, why that is a pretty strong prison too?

Jones: I am an honest man.

Garrow: I believe in the third prison you was so bad a fellow, that the keeper himself got some of his own people to bail you, to get rid of you, and in order that you might not corrupt the whole gaol?

Jones: Right, Sir! Very right, Sir! Very right, Sir!

In the event, the judges, Mr. Justice Gould and the recorder of the City of London, told the jury that in law reasonable force might be used by a gaoler to prevent a riot in a prison and, on that direction, the jury found the accused not guilty. Nothing was said about Stevenson not being a gaoler or, if force was to be used, how much force was reasonable in the circumstances. But, in attacking Jones in a forthright manner, Garrow had cast doubt upon the prosecution case in the eyes of the jury and it appears he was successful.

"Being nervous and cross-examined by Mr. Garrow," by Rowlandson.

**By permission of the Yale Center for British Art, Yale University.
Paul Mellon Collection.**

Three years later Garrow defended Thomas Duxton on a charge of burglary of goods worth £3. 3s – a capital offence.[27] The owner gave evidence of the theft and a fence named Francis Fleming testified that he had bought the goods from Duxton. The case against the prisoner seemed clear. However, in response to questioning by Garrow, Fleming admitted that he did not keep books relating to stolen goods and gratuitously added that he was thinking of settling in another way of business as he was proposing to get married. Garrow immediately took the offensive.

> **Garrow:** It is very unlucky for the family you meant to honor with your alliance; you are the same Mr. Fleming that has been a receiver of stolen goods for six months?
>
> **Fleming:** I am the same Fleming that was examined before you on a similar

---

27. OBP Online. (www.oldbaileyonline.org) 12 December 1787. Ref: t17871212-78.

occasion.

Garrow: Now my honest, worthy friend, Mr. Fleming, how happened it that you kept this a secret all the summer months from July down to December?

Fleming: I did not mean to disclose it, unless I had been compelled to it.

Garrow: Unless you had been compelled to it by the danger of the gallows; I dare to say you was charged with nothing when you made this disclosure?

Fleming: To my knowledge I was not; I know the situation I am in.

Garrow: Hear the question and answer it.

Garrow then pointed out to Fleming that being in possession of stolen goods he was likely to be hanged unless he could fix possession on another person. He then continued, "Did you not do this to save your own neck; did you not make the disclosure to save your own life?"

Fleming: I suppose I must answer, Mr. Garrow, in the affirmative, for I know no better: I certainly made this disclosure to save myself.

Garrow: Then you are now swearing, in order to fix this danger on somebody else to save yourself.

Fleming: I apprehend, Mr. Garrow, I am still in the same danger if I do not fix on the right person.

As a consequence of this devastating cross-examination, and against the prosecution evidence, the jury found Duxton not guilty.

Garrow's practice, declares Beattie, illustrated a more committed advocacy of cases in the courtroom and a new emphasis on [prisoners] rights."[28] The significance of the last point cannot be over-stated in its application to the modern doctrine of human rights. Equal justice was being sought and according to a contemporary, "in the eye of reason and in the contemplation of English law, the life and liberty of His Majesty's subjects, are of as great value and estimation, as those of the most exalted."[29] Beattie goes on to say of Garrow that, "in his aggressive behavior, in his insistent and pressing and revealing cross-examinations of prosecution witnesses, in his challenges to the rulings of the bench, he represented a new phenomenon. Even his critics acknowledged his abilities and his pre-eminence at the bar."[30]

Defendants themselves were now encouraged to say less and rely upon their

---

28. J.N. Beattie. `Scales of Justice.' *Op. cit.* p. 238.

29. R.W. Bridgman, (1804) *Reflections on the Study of the Law.* Cited by D. Lemmings. (2000) *Professors of the Law:Barristers and English Legal Culture in the Eighteenth Century.* Oxford University Press. p. 225.

30. J.M. Beattie. `Scales of Justice', *Op. cit.* p. 247.

counsel to deal with everything for them. In one case at the Old Bailey, when a prisoner in reply to a question said, "I leave it to my counsel," Garrow responded that, "You understand we cannot say anything to the Court or Jury in your defence, we can only examine witnesses." But, when the prisoner then asked a witness a question the judge, Mr. Baron Hotham supporting Garrow, told him, "God forbid that you should be hindered from saying anything in your defence, but if you have only questions to ask, I would advise you to leave them to your counsel."[31]

Whereas in earlier cases the prisoner, the judge and members of the jury had all been able to join in the proceedings with questions and comments, now the dynamic of the jury trial was altered. Counsel began to silence his client, at least until the prosecution evidence had been fully disclosed.[32] In a trial in 1784 Garrow's client, the prisoner, spoke up during Garrow's cross-examination of the accused, saying "I wish to put another question to [the prosecuting victim]." Garrow interrupted to say "Send the question to me in writing."[33]

This was part of the process whereby counsel radically changed the criminal trial and broke down the judge's mastery of the proceedings. "Over the course of the eighteenth century," says Langbein, "our criminal procedure underwent its epochal transformation from a predominantly non-adversarial system to an identifiably adversarial one."[34]

RULES OF EVIDENCE

Rules of evidence were evolving during the years that Garrow practised in the criminal courts. Where a rule could benefit his client, Garrow insisted that it be strictly followed. Very early in his career, Garrow acted as defence counsel for John Hinxman who was charged with stealing property from his employers. This trial is of interest because the outcome of the case hinged on the strict application of a rule of evidence. It also shows the harshness of the criminal law at that time for what today would be a petty crime – the stealing of a few minor items including a handkerchief.[35]

Upon being dismissed from his job, Hinxman was caught with a locked box as he departed the store. The prisoner confessed, although his confession may have been urged by his employer in the hope that he might receive mercy. At issue were some

31. OBP Online. (www.oldbaileyonline.org, 15 October 2004) 10 December 1783. Trial of Jacob Thompson for Theft. Ref: t17831210-148.
32. D.J.A. Cairns. *Advocacy and the Making of the Adversarial Criminal Trial 1800-1865. Op. cit.* p. 30.
33. OBP Online. (www.oldbaileyonline.org, 7 January 2005) (21 April 1784 Trial of Humphry Moore for theft from a dwellinghouse. Ref: t17840421-92.
34. J.H. Langbein. (1983) `Shaping the Eighteenth Century Criminal Trial: A View from the Ryder Sources.' Chicago, *University of Chicago Law Review.* p. 123.
35. OBP Online. (www.oldbaileyonline.org) 26 May 1784. Trial of John Hinxman. Ref: t17840707-62.

pieces of silk, some socks and one handkerchief. Theft of this property was a serious offence with draconian consequences if Hinxman was proved guilty as charged.

Garrow immediately went on the attack, identifying significant procedural errors and difficulties with the evidence of the prosecutors. Even though Hinxman had confessed, Garrow was able to get the jury to return a verdict of not guilty. Garrow's style in defending even guilty people is demonstrated in the records of this case.

Garrow: Was that confession reduced into writing?

Wood: I fancy it was.

Garrow: Then you must not talk about it? Your Lordship I humbly submit will not hear any thing about that confession.

Court to Wood: Can you or can you not say from your own knowledge, whether it was taken down?

Wood: I cannot say, it possible might. ....

Garrow: ... I understand the Court to say ... that it was the duty of a Justice to reduce everything into writing, for that the neglect of the magistrate should not operate against the prisoner at the bar, who may have said something, which, if reduced into writing, might appear in a different light ... monstrous mischief to prisoners might happen if part is to be kept back, and a witness who is unwilling to disclose the whole truth should come and give an oral evidence in part.

Court: The Justices have no right to ask a prisoner to confess, but if the prisoner does confess, it should be taken down no doubt of it.

Mr. Reynolds. Here is no confession returned.

Garrow then cross-examines Wood, one of the owners and the prosecutor, on how he claimed the contents of the box were in fact his property, implying that Hinxman could have bought it elsewhere or even in Wood's own shop. They were technical points focusing on possibilities, avoiding any discussion of the probability that Hinxman did steal from his employer.

Garrow: I ask you whether these stocking might not be matched? (i.e., available elsewhere)

Wood: I do not suppose they might.

Garrow: Do you believe upon your oath that they could not?

Wood: I never saw any more of the same, I swear upon my oath they are my property.

Garrow: I shall repeat my question till I get an answer; upon your oath do you believe there is a possibility they might be matched?

Wood: They possibly might, I do not know that they might, I never saw any like them. I will not swear that there are none of the same sort, but the person I bought them of had no more.

Garrow: Give a reason for your certainty, as that will go to your credit?

Wood: He very possibly might ...

Garrow: For God's sake, Sir, have a little regard to your oath and character?

However Garrow did establish through cross-examination that Hinxman did buy similar material from his employer. This focused the examination on the ownership of the handkerchief, and whether Hinxman had the right to sell himself something from the store.

Garrow: You mean to swear, that a man entrusted to sell handkerchiefs to himself or anybody else could not have done so?

Wood: It is not possible for a man to sell goods to himself.

Court: It is very odd that he should.

Garrow: But it is no theft, it may perhaps be an impeachment of the prudence of the prisoner, but not of his honesty.

There had been some discussion that the other owner, Mr. Harvey, had made promises to the young man if he confessed, but Mr. Harvey claimed to be sick at the time of the trial so he could not testify or his testimony be cross-examined. Another employee stated that he overheard Hinxman say that he had done the thing that was wrong, and he hoped they would be merciful. This apparently did not sway the jury. Hinxman called four witnesses who spoke of his very good character, and the jury gave a verdict of not guilty. It is doubtful that Hinxman could have defended himself, and saved himself from the gallows or from transportation without help from Garrow.

In addition, defence counsel exploited cross-examination and legal arguments to challenge suspect evidence that might unduly influence jurors, such as hearsay, confessions, and the evidence, often relied upon by the authorities at this time, of "thief-takers prosecuting for rewards and accomplices testifying under promises of non-prosecution."[36] In doing so they set in motion the establishment of rules of criminal evidence that were to prove of vital importance in the protection of prisoner's rights. Garrow played a prominent part in this process and examples will be seen in the extracts from some of his cases which follow. It is interesting that in earlier times prosecution witnesses had always been allowed to introduce hearsay evidence - an indulgence not allowed to the defence. "How very partial they had been in giving, and permitting evidence to be given by hearsay ... which they would not permit in his defence" said Sir John Hawles, later Solicitor-General.[37]

As we shall see, Garrow was a pioneer in using cross-examination as a means to comment on the evidence, refute or discredit the prosecution case and aggressively battle for the accused.[38] Such tactics were characterized by Stephen as the "most remarkable change" in the character of criminal trials, although he admitted that he could not trace their origins.[39]

THE GROWTH OF ADVOCACY

According to Landsman the 1780s were the years when a huge leap in counsel participation seemed to occur.[40] The scale of the upheaval is also shown by King who found that whereas between the 1730s and the early 1780s defence counsel were involved in a minimum of around 10 per cent of London cases, after 1780 between a quarter and a third of prisoners had counsel while in provincial practice a similar change was occurring. Furthermore, he continues, "all these figures are considerable underestimates since the presence of counsel was only noted if they made decisive interventions."[41] Not surprisingly, by 1836 Henry Brougham was able to claim that it was an, "unquestionable proposition that advocacy is indispensably necessary to the administration of justice."[42]

In the mid-eighteenth century trials began with the reading out of the charge against the defendant, followed by the opening statement of the prosecution counsel, if present.[43] Speeches of defence counsel were often omitted from the record of

36. D.J.A. Cairns. `Advocacy and the Making of the Adversarial Criminal Trial 1800-1865.' *Op. cit.* p. 30 and see Beattie. `Scales of Justice:' *Op. cit.* pp. 233-34.
37. Sir J. Hawles. (1689) *A Reply to a Sheet of Paper, entitled, The Magistry and Government of England Vindicated.* London, p. 13. Cited by Shapiro. *Op. cit.* p. 223.
38. P. King. *Crime, Justice and Discretion in England 1740-1820. Op. cit.* p. 228.
39. J. F. Stephen. (1883) *A History of the Criminal Law of England. London, Routledge/Thoemmes Press.* vol. i. p. 424.
40. S. Landsman. `The Rise of the Contentious Spirit. Adversary Procedure in Eighteenth Century England.' New York, 75 *Cornell Law Review.* p. 524. note. 126.
41. P. King. *Crime, Justice and Discretion in England 1740-1820. Op. cit.* p. 228.
42. H. Brougham. (1836) Review of *A Popular and Practical Introduction to Law Studies* by Samuel Warren. 64 *Edinburgh Review.* Edinburgh, Longman, Ross & Ors. p. 163.
43. www.oldbaileyonline.org/proceedings/value.html

the proceedings,[44] but according to Beattie, on the information available, by the year 1786 "close to two hundred men and women on trial for felonies at the Old Bailey had the help of lawyers. And although that was still only a fifth of those tried that year, it represented a remarkable and sudden increase in the number of cases defended by counsel."[45] Whilst the percentage of cases where defence counsel appeared stood at 0.5 per cent in 1740, it had risen to 36.6 per cent by 1795.[46] At the same time the lawyers themselves were becoming more pro-active in their determination to cross-examine more effectively, to impress the jury and to discredit the prosecutor.[47] Beattie found that in Quarter Sessions and Assizes in Surrey and Sussex, counties close to London, trial juries found prisoners not guilty in 35 per cent of property offences in the latter part of the eighteenth century.[48]

Successful criminal counsel, like Garrow and Erskine, had intruded into the criminal trial and had begun to forge a link with juries that had a large impact upon them, often to the discomfort of the judges, and it certainly increased the number of acquittals. The change is described by Landsman in the following words:

> [t]he parties, or more accurately, highly skilled advocates on their behalf assumed ever greater responsibility for interrogation, while the judges retreated from inquisitorial activism and accepted a far more neutral and passive role. Rules of evidence and procedure multiplied and a contentious mechanism arose. Directed by the litigants, emphasizing bi-party examination and regulated by a strict set of forensic prescriptions, the structure clearly conformed to an adversarial pattern.[49]

Hence, in the eighteenth century, "[r]ather than undertaking an exercise in finding the truth for the case as a whole, English criminal procedure developed the dialectic method of cross-examination to establish whether a case could be proved against a specific defendant.[50] But such cross-examination of itself was more likely to extract the truth than the earlier "no counsel" system where prosecution evidence frequently went unchallenged.

Counsel's Pugnacity

Another case which illustrates Garrow's aggressive style was heard on 29 June 1785 when Catherine Molley was charged with simple grand larceny in stealing property

---

44. *Ibid.*
45. J.M. Beattie. (1991) `Garrow for the Defence'. *Op. cit..* p. 50.
46. Beattie. (1991) `Scales of Justice: Defence Counsel and the English Criminal Trial in the Eighteenth and Nineteenth Centuries'. *Op. cit.* p. 227. Original data from Old Bailey Sessions Proceedings.
47. *Ibid.*
48. J.M. Beattie. *Crime and the Courts. Op. cit.* p. 411.
49. S. Landsman. (1990) `From Gilbert to Bentham: The Reconceptualization of Evidence Theory.' In 36 *The Wayne Law Review*. University of Oregon School of Law. p. 1150.
50. D. Dwyer. (2003) Review of Langbein's *The Origins of Adversary Criminal Trial*. 66 *The Modern Law Review*. Oxford, Blackwell Publishing. p. 943.

from John Thorne.[51] Thorne gave evidence that the prisoner had been his servant and had stolen a number of articles from his home. Garrow cross-examined him.

> **Garrow:** I fancy I shall make an end of this business, by a word or two with this old gentleman; you thought it was a good thing to get her bailed, then you had her?
>
> **Thorne:** I had nothing but honour and honesty in me.
>
> **Garrow:** That is certain, my old buck!
>
> **Thorne:** She had left my service about a year and a quarter.
>
> **Garrow:** How many of your apprentices boarded and lodged with her by your desire?
>
> **Thorne:** There was one, and I gave a bond that he should be at liberty in five years.
>
> **Garrow:** That is, in defiance of law, did this young man live with her?
>
> **Thorne:** He did live with her, he cohabited with her.
>
> **Garrow:** Is she not a married woman?
>
> **Thorne:** I do not know that.
>
> **Garrow:** What do you believe?
>
> **Thorpe:** He lay out of my house, and lay with her.
>
> **Garrow:** So that a year and a half after you took her up for stealing these things.

This was clearly a curious, as well as aggressive, cross-examination but it probably influenced the jury who found Molloy not guilty. Again, Garrow had thrown doubts on the prosecution case by attacking the character of the witness.

Another example occurred on 14 September 1785 when William Bear and William Davis were indicted for feloniously stealing from a barge on the Thames 31 deal boards valued at £4.[52] One of the witnesses who gave evidence for the prosecution was John Hyser. Immediately after he was sworn and before his examination commenced Garrow, defending, interposed saying, "Stand up little honesty."

No objection was raised by either the prosecuting counsel or the court. Hyser testified that he helped Bear and Davis take the boards from the barge. At the end of his evidence prosecuting counsel, William Fielding (the son of Henry Fielding the

---

51. OBP Online. (www.oldbaileyonline.org, 7 January 2005) 29 June 1785. Trial of Catherine Molley. Ref: t17850629-13.

52. OBP Online. (www.oldbaileyonline.org, 12 January 2005) Trial of William Bear and William Davis. Ref: t17850014-80.

novelist and magistrate) asked, "Now young man, upon your oath, is it all true that you have told the Court?" and received the reply, "Nothing but the truth."

Immediately on his feet, Garrow asked, "What is it my friend is afraid of, that you will not tell the truth, why you are an honest lad and came to speak the truth?"

"Yes" replied Hyser. Questioning him further Garrow ascertained that the witness had come to court from prison and the following exchange then took place:

Garrow: Oh! In custody! That was what made my friend so fearful, why what are you in custody for my man? Speak out, don't be bashful.

Hyser: Yes.

Garrow: Is it upon account of this affair?

Hyser: I suppose so Sir.

Garrow: What, somebody was wicked enough to suppose you stole them? (No answer)

Garrow: Why you could speak fast enough just now, now you are as mute as a mackerel, now I am come to speak to you, why don't you speak out, did not somebody take you up about these deals?

Hyser: Yes Sir.

Garrow: Now I ask you upon your oath, (God knows you don't mind that) did not your master turn you away?

Hyser: I went away, they did not take me up, and he wanted to persuade me from going to sea.

Garrow: As the only way of preventing you from being hanged: now whose stitch of bacon was it you stole?

Hyser: I never stole any bacon.

Garrow: Can you state the name of any human being, that you have done one honest day's work for these six months?

Fielding to Hyser: Why do you not answer my friend by asking him the same question?

Garrow to Fielding: I have held many briefs of yours during that time.

Despite the closeness to *Alice in Wonderland* scenarios in some of these exchanges, the judge, Mr. Baron Hotham, made no attempt to intervene and at the end of the trial Bear, against whom the evidence was clear, was found guilty and Davis was acquitted.

An example, not only of Garrow's aggression towards prosecution witnesses but also of his humanity to those found guilty, is revealed in a case in 1789 in which the prisoners were charge with having stolen goods worth 32 shillings.[53] Garrow cross-examined a prosecution accomplice witness, James Roche. Here in the one case is revealed Garrow's attitude to the evidence of accomplices, pious perjury by the jury and an example of the jury being allowed, indeed encouraged to change its mind.

Garrow: You are a thief?

Roche: Yes, Sir.

Garrow: Will you swear that you never was a thieving before?

Roche: I will swear that I never was a thieving before in that there fact, never before.

Garrow: Aye, in that there fact … How came you to find your way into the loft, if you had not been in Wright's house before?

Roche: Because I ran up frighted, there was a way broke open, I could not miss it.

Garrow: That was into the plant, was it not?

Roche: I do not know.

Garrow: Where is Mr. Wright's plant?

Roche: I do [not] know.

Garrow: Upon, your oath, is that not the plant?

Roche: I cannot tell'

Garrow: You know what I mean?

Roche, Yes, anyone knows what is meant by that.

Garrow: There are very few honest men in Court that know beside myself, what is a plant my honest friend?

Roche: I suppose you mean putting things away.

On the evidence of the accomplice the two prisoners were found guilty and sentenced to death. Garrow then addressed the judge arguing that there was no evidence against them on the capital charge apart from that of the accomplice. Stressing the importance of mercy, he suggested that if they saw fit the jury should be allowed to mitigate and change their finding.

---

53. OBP Online. (www.oldbaileyonline.org) Trial of John Merryman and William Pickering for house-breaking. 3 June 1789. Ref: t17890603-66.

The judge, Mr. Baron Perryn, thanked Garrow for his observations and told the jury that it was always his wish that mercy be mixed with the exercise of justice. The judges, he said, were of the opinion that an accomplice was a competent witness but his credit was to be left to the jury. Garrow then said to the jury: "Gentlemen, the verdict is not yet recorded, and I am sure it will reflect no discredit on the Jury to alter their verdict, particularly after the humane observations from the learned judge."

On this the jury changed their verdict and found the defendants guilty only of stealing 4s.10d from a dwellinghouse, which was not a capital offence. Nevertheless, they were transported for seven years which, awful as it was, must be regarded as an improvement on the gallows.

In another trial in the same year, Peter Miller, a boy aged nine, was indicted for feloniously stealing from Thomas May a sum of 10 shillings.[54] May gave evidence that Peter had helped him on with his coat and stolen 10 shillings in coins from its pocket and the boy had later admitted it. In response to a question, he told the judge that no one had told him that it was a capital charge. Persistently Garrow returned to the point, asking with incredulity whether he really did not know that if the boy was convicted he would be hanged.

After tenaciously pursuing the witness with the question, he then asked him if he had been told that on a conviction he would receive a reward of £40. May replied that he had been told so but he could not remember by whom. When May pleaded his poverty, Garrow asked, "Is your memory affected by your poverty?". On the witness answering, "No" Garrow responded with, "Is your head affected?" May replied that it was a good deal to which Garrow said, "You'll be mistaken this time as to the reward." The jury agreed and found the boy guilty of stealing 10 pence which was not a capital offence. For that he was sentenced to be whipped.

Garrow was, "not always popular … but his aggressive advocacy, his knowledge of complex evidential rulings and his systematic scrutiny of the prosecution case could be very influential."[55] And, indeed, his overall success was such that at this time his fee for defending Joshua Palmer for receiving stolen goods valued at £200,000 was rumoured to be the enormous sum of 200 guineas[56].

A contemporary, Thomas Hague, described him as pert, vulgar and garrulous, saying that the, "brutal insolence" and "wanton scurrility" he employed in cross-examining witnesses "wounded private feelings, insulted the dignity of the court and violated public decorum; more important, it tended to upset the ends of justice."[57] Such sentiments are, no doubt, exaggerated since Hague was bitterly

---

54. OBP Online. (www.oldbaileyonline. Org) 22 April 1789. Trial of Peter Miller for theft. Ref: t17890422-92.
55. P. King. *Crime, Justice and Discretion in England. Op. cit.* p. 229.
56. *The Times.* 23 January 1800.
57. T. Hague. (1812?) *A Letter to William Garrow, Esquire, in which the Conduct of Counsel [especially W.*

hostile to Garrow and prone to hyperbole. Nonetheless, Garrow could, on occasion, be too aggressive and too insensitive. However, that was rare and was a small price to pay for his contribution in establishing adversary trial.

Garrow] in the cross-examination of Witnesses, and commenting on their testimony, is fully discussed and the licentiousness of the bar exposed. London, J. Parsons. pp. 3, 6.

CHAPTER 4

Early Trials

In an age when the rights of individuals were growing in importance, the focus of the criminal trial became "the defence of the individual against the power of the state, rather than the state finding the offender on behalf of the victim."[1] As Beattie puts it in regard to Garrow, who exemplified the transition, "He placed a new emphasis on defendants' rights, indulged in aggressive behaviour, was insistent and pressing in cross-examining prosecution witnesses, challenged the rulings of the Bench, and his presence dominated in the courtroom."[2] His importance lies in the fact that he was the first to develop such techniques and skills and in doing so changed the nature of the trial into adversariality.

DEDICATION TO THE DEFENCE OF CLIENTS

As we have seen, it is in reading the court proceedings that one gets a penetrating feel for Garrow's work. It is in his early cases that one first witnesses his new and aggressive practice in the examination and cross-examination of witnesses and of his dedication to the defence of his clients. The records of these cases from the Old Bailey for the years from 1784 to the early 1790s can be found and studied. Hundreds of them in which Garrow defended or prosecuted individuals are now readily available online from the website *The Proceedings of the Old Bailey, London 1674 to 1834*. As Garrow branched out onto the assize circuits, detailed records of the cases are also occasionally available. In addition to trials mentioned in *Chapter 3*, examples of Garrow's courtroom style are presented here from his early cases.

Modern scholars focus on these early cases in which crimes typical of the common people of London were tried. It was in this short period of time that those charged with felonies started in increasing numbers to depend on defence lawyers to aggressively defend their lives. Some of the common types of crimes in which defence counsel were employed were assault, bigamy, burglary, coining, embezzlement, forgery, highway robbery, larceny, manslaughter, murder, pickpocketing, rape, receiving stolen goods, returning from transportation, riot, robbery, shoplifting and treason. It was in this setting that the adversary trial system grew. During this period defence counsel not only changed the way the trials were conducted, and how the accused were defended, they continued the process of defining rules of evidence,

---

1. D. Dwyer. (2003 Review of Langbein's *The Origins of Adversary Trial*. 66 The Modern Law Review. p. 943.
2. J.M. Beattie. (1991) "Scales of Justice: Defense Counsel and the English Criminal Trial in the Eighteenth and Nineteenth Centuries." *Law and History Review*. University of Illinois Press. pp. 238 and 247.

such as the hearsay rule, self-incrimination, involuntary confessions, and the use of accomplice evidence. Because detailed records are now readily available, this period can be more easily studied then in the past. What follows includes a small sample of these cases.

Oil of Garrow by Romney (reproduced by Ward & Roberts II) 1785
© The Trustees of the British Museum

INITIAL SUCCESS

One of Garrow's first trials at the Old Bailey was his prosecution of John Henry Aikles for obtaining by false pretences a bill of exchange on 14 January 1784.[3] Although he had been called to the Bar only two months earlier, it was in this case, although acting for the prosecution and not the defence as he preferred, that Garrow established his successful entry into the field. It also, that early, gives the flavour of his style and tactics that were to bring him renown as a barrister. It was in the Aikles

---

3. OBP Online. (www.oldbaileyonline.org) 14 January 1784. Ref: t17840114-80.

case he had quickly set himself apart from other counsel with his aggression and irony at the prisoner's expense.

This is recalled in *The Judges of England* by Edward Foss.

> A clever swindler, Henry Aikles, was indicted for stealing a bill of exchange, which he had obtained under the promise of getting it discounted; instead of doing which, he had converted it to his own use. His counsel contended confidently that this was no felony, and it was considered a very doubtful point; but the acuteness of Mr. Garrow's reply, and the readiness and cogency of his arguments, so far satisfied the judge, that he left the question of fact to the jury, who convicted the delinquent; and on a reference to the twelve judges, they coincided with Garrow's view of the law.[4]

In this case, Garrow was opposed by two of the most experienced and able practitioners of the day, a Mr. (afterwards Sir John) Sylvester and Mr. Fielding. In his comments to the court, Garrow was able to clarify a confusing point of criminal law. Later, he wrote in the margin of his copy of the case record that he attributed the recognition he received in this case to be that "which chiefly occasioned my success in life."

A bill of exchange is a form of negotiable instrument, a means of securing a temporary loan. To immediately receive a sum of money the person signs the bill which requires him to pay on demand, or at a fixed future time, a given sum of money to, or to the order of, a specified person or to bearer. It was alleged that Aikles had stolen a bill valued at £100 from a Samuel Edwards, by promising to pay to Mr. Edwards its face value, less a small commission. Aikles took the signed bill but did not hand over the money. When the bill was handed to him, he claimed the money was at his apartments and Edwards sent a Mr.Croxall with him under instruction not to leave him without the money. However, Aikles got away without providing the money, and apparently sold the bill to another party who had the right to demand payment. The question before the court was whether Aikles had feloniously stolen the bill valued at £100.

In opening the case to the jury, Garrow spoke with heavy irony of Aikles as "one of those virtuous and benevolent men, who have discovered the secret of acquiring large fortunes, and of supporting elegant houses and superb equipages by acts of patent philanthropy, and the most enlarged benevolence." He concluded his opening remarks:

> I assure myself, that having heard [the] facts ... you will feel great pleasure that it has become your duty to diminish, by one at least, a nest of vermin, who have but too long infested this metropolis, to the utter ruin of some of the first families in the kingdom.[5]

---

4. Foss, Edward. (1864) *The Judges of England: with Sketches of their Lives and Miscelaneous Notices Connected with the Courts at Westminster from the Time of the Conquest.* London, John Murray. vol. ix. pp. 87-8.
5. OBP Online. (www.oldbaileyonline.org) 14 January 1784. Ref: t17840114-80.

After presenting evidence and defending it, in his closing statement Garrow spoke to the judge about the law and recent precedents. In effect his statement was also to the jury, and he spoke in a manner that the jury would clearly understand. He describes a theoretical example and then a series of recent cases which he considers to be similar and precedent setting. In part he states:

> My Lord ...The case which we are now arguing is precisely like the case of a man who goes to Smithfield Market and chooses a horse, the owner delivers him the horse for the purpose of trying his paces, and the stranger rides away with the horse; if I was to address myself to the common understanding of any man who hears me, and was to ask in whom the possession in the horse resided, he would answer, that the actual possession ... was determined by his delivery to the stranger; but the law has said, that this possession having been acquired with a felonious intent ... such a taking is a felony.
>
> What was the case of Sharpless at this place about nine years ago? It was the fashionable trick of that day (for every period has its fashions in artifice) to go to a goldsmith's and to order a quantity of his goods to be sent home; and it was the caution of the day for the goldsmith to direct his servant not to leave the goods without the money, but on some pretence Sharpless sent back the servant and kept the goods, and the Judges held that this was felony, though it would be difficult to prove that the goldsmith had any actual possession of his goods after they were delivered by his servant to the stranger.
>
> I have had the honour of stating to your Lordships one case of horse-stealing, there is another, which has received a solemn determination of all the Judges of England within a very short time, which is conclusive of this case. A man hires a horse on pretence of taking a journey into Essex, in point of fact, he never takes such a journey but sells the horse; this has been determined to be felony. ....
>
> I shall ... conclude with stating one very recently determined, and which, if it stood alone, might serve as an answer to the objection of my friend Mr. Fielding. A man goes to a publick house and orders a pot of beer and change for a guinea to be sent to the house of Mr. Stiles, and when it is brought, he sends the servant back on some pretence, takes the change and goes off; permit me to ask whether the publican who remained in the bar of his house, had any more control over, or possession of his money, than any man who hears me; and yet your Lordships have held, and held with great wisdom, that this taking is a felony ....
>
> Mr. Silvester asks, When did the felony commence? I answer precisely at the same period of time, at which it commenced in the cases which I have had the honour of submitting to the Court; in the case of the horse-stealer, it commenced at the instant in which he put his foot into the stirrup with an intent to steal the horse; so here the felony commenced at the instant in which the prisoner got the note into his hands, with a felonious intent to convert it to his own use.[6]

Clearly Garrow had commenced his career in a manner in which he intended to continue over the succeeding years and which brought him a great deal of work, fame and wealth. The trial record shows that he revealed a clear understanding of the law of larceny, was forthright in his assault on the character of the accused and carefully drew in the jury. Whilst defence counsel were not permitted to address the jury, prosecuting counsel were, although usually only in opening their case. In

---

6. *Ibid.*

this trial, however, Garrow, went further and after all the evidence had been given, said, "My Lord, I should leave this case with the utmost pleasure to the Court, but that all arguments of this sort are addressed to the Jury, and are intended to have their operation there, it therefore becomes my duty to trouble your Lordship with a few words by way of reply." It was a new and effective oblique approach to the jury which he was to continue to use, mainly in defence, throughout his career as an advocate. Here we get a real feel, in Garrow's own words, for the electric effect he had in the context of the criminal courtroom.

On the facts of the case, and no doubt influenced by Garrow's tactics, the jury found Aikles guilty as charged and he was sentenced to death, although later he was conditionally pardoned with the sentence changed to one of transportation. Curiously, in September 1785 when Aikles was found at large in London having avoided being transported and faced the gallows again, Garrow appeared for him and used legal arguments and Aikles ill-health to secure his release.[7] It is not clear from the record whether Aikles was then entirely free or whether he was transported for his original offence with the bill of exchange.

Most of Garrow's cases in these early years were crimes of the common people, and because of the bloody code in England, many were felony crimes where a conviction carried with it a sentence of death or transportation.

AGGRESSIVE STYLE

Garrow often used aggressive and bruising cross-examination of prosecution witnesses to get at the truth. This was especially true when the witness was a thief-taker, a person attempting to prosecute an innocent defendant on trumped-up charges to get a reward from the state if the accused was convicted.

Garrow defended James Wingrove on a charge of theft with violence in the course of highway robbery.[8] If convicted Wingrove would be hanged. William Grove had charged Wingrove with the crime and gave evidence to support the charge. In cross-examining Grove with a series of hostile questions, Garrow got him to admit to a fuller explanation of events. Two other men had been robbed. Under merciless and lengthy questioning by Garrow, Grove admitted that they were smugglers and had made no claim to having been robbed by Wingrove when taken before the examining justice the morning after the robbery. It became clear to the jury that Groves had perjured himself in an attempt to get a reward. This case provides examples of Garrow's aggressive cross-examination style:

7. John Hostettler. (2006) *Fighting for Justice: The History and Origins of Adversary Trial.* Winchester, Waterside Press. p. 100.

8. OBP Online. (www.oldbaileyonline.org) 26 May 1784. Trial of James Wingrove. Ref: t17840526-117.

Garrow: Who were these two men, let us hear a little about them?

Grove: They are not here, they live at Sunbury, one is Humphries and the other Marchant.

Garrow: What business are they, are they not a sort of moonlight men?

Grove: It was not moonlight.

Garrow: Are they not a couple of smugglers?

Grove: They may be as far as I know.

Garrow: So they told you they had been robbed?

Grove: Yes.

Garrow: Did they give any charge against Mr. Wingrove?

Grove: I do not know what you mean by charges.

Garrow: I believe you do, you are pretty well used to charges; did these two smugglers of yours give any charge against this prisoner?

Grove: They are no smugglers of mine.

Garrow: They are friends of yours?

Grove: They are no friends of mine.

Garrow: They, these two fellows, did they make any charge against Mr. Wingrove for robbing them?

Grove: Yes, they did make a charge.

Garrow: Do not shuffle, Master Grove.

Grove: I do not know what you say.

Garrow: I will make you know directly; upon your oath, did not these two men attend the next day at Mr. Taylor's and say that Mr. Wingrove was not one of the men who robbed them?

Grove: He is the man that robbed me, I will tell you the truth, he was the man that robbed me, I did not hear them say that he was not the man.

Garrow: That they swore?

Grove: Yes.

Garrow: Was he committed for robbing them?

Grove: No, he was committed for robbing me.

Garrow: Who were the two men that robbed you a little while ago?

Grove: I never was robbed before.

Garrow: No, Mr Grove!

Grove: Yes, I have been robbed, but I do not know who they were, and pilfered and too much robbed.

Garrow: I will put it now most unequivocally to you, and ask you upon your oath, whether you have never said to Mr James Clarke by name, that you had been robbed some time since by two men, whom you have not prosecuted, who lived at Brentford; that they were good friends, and that if you called on them at any time, you could have a guinea of them?

Grove: No, never in my life; no, no, they mistook, they came to me and wanted me not

At this point Grove was interrupted and in the end he capitulated and admitted that the two men had not made a charge. Eventually, Garrow came to the question of the statutory reward for the conviction of a highwayman, and Groves' identification of Wingrove as the man who had robbed him.

Garrow: You know it is not every day that one gets forty pounds for hanging a man; had you no conversation at "The Cock" at Staines about the reward for conviction?

Grove: You ask a hundred questions, I will answer you what I know; no, not about no reward, I have been there, and there they have been asking me about it, that is, we drank together, and I said to him, as I might say to you, I do not know anything about it. I did not say any such thing. I never said anything about any reward, that I can say. I have said nothing about no reward.

As Garrow could not address the jury, Wingrove (unusually when counsel was appearing) made his own defence and, more normally, called a number of witnesses to speak of his good character.

The jury found him not guilty and Garrow applied to have Grove committed for perjury. He suggested that he would prosecute him at his own expense but Wingrove would not bring such a charge. It is almost certain that the Groves' (father and son) prosecuted Wingrove to obtain the reward; indeed the judge told them that they had rashly charged a man where there was a reward. Not surprisingly, when thief-takers prosecuted maliciously for this purpose Garrow always cross-examined them at length and with vigour to reveal their true natures to the jury.

Alongside so-called thief-takers seeking blood money, however, were true thief-takers whom Garrow treated with more respect. These were the Bow Street Runners who, as peace officers, served the stipendiary magistrates at Bow Street, Sir Henry Fielding, novelist and reforming JP, and his blind brother Sir John Fielding, known as the "Blind Beak of Bow Street." These officers were the real thief-takers and were not regarded by Garrow with the same contempt as the disreputable kind.[9] In fact, by 1815 they comprised 70 plain-clothed foot runners and a uniformed horse patrol called "Robin Redbreasts" or "Raw Lobsters" because of their scarlet waistcoats. Despite these nicknames they had a real effect and showed that control of street crime was possible.

EXPOSING THIEF-TAKERS

A series of cases will be presented in which Garrow challenges both professional and first time thief-takers and makes sure that the juries are fully aware of the possibility of perjury. In the first case, Garrow defended three men, William Eversall, William Roberts and Joseph Barney who were charged with violent theft and highway robbery.[10] Specifically they were charged with assaulting John Troughton and putting him in corporeal fear and danger of his life. And they stole his hat. The issue was, did the scuffle in which Troughton lost his hat also put *him* in corporeal fear and danger of *his* life? Or was Troughton enhancing the danger he experienced to get a reward? If it were simple robbery he would get no reward. On the other hand, if the struggle could be established as violent theft, a conviction would produce a reward.

John Troughton, the person assaulted, was the prosecutor, and gave evidence of what happened. He described it in these words: "I met the three prisoners in a narrow alley,… they collected themselves into a body about two or three yards before me, and … one of them, I believe Barney, had something in his hand, which he threw into my eyes." Asked what it was, he stated "Snuff or tobacco dust … they said afterwards at the watch-house it was tobacco dust"… He said, "I took hold of one on them." … "We struggled till we got into Golden-lane, then they all surrounded me, and I received some blows about my face and head; I defended myself as well as I could; one of the blows drove me against the public-house, I staggered against the wall, I did not fall down; and in that position one of them took off my hat and wig; I picked up my wig, I suppose it fell out of my hat, and my hat was gone almost instantly; I call (the) watch, and stop thief, seeing they took different ways.….. he was never out of my sight … I took hold of him, and after some little struggle I brought him back with me; by the alarm of the watchman's-rattle, a

---

9. See J.M. Beattie. (2007) "Garrow and the Detectives: lawyers and policemen at the Old Bailey in the late eighteenth century." 11(2) *Crime, History and Societies.* Geneva, Switzerland, pp. 5-24.
10. OBP Online. (www.oldbaileyonline.org) 7 May 1788. Ref: t17880507-3.

gentleman had stopped Roberts, and a watchman had taken Eversall." Asked if he ever got his hat again, he answered "yes".

In Garrow's cross-examination of John Troughton, the following exchange took place:

Garrow: This was a dark alley; the first thing before you observed the men was something was thrown in your eyes?

Troughton: Yes

Garrow: How is it that you with tobacco dust in your eyes, in a dark alley, knew these people?

Troughton: When I came to the bottom of the alley after the struggle, they all came around me; there was a lamp over my head; Barney and Roberts attacked me in front.

Garrow: You have cleared your eyes of the tobacco dust; and the thief-takers have thrown some gold dust in your eyes?

Troughton: There is no thief-takers in the business.

Garrow: You know there is a reward of three forty pounds, if the prisoners are convicted?

Troughton: To be sure, I know that, but I don't come here on that account.

Garrow: Did not you say before the Justice that you did not know whether your hat fell off in the struggle, or was taken off?

Troughton: I don't know that I did.

Garrow: Upon your oath, did not you tell the Justice, that you did not know whether it fell off, or was taken off?

Troughton: I cannot tell, I don't know that I did, I might say so.

Garrow: Who told you, if you should swear so here, these men could not be convicted so as to get the reward?

Troughton: Nobody.

The cross-examination continued as Garrow tried to establish that Troughton was uncertain how he lost his hat while Troughton attempted to establish it was knocked off. The hat was found on one of the prisoners. Garrow called four witnesses to give good character evidence, and the jury found all three prisoners not guilty.

This very brief trial gives a glimpse into criminal trials of that period, and the emerging role of the defence counsel in that scene. Stealing a hat could be a capital offence if the accosted person could successfully claim he felt his life threatened. A government award of 40 pounds a head for a conviction - a very large sum for the common people of London - was a powerful incentive to try to make that case. Evidence given by someone labelled a "thief-taker" was considered by most juries with suspicion. And in addition, juries were reluctant to give a guilty verdict when the crime was trivial and the punishment death or transportation. In these cases juries were looking for opportunities to give "not guilty" verdicts, and Garrow was skilled in creating uncertainty.

In another case, John King was charged at the Old Bailey on 24 April 1790 with violent theft and robbery.[11] This case demonstrates how trials, even those where the death penalty was at play, often took only a few minutes. Garrow's defence of his client could be achieved with a few carefully constructed questions or observations during the cross-examination of a witness. King was indicted for feloniously making an assault on John Myers, putting him in fear, and feloniously taking from him, against his will, five guineas, three half guineas two half crown pieces and a shilling, and a piece of a watch. In the trial it was quickly established that Myers was unaware that his pocket had been picked until a few moments after the event. And King, was very much indisposed at the time of his arrest. Garrow, in his examination of Myers made this as clear as day.

The next witness was George Allen, the constable who was on the spot at the time and arrested John King. George Allen makes a statement:

> I know the prisoner very well; I saw him and Mr. Myers together.... Mr. Myers was in the crowd; the prisoner was behind him; there was a great crowd and a pushing; just as he came to the end of the passage, where it was wider, Mr. Myers said, God bless me! I have lost my money, I am robbed; as soon as he said so, I said this is the man that robbed you; I saw him pushing up behind him in the crowd; and being the nearest to him, I caught hold of the prisoner.

At this point Garrow started his cross-examination:

Garrow: What way of life are you in?

Allan: I am constable.

Garrow: We see you very frequently every where?

Allan: Very frequently ....

Garrow: I take it for granted, this is under your advice, that this is laid to be a highway robbery? ....

---

11. OBP Online. (www.oldbaileyonline.org) 24 April 1790. Ref: t17900424-16.

Garrow: You know it makes the difference of forty pounds, that you are to have your share? ... Do you understand that?

Allan: Yes.

Garrow: Was it a loose great coat?

Allan: Yes, and a right hand outside pocket.

Garrow: Now I am going to ask you a question: Do not you know that it frequently has happened, both at the theatre and other public places, that after an alarm has been given, the thief very often puts the money into an honest man's pocket?

Allan: I do not know it.

The prisoner called two witnesses to his character, and the jury found him not guilty.

With this case, Garrow quickly and clearly established the probability that the professional thief-taker had orchestrated a situation in which the man's pocket was robbed, the contents slipped into the pocket of another person, who was immediately apprehended, and charged with the crime of robbery, or violent theft. By capturing the alleged robber, and then giving damming evidence in the trial, he would clearly be entitled to the forty pounds if the prisoner were found guilty. In these quick-paced trials, Garrow, with only a few words, made the situation crystal clear, and the jury understood the game of the thief-takers. This defence counsel support was viewed as a new source of help for the accused facing felony charges.

Another trial illustrates Garrow's aggressive style of defence, especially if those bringing the charge could be viewed as thief-takers. This was the trial of Robert Mitchell for highway robbery.[12] The prosecutor was a Simon Sheppard from whom in cross-examination Garrow obtained an admission that twice before he had prosecuted for robbery, and had secured a conviction in one of the cases. In this present trial Sheppard claimed Mitchell and two others had attacked him with a knife and stolen money from him. Garrow rose to establish the defence by cross-examination:

Garrow: Here my old friend, a word with you; so they beat you for half an hour?

Sheppard: They beat me like a dog.

Garrow: Was it with a knife that they beat you?

---

12. OBP Online. (www.oldbaileyonline.org) 8 December 1784. Trial of Robert Mitchell. Ref: t17841208-181.

Sheppard: No, with their fists, and kicked me with his foot, he knocked out my teeth with the toe of his shoe; one tooth, Sir.

Garrow: What sort of knife had he?

Sheppard: A long snig-a-snee knife, a spring knife.

Garrow: He took it out deliberately, and opened it before all the people?

Sheppard: Not before all the people, but before the people in the yard.

Garrow: How often have you had the misfortune to be robbed in your life?

Sheppard: Four or five times.

Garrow: So I thought: how often have you been a witness here of robberies on your own person?

Sheppard: Two times.

Garrow: How many of the people you have prosecuted have died in Newgate?

Sheppard: Only one.

Garrow: Upon an average, how many prosecutions had you in the course of the last two years?

Sheppard: One before this.

Garrow: They have been both within the year?

Sheppard: Yes.

Garrow: Did you convict the last man?

Sheppard: Yes.

Garrow: What did you get for it?

Sheppard: I cannot tell, I got nothing at all.

Garrow: Upon your oath, Sir, what did you get, do not you remember what was added to the stock of sixty you had before?

Sheppard: Please you, my Lord, only my expenses.

Garrow: Do you mean to swear you had no more allowed you but your expenses?

Sheppard: Lucas is dead.

Garrow: Then you will not get above forty if you convict now, my old friend, you will not get eighty this time?

Sheppard: No

Garrow's withering attacks on the prosecutor achieved what he wanted, namely to influence the jury which speedily found the prisoner not guilty.

JURY NULLIFICATION AND PIOUS PERJURY

Garrow's aggressive style of cross-examination could uncover circumstantial information that motivated juries to bend the rules and reduce the severity of punishment. This is called "nullification and pious perjury". Nullification occurs where a jury act according to their consciences or where they appear to nullify the law or the evidence in a case. Pious perjury was where the jury reduced the value of goods stolen, sometimes substantially, in order to circumvent the death penalty when it was considered to be too harsh a punishment and out of proportion to the offence.

One such case of the latter occurred in 1784 when Garrow defended Elizabeth Jones and Mary Smith on charges of shoplifting goods valued at 14 shillings.[13] A witness named Lewis who helped to apprehend the two women swore that when arrested they begged for mercy. Garrow cross-examined him.

Garrow: I believe you have some reason to know some of the rules of evidence?

Lewis: Why, Sir?

Garrow: I believe you have been here pretty often in the character of prosecutor and witness?

Lewis: Frequently, and if I have an opportunity I may appear against more; but I never came without a safe conscience to this Court.

Garrow: You have a good deal of leisure time on your hands I take it for granted?

Lewis: I could perhaps fill up my time sometimes better than I do.

Garrow: Answer my question, Sir, you have heard it?

Lewis: I have sometimes leisure time upon my hands.

Garrow: It so happened you had a good deal of leisure at this time?

Lewis: I was attending these women in my shop the day before.

Garrow: Now you have told us, that when they [the prisoners] were carried back to Mr. Gray's shop, they put their hands together and asked for mercy and acknowledged the fact; I wish you to state the very expression?

Lewis: They wrung their hands, and hoped for mercy.

---

13. OBP Online. (www.oldbaileyonline.org) 15 September 1784. Ref: t17840915-68.

Garrow: Was that all they said?

Lewis: I cannot recollect every word.

Garrow: Then that is what you meant when you said they acknowledged the fact?

Lewis: I consider that as an acknowledgment.

Garrow: Then when you told my Lord, that these women had acknowledged the fact, you meant to refer to their having said that they desired mercy?

Lewis: They begged for mercy.

Garrow: That is what you call acknowledging the fact, Sir, is it? That is a little extraordinary.

There was too much evidence against them for the prisoners to be acquitted but by his cross-examination Garrow gave the jury an opportunity to indulge their inclinations by giving a partial verdict and they found them guilty of stealing fans worth 4s. 10d. By putting the value of the stolen fans below five shillings the jury, in a fine example of "pious perjury" avoided the women being sent to the gallows and they were each sentenced to be privately whipped and confined to hard labour for twelve months in a House of Correction. When capital punishment existed for many property crimes juries would frequently reduce the charge and thus lessen the sentence, often from death to transportation or, as in this case, to whipping and imprisonment. The term "pious perjury" was coined by Sir William Blackstone who wrote that "the mercy of juries often made them strain a point, and bring in larceny to be under the value of twelve pence, when it was really of much greater value … a kind of *pious perjury.*"[14]

DISPUTES WITH THE BENCH

Garrow was prepared to do battle with the judges on the court bench as he pressed forward the role of counsel for the defence of his client. In the case of William Bartlett, charged with theft on 11 January 1786,[15] he objected to a prosecution witness, John Rasten, being sworn. He argued that as he was deaf and dumb he

---

14. Sir. W Blackstone. (1830) *Commentaries on the Law of England.* London, Thomas Tegg. vol. vi. p. 248.

15. OBP Online. (www.oldbaileyonline.org) 11 January 1786. Trial of William Bartlett. Ref: t1786111-30. The exchange between Garrow and the judge is not reported fully in this Old Bailey Proceeding but is quited by Beattie from the Sessions Papers held at Harvard University at pp. 247-8. Beattie. "Scales of Justice" *Op. cit.* pp. 264-5. Note 66. Beattie claims that the absence of this material is a reminder of how limited the Old Bailey Papers are as a source for the history of trial. However, there is supplemental material in the Old Bailey Proceedings under ref: t17860111-1 which Beattie does not mention. It includes the whole altercation between Garrow and the judge as well as Garrow's motion to the judge.

could testify only through an interpreter, his wife, to whom Garrow also objected. Mrs Rasten claimed to be a satisfactory interpreter because, she said, she would look up to heaven to show her husband that he should answer seriously. The dispute between counsel and Mr Justice Heath then arose.

Garrow quoted from Sir Matthew Hale that a deaf mute was presumed to be an idiot and could not communicate with the court. The judge said he remembered a deaf and dumb man being sworn in the court of common pleas and he accepted that sign language was sufficient, although Garrow continued to disagree. This led to the following exchange:

Heath: You must not interrupt; your objection is premature.

Garrow: My Lord I was not objecting. I was going on with my Examination and your Lordship did me the honour to interrupt me.

Heath: You will examine your Witness with some degree of decency. Your conduct and behaviour are very improper. What you do here is by permission of the Court in a criminal case.

Garrow: My Lord, I object to the Witness being examined and I take the liberty to state my objection to the Court.

Heath: You must examine your Witness.

Garrow: I have a right to my Objection.

Heath: If you do not examine your Witness you shall sit down.

Garrow: My Lord, I shall not sit down.

Heath: Then I shall commit you.

Garrow: So your Lordship may.

Heath: Then I certainly will commit you.

Garrow: There is a point of Law to be argued.

Heath: There is no point of Law and if there was you are to be Assigned to the Court but you are to behave with Decency.

Garrow: So I do my Lord. I have not been used to be interrupted. I am here to argue points of Law for the prisoner.

Heath: You have no right until you are Assigned.[16]

---

16. Prior to the Prisoners' Counsel Act, 1836, defence counsel were not instructed by the prisoner to argue points of law but were assigned by the court to do so, even if not requested by the prisoner. The point of law could be raised by the prisoner, the judge or any barrister present in court. D.J.A. Cairns. (1998) *Advocacy and the Making of the Adversarial Criminal Trial 1800-1865*. Oxford, Clarendon Press. pp. 46-7.

Garrow: If you tell me so my Lord, I sit down.

Heath: I tell you so.

Garrow: I sit down.

Later, Garrow asked Mrs Rasten, "Suppose you was to tell him [her brother] that Mr Lamardi had arisen into the Air in a Balloon, how sho'd you communicate that idea? Her reply was, "Oh very well" which seemed sufficiently to prove Garrow's point. Ultimately, Garrow made a long speech to the judge in the hearing of the jury. He pointed out that even if the witness and the interpreter could converse that did not prove the witness was capable of understanding complex ideas, particularly the principles of the Christian religion that underlay the binding power of the oath. He then added, "My Lord, I wish I could also address the jury on this trial. I should be glad to ask them whether they should choose to convict a man of felony upon the testimony of a man with whom they could not hold a conversation". Bearing in mind the presence of the jury, he concluded with an apology for what might have been considered his earlier "intemperance or indecency", adding that by his zeal on behalf of his client he had intended no disrespect to the "great and brave and venerable and learned judges of the law of England". In the event, on the evidence of the witness, Bartlett was convicted and transported for seven years.

Although in this trial, Bartlett was convicted, Garrow was allowed to give him aggressive though limited assistance. By this time lawyers were well on the way to capturing the courtroom and the process could not be reversed. In the words of Langbein:

> The judges of the 1730s who turned common law criminal procedure down this path had no way of knowing that defence counsel would overcome the limitations that the judges placed upon him, indeed, that defence counsel would recast the dynamic of the criminal trial so fundamentally that the judges would ultimately cede mastery of the criminal trial to counsel.[17]

And, not only did defence counsel recast the dynamic of the criminal trial, but in doing so they also had a positive impact not just on the outcome for prisoners but also upon their broader rights.

NEWSWORTHY TRIALS

One newsworthy trial concerned the case of Mrs. Weltjie accusing Betty Callaway of assault.[18] The *Public Advertiser* reported the case tried on 29 October 1792 in which

---

17. J.H. Langbein. *The Origins of Adversary Criminal Trial. Op. cit.* p. 177.
18. Lucy Werkmeister. (1963) *The London daily press 1772-1792*. Lincoln, University of Nebraska Press. pp. 128-9.

Garrow represented Mrs. Weltjie against her husband's "servant," Betty Callaway, accusing her of assault. What makes this case interesting now and at the time it was prosecuted was that Mr. Weltjie was a personal associate of the Prince of Wales. The Prince's association with Mr. Weltjie, as previously depicted in the press, had already been the subject of criticism and embarrassment to him. Now the Prince would be subjected to ridicule again. In taking the case, Garrow dramatized the quality of the domestic life of the Prince's friend:

> .... the plaintiff, Amelia Louisa Weltjie, who described herself as the wife of 'Mr. Weltjie, a person who some time since held a lucrative situation under ... the Prince of Wales,' accusing Betty Callaway, 'Mr. Weltjie's servant,' of assault. William Garrow, who represented Mrs. Weltjie, charged that for years she had been 'ill-treated by her husband,' frequently 'turned out of doors by him and otherwise been treated with brutality,' but the situation had worsened during the summer, he said, when, although she was very ill, her husband would not permit the servants to care for her or even to change her bed linen.

On 2 July she had risen and, waiting until the kitchen was clear, had stolen some clean sheets from the laundry; but, as she was returning to her room, she was viciously attacked by Miss Callaway. When she complained to her husband, he defended the servant, stating that she had acted on his instructions, and refused to dismiss her. Mrs. Weltjie thereupon took her to a magistrate, but Weltjie followed, provided bail, and escorted the servant back home.

> 'Happy' said Garrow in conclusion, Weltjie was not 'an Englishman,' but only 'an arrogant purse-proud foreigner, who had got rich in the service of the most illustrious subject of the country.'

The jury found Miss Callaway guilty, and she was sentenced to two months imprisonment. There was no fine because, said the magistrate, Weltjie was so "gallant" that he would have paid it for her.

Another case that created public interest then and now is:

Baron Hompesch v. the Farmer and his Dog

This case illustrates how the landed gentry and gentlemen were especially threatened by Garrow's courtroom tactics, which they experienced as a threat to their honour. Baron Hompesch became so angry at Garrow because of his courtroom style that he challenged him to a duel.

Baron Hompesch was a Swiss nobleman and an officer in the British army. He had rented an estate in Kent and charged his neighbour, farmer Sherwood, with hunting game on his land with a dog. This was a violation of the game laws. Garrow defended farmer Sherwood, and in his defence he brought in the farmer's dog to establish that it was merely a sheep dog. In doing so he made fun of the Baron, stating that his cause was supported by two witnesses, the Baron and the dog, "of which the last was certainly an honest witness." John Beattie was the first to reintroduce this story to modern readers, and noted that Garrow did not accept the challenge of a duel but, "merely sheltered himself under the shield of the law".[19] Beattie also noted that the Baron then wrote a letter to the Prince of Wales denouncing Garrow and stating that Garrow was, "henceforward unfit to be received in company of gentlemen".

An account of this case was published by Thomas Hague in 1808 in a letter widely circulated in London at the time. Because the purpose of Thomas Hague's letter was to criticize vehemently Garrow's behaviour in the courtroom, a different view of the case is presented. Hague's description of the case is quoted in detail since it gives an in depth account of Garrow's courtroom behaviour, and how Garrow was treated by the press:

The witness called to prove the fact was Baron Hompesch. The Baron stated, that the defendant used the lands of a Mr. Chambers, who was then a prisoner at Verdun, and whose manor he (the Baron) rented. He saw Sherwood (the defendant) on the 6th of February last, in a small cover near Sittingbourne, with a gun on his shoulder, and a dog following; the dog was between a setter and a sheep dog. He said to him, Farmer Sherwood, you have been beating the cover. He replied, What if he had? The Baron answered, Who gave you leave? He replied, he had taken leave and what was it to the Baron? The Baron answered, it would appear hereafter what he had to do with it.

> Upon cross-examination the Baron said, he should know the dog again if he saw it; it was something like a sheep dog, but Farmer Sherwood had told him it was one of the best dogs in the county for an hare, and he had been offered a great deal of money for it. He admitted, that formerly he and the defendant were upon good terms; that the defendant came to him, and drank some times with him; and they played sixpenny whist together, at the Baron's house, until one evening the defendant's wife came, and gave him a good trimming; she boxed her husband's ears, and made him immediately go home.

A few days afterwards, the Baron admitted, he sent the defendant a small present, consisting of a little wine to refresh his spirits after the beating his wife gave him, and a very neat ornamented horsewhip with ribbands, which he recommended as a good alternative medicine for his wife. He, however denied, that he had written any libel on the defendant, or had behaved with indecency to any lady, which was the subject of the present complaint; but Mr. Garrow assured him, he should hear something of the kind before the assizes were over. The dog was then produced in court, which the Baron admitted to be his old acquaintance, as an evidence to prove that he was no lurcher.

---

19. J.M. Beattie. (1991) "Garrow for the Defence". *History Today*. History Today Ltd., p. 53.

Mr. Garrow, for the defendant, made a most animated address to the Jury. He said, the cause had been supported by two witnesses, the Baron and his dog, of which the last certainly was an honest witness; and with respect to the former, as he called himself, "*His Excellency the Baron Hompesch*," he supposed he had a just and legal claim to the title, but he insisted, the jury ought not to convict the defendant on his evidence, because it was most clear there were other motives in his mind than the mere desire of enforcing the law.

He adverted with great force to the virtues which ought to adorn high rank and fortune; and dwelt with energy on the conduct of his *Excellency* the Baron, in sending a horsewhip to a man for the purpose of chastising his wife; if he had himself received a good drubbing from the strong arm of the Kentish farmer, he would have had his deserts.

He said, that there was no evidence whatever, that the defendant used his gun for the destruction of game; at these times every man ought to have his gun; and as well might you convict a professed duelist of a design to commit a footpad robbery, because he had a brace of hair-trigger pistols in his pocket. "[And he] made assertions which were likely to make the Baron an object of some suspicion and contempt in his neighbourhood as a foreigner."[20]

The letter Hompesch sent to the Prince of Wales is contained in *The Correspondence of George, Prince of Wales 1770-1812*, edited by Aspinall (1971). The spelling is as Hompesch wrote it.

Battersea Fields, 30 Aug. 1807

After the so unworthy, thorough ungentlemanlike conduct of Mr. Garrow, every forbearance, even the offer of submitting the case to referrees having vainly been held out to him, I feel myself compell'd officialy to denounce to the First Gentleman of the land that Mr. Garrow (after grossly insulting a British General Officer in public court) was there branded with the appellation of an infamous lyar, and publicly and tamely having received the lie, cowardly shrunk from a manly satisfaction and swearing the peace, meanly sheltered himself under the shield of the law; that in consequence allready members of the military corps waited on their Colonel to have Mr. Garrow expelld, but he had previously quitted the corps; that as a paltry lyar, coward and poltroon he is deemed henceforward unfit to be received in company of gentlemen or men of honor ever to associate with him.[21]

This was not a trivial trial about trespassing. It was about the charge of violating the game laws, going onto the estate of the landed gentry to shoot rabbits or birds...an offence which often called for penalties that today would seem sadistically severe.

---

20. T. Hague. (1808) *A Letter to William Garrow, Esq. In which the Conduct of Counsel in the Cross-Examination of Witnesses, and Commenting on their Testimony, is fully discussed, and the Licentiousness of the Bar Exposaed.* London, R. MacDonald. pp. 11-21.
21. A.Aspinall. (1971) *The Correspondence of George, Prince of Wales 1770-1812*, vol. v. 1804-1806. New York, Oxford University Press. pp. 207-8.

Mrs. Day's Baby

Another trial that captured the attention of the public was "The Case to Determine if Mrs. Day is the Baby's Legitimate Mother."[22] During the summer assizes in the County of Huntingdon in 1798-1799 there was a case which was described in *Public Characters* under the title "Mr. Garrow." In addition to the drama of this case, the author describes what Garrow had achieved in reputation during the early phase of his career.

The cause was tried before Mr. Justice Heath concerning the legitimacy of the gentleman of the name of Day. What appeared in the case was that Mrs. Day, being a Staffordshire woman, and advanced in pregnancy, left her husband's residence, at Kimbolton in Huntingdonshire, to lie in with her relations in Staffordshire. It appeared that Mrs. Day either miscarried or lost the child upon whom an estate of five or six hundred pounds per annum was settled. It was being charged that Mrs. Day, needing a substitute infant, returned to her husband in the beginning of March with a child she claimed was her own. Many years then passed before the issue of Mr. Day's legitimacy was challenged in court.

There is no doubt that it was the intention of Mrs. Day to return to her husband with *a child* and it appeared that she had actually applied to different persons, and particularly to the workhouse at Wolverhampton, for one. Garrow's task was to cross-examine the woman who supposedly sold a child to Mrs. Day, and who now claimed that the child she sold was the same person now called Mr. Day whose legitimacy was in question.

The adroitness with which Garrow cross-examined this woman left no doubt that the child Mrs. Day carried home was a substitute, but that the woman who claimed to have sold the child to Mrs. Day had given false testimony. The age of her child did not match the age of the child Mrs. Day presented to her husband. The jury, however, gave their verdict in favour of the legitimacy of the heir on other grounds.

Mrs. Day certainly had a child, as she herself suckled the child with which she returned to her husband; but it happened that many witnesses who would have had critical information had subsequently died. This included the mother and the persons who had attended her lying-in, so that no positive proof could be obtained of the delivery, and the whole of the case rested upon the conversation held by the neighbours among themselves and with the mother at her return, together with the acknowledgment of the child by the father.

This case filled the whole country with gossip and attracted a crowd in the court of a size seldom witnessed. The ingenuity Garrow employed to show that, even supposing the child with which Mrs. Day returned to her husband - which he, *"good, easy man"*, believed to be his own - was in fact a substitute, yet it was not

---

22. See *Appendix 3* to this work, *Public Characters*.

possible that it could be the same child sworn to by the woman. That child would have been fifteen weeks old, whereas the child that was brought back by Mrs. Day, and alleged to be hers, was only five weeks old when she returned to her husband in Huntingdonshire. So that child could not possibly be the witness's child.

The author of this account then states:

> The difficulty with which Mr. Garrow established these facts, and the great art with which he, extracted them from a woman who was so well trained and prepared in her story, afforded to a young barrister the finest lesson of cross-examination. No scene in any dramatic author was ever more interesting than the one, which we have now described, appeared to all that saw it.
>
> The court was in a dead silence during the examination, which lasted about three hours; Mr. Garrow's eyes were scarcely once off the witness; they seemed to penetrate into her very soul, and lay open the inmost workings of her mind. She was as collected as himself for some time, but her firmness at length gave way; he broke in at last upon the truth of the story, and, finally, made her so palpably confute herself, that his victory was complete.

In this account the author continued to discuss Garrow's place in the way law was being practiced in his contemporary England.

> This was the greatest triumph, in our recollection, of Mr. Garrow's talent of cross-examination; and independent of the peculiarity of the story, we have related it in order to impress upon the gentlemen of the law the importance of cultivating an art, which, in matters not only of life and death, but where great masses of property are concerned, is able to effect so much.

These trial records of this early period in Garrow's long legal career show the qualities that he was known for in his day, and remembered for immediately after his death. It is this early period that is of interest to the scholars of the development of common law. However, to understand the man who is being credited with significant contributions to the emergence of the adversary trial, other aspects of his long life will hold some interest.

CHAPTER 5

Adversary Trial and Human Rights

Apart from the example given by the Treason Trials Act of 1696, three factors are generally put forward to explain the entry of defence lawyers in criminal trials in the eighteenth century. The first is the creation of a rewards culture for bounty hunters. This commenced with a statute in 1692[1] which provided for a bounty of as much as £40 a head for thief-takers and was aimed at the capture and conviction of highwaymen in particular.

PRESSURES FOR DEFENCE LAWYERS IN CRIMINAL TRIALS

The Act of 1692 providing for bounties was followed by three others which extended the bounty provisions. Furthermore, there was a perceived increase in criminal activity which gave rise across the country to Associations for the Prosecution of Felons which not only paid the expenses of criminal investigation and prosecution for victim members but also offered rewards for information.[2]

Such rewards by these associations and the government, whereby conviction of a highway robber could be worth £140 to a thief-taker, rising in multiples where there were co-accused,[3] were a free-market "solution" to rising crime and proved to be a potent inducement to perjury and false prosecutions. For example, in 1732 a John Waller, was convicted at the Old Bailey of a misdemeanour in attempting to prosecute a person falsely for a highway robbery in order to collect the reward. Evidence was adduced that Waller had succeeded in bringing such prosecutions in other counties. He was convicted and sentenced to be pilloried. When he was exposed in the pillory at the Seven Dials (today's Cambridge Circus in London), Edward Dalton, the brother of one of his victims set upon him and beat him to death.[4]

Indeed, solicitors, who often managed the prosecution associations, arranged not only the investigations of crimes but also controlled the prosecutions themselves and sometimes attempted to bribe jurors.[5] Moreover, prosecution counsel "began to appear in a small number of cases, especially murder trials, in the second and third decades of the eighteenth century, followed by a more substantial increase in numbers" in later years.[6]

---

1. 4 & 5 W. & M. c. 8. s. 2.
2. J.H. Langbein. (2003) *The Origins of Adversary Criminal Trial.* Oxford, Oxford University Press.. p. 133.
3. J. N. Beattie. (1986) *Crime and Courts in England 1660-1800.* Oxford, The Clarendon Press. pp. 50-9.
4. J. 18 Geo. III, c. 19. Ss. 7-9. J.H. Langbein. *The Origins of Adversary Criminal Trial. Op. cit.* p. 152.
5. Langbein. *Ibid.* pp. 136-40.
6. D. J.A. Cairns. (1998) *Advocacy and the Making of the Adversarial Criminal Trial 1800-1865.* Oxford, The

Langbein, supported by David Lemmings,[7] has concluded that together the use of prosecution counsel at trial, the reward system and the Crown witness system of using accomplice evidence, all prompted the judges to allow counsel to assist the felony defendant.[8] But this unqualified view is not accepted by other academics and should not obscure the vital function played by the lawyers in the change to adversary trial.

A second factor, put forward by Landsman, as leading to the introduction of defence lawyers in trials for felony, was the conduct of campaigns through the criminal courts by political reform movements such as those of John Wilkes in the mid-eighteenth century and the anti-slavery campaigners at the end of that century.[9] The people involved in these movements were keen to engage defence counsel,[10] and the latter were sometimes happy to act for political reasons.

It is also likely, however, that a hope of high income and fame were at least contributing factors. With Garrow, for example, although criminal work was not generally as well paid as civil work his practice, and no doubt his income from it, were extraordinary. One has only to look at the fee of 200 guineas he was believed to have received for one case in 1800 when fees were generally two or three guineas for a brief.[11]

Garrow was certainly a Whig in the early years of his career (he joined the Whig Club on 26 June 1784). However, his actions in the House of Commons suggest that he was not motivated by concerns for an overhaul of the legal code. Indeed, as far as criminal law is concerned it was otherwise. In the House of Commons, he opposed Romilly's proposed reforms of the outdated and harsh criminal law in strong terms. He believed that discretion in punishment was sufficient and safe with the jury, the judiciary and the Crown and claimed that in thirty years experience of the criminal law he had not met with six instances in which he would have differed from the jury's verdict.[12] He also declared that, "[t]he severity of the law was not too much for some cases; for the utmost rigour was sometimes called for out of mercy to society."[13] It is significant that when offered a position as a law officer he immediately changed his political allegiance and on behalf of Pitt's government prosecuted law and constitution reformers for sedition. Prior to that, however, his concern, not

Clarendon Press. p. 29.

7. D. Lemmings. (April 2005) 'Criminal Trial Procedure in Eighteenth-Century England: The Impact of Lawyers.' 26(1) *The Journal of Legal History*. London, Routledge. pp. 65-9.

8. J.H. Langbein. *The Origins of Adversary Criminal Trial. Op. cit.* p. 4.

9. S. Landsman. (1990) 'The Rise of the Contentious Spirit: Adversary Procedure in Eighteenth Century England.' New York, 75 *Cornell Law Review*. p. 583.

10. *Ibid.* p. 581.

11. A.N May. (2003) *The Bar and the Old Bailey 1750-1850*. Chapel Hill, University of North Carolina Press, p. 84.

12. *Hansard.* [24] cols. 567-72.

13. *Ibid.* (February 1813) col. 571.

only for his fees, but also for his clients' rights and liberty were at the forefront in his professional career at the Bar.

The third reason put forward for the entry of defence lawyers into criminal trials is the creation of rules of evidence. However, since it was the presence of lawyers in trials that enabled them to advance rules of evidence, that is putting the cart before the horse. It was after the birth of adversariality that the "best evidence" rule, the rule against hearsay and other rules of evidence grew at the insistence of Garrow and other defence counsel so that by the middle of the nineteenth century books dealing with exclusionary and adversary rules existed in some numbers.

Significantly, Landsman sees the growth of rules of evidence as being used as a tool by Old Bailey lawyers in their efforts to control the litigation process and take over the criminal courts,[14] This is contrary to Langbein's view that the judges created the law of criminal evidence without being prompted, although even he accepts that, despite his considering that it was a judicial creation, "it played into the hands of the lawyers, by opening to oversight and demand of counsel matters of trial conduct that had previously been the preserve of judge and jury."[15]

Other impulses, says Landsman significantly, included "the rise of dynamic individualism and the growth of a market economy."[16] He concludes that "[t]he adversary system with its emphasis on the action of individual litigants was well suited to the economic and social needs of such a time."[17] It should also be added that, together with the rule of law, it is sometimes an important factor in securing the proper functioning of the market economy.

RIGHTS OF THE INDIVIDUAL

Although the "no counsel" rule was still in force in the late seventeenth century, by this time change was in the air. Although the larger picture was to a great extent unremarked to contemporaries, technology was beginning to transform the agricultural and industrial fabric of the country alongside the final ending of the "divine right" of monarchy and the enactment of the Bill of Rights following the Glorious Revolution. Institutions and fundamental aspects of social structure that had been taken for granted were found to be artificial and amenable to change. The American and French Revolutions, together with the Enlightenment, set in motion a whole range of new forces and ideas in politics and economics[18] and elicited a new aware-

---

14. S. Landsman. (1990) `The Rise of the Contentious Spirit: Adversary Procedure in Eighteenth Century England.' *Op. cit.* p. 564.
15. J.H. Langbein. *The Origins of Adversary Criminal Trial. Op. cit.* p. 5.
16. S. Landsman. `The Rise of the Contentious Spirit: Adversary Procedure in Eighteenth Century England.' *Op. cit.* p. 602.
17. *Ibid.* note 548.
18. E.J. Hobsbawm. (1962) *The Age of Revolution: Europe 1789-1848.* London, Weidenfeld & Nicolson.

ness of the rights of the individual against the state.

England was changing rapidly and, in a sense, the political events that gave rise to the Glorious Revolution in opposition to royal and aristocratic power acted as a midwife in bringing into the world a new philosophy stressing the importance of the individual in society. And people themselves demanded the right to a fair trial and a presumption of innocence.[19]

But there were other fundamental and far-reaching adjustments also taking place that would alter the cultural face of society world-wide. In particular, the Industrial Revolution, the growth of the market, the Enlightenment and the American and French Revolutions, with their *Declarations of Rights,* each evoked powerful responses in bringing to light the importance of individual human rights. In such circumstances adversariality, alongside the criminal jury, became a crucial component of the judicial system, a safeguard against abuse of power or maladministration by the state.

It was in this situation that lawyers in England (and some from Scotland), consciously or unconsciously, acted in a manner that developed adversary trial and its accompanying rights for prisoners. Indeed, such a form of trial extended process rights to all prisoners and "the proposition that the Crown in a criminal prosecution was an adversary on equal terms with the humblest subject was startling and far-reaching in its application. The same lawyers who achieved this practical transformation from deference to debate went on to elevate the doctrine to a full-blown political ideology in the revolutionary creeds of the late 18th century."[20]

ADVERSARY TRIAL IN A CHANGING WORLD

The three practical explanations for the entry of defence lawyers into criminal trials given earlier may or may not be convincing, says Vogler. There has been, he says, "a strong tendency in the recent academic literature to see the whole creation of adversariality as merely an *ad hoc* development".[21] But, he continues, "whilst the practical reasons may have been important and may go some way to explain the chronology of change, it is not unreasonable to link the birth of adversariality" with wider movements in Britain and the world.[22] After all, it was a period of breathtaking commercial expansion and demands for political and economic freedoms and individual liberty. And, "by directing political attention to individuals and their rights ..." says Shapiro, "the Whig political theory shifted attention from the pros-

---

19. A.H. Shapiro. (1993) `Political Theory and the Growth of Defensive Safeguards in Criminal Procedure. The Origin of the Treason Trials Act of 1696.' Illinois, 11(2) *Law and History Review.* American Society of Legal History.
20. R. Vogler. (2005) *A World View of Criminal Justice.* Aldershot, Ashgate Publishing. p. 131.
21. *Ibid.* p. 142.
22. *Ibid.* pp. 142-3.

ecutor to the defendant," who had a right and duty to resist arbitrary and illegitimate authority.[23]

This theory, based on the authority of the philosopher, John Locke, "greatly enhanced the trial reformer's appreciation of the defendant's predicament and the vulnerability of the innocent."[24]

Moreover, "It is not unreasonable," adds Vogler, "to link the birth of adversariality with the more profound shifts in contemporary understanding of the world and the political economy which followed from the Glorious Revolution of 1688."[25] He argues that during the period prior to 1688, the bloody judicial retribution of judges such as Jeffreys and Scroggs brought the rights of criminal defendants to the heart of the Whig political agenda. As a consequence, the Whig ascendancy of Hanovarian England was content with the disempowerment and growing neutrality of the trial judge.

Vogler refers to the strange birth of the adversarial principle and this occurred without its significance being appreciated at the time or, indeed, until recently. Clearly there were the practical causes for its origin as outlined above and they each played a significant part in its birth. But the period of the rise of adversary trial was one of a profound transformation in society which was undermining the earlier trial procedure and helped determine the direction which the new procedure took.

For the prisoner in the dock charged with felony and weighed down by rules that, unless the jury showed mercy or he had "benefit of clergy"[26], meant his life was in serious danger, the change to adversary trial was a momentous transformation. And, it not only flourished in England but was widely and quickly adopted in other countries where it had a vital impact on criminal procedure around the globe.

These momentous upsurges in English national life, and the intellectual ferment they aroused, together with the philosophy of John Locke and the English Bill of Rights of 1689, foreshadowed human rights becoming an integral part of the legal, moral and political fabric of civilized society in which today the courts play "a leading role in resolving human rights controversies and developing human rights norms."[27] In this development of adversary trial played a critical part and also enhanced the concept of due process of law.

---

23. A. H. Shapiro. `Political Theory and the Growth of Defensive Safeguards in Criminal Procedure: The Origins of the Treason Trials Act of 1696.' *Op. cit.*. pp. 228, 233.

24. *Ibid.* p. 236.

25. R. Vogler. *A World View of Criminal Justice. Op. cit* p. 142.

26. A device whereby a convicted felon would be set free if he or she could read the first verse of psalm 51 (the so-called "neck verse").

27. Steiner & Alston. (1996) *International Human Rights in Context: Law, Politics, Morals.* Oxford, Clarendon Press. pp. v-vi.

HUMAN RIGHTS

Intrinsic to the nature of adversary trial is that it is rights-based. As we have seen, it emerged in early eighteenth century England alongside the right of prisoners to engage counsel to assist in their defence in felony trials. Once established it quickly spread to countries where the common law had been introduced - mainly English colonies, including those in North America. It contrasts with the Roman-canon inquisitorial system in operation in other parts of the world, particularly Europe. Differing from the battle between opposing counsel in adversary trial, the continental system imposed on the judge a duty to inquire into the circumstances of the case with a view to uncovering the truth. In fact, his powers were so extensive that his authority had to be limited by evidentiary strictures under which, according to Stephan Landsman:

> He could convict a criminal defendant in only two circumstances: when two eye witnesses were produced who had observed the gravamen of the crime, or when the defendant confessed. Circumstantial evidence was never sufficient in itself to warrant conviction. These evidentiary rules made it impossible to obtain convictions in many cases unless the defendant was willing to confess. Roman-canon process authorized the use of torture to extract the necessary confessions. Thus, torture became a tool of judicial inquiry and was used to generate the evidence upon which the defendant would be condemned.[28]

This system was adopted on the continent following the abolition of trial by ordeal by the Lateran Council of the Roman Catholic Church in 1215.[29] At that time in England Henry III was an infant and, lacking strong leadership from the King's council, the judges hesitated before finally, in 1219, turning the presenting jury into a jury of fact finders who could determine guilt or innocence. They thereby avoided both the all-powerful judge and the use of torture at common law.[30]

Over succeeding centuries, the criminal trial jury in England changed its character but remained a fact-finding body whilst criminal law procedure made the parties responsible for producing all the evidence on which the jury would base its verdict. In time, it was the conflict between the parties that was the basis on which the procedure of adversary trial would be built. But this did not come about until lawyers were permitted to cross-examine witnesses in a manner in which they came to dominate the courtroom.[31]

As Landsman has written elsewhere, "[t]he fundamental expectation of an adver-

---

28. S. Landsman. (1983) `A Brief Survey of the Development of the Adversary System.' 44 (1) *Ohio State Law Journal.* p. 724.
29. J. Hostettler. (2004) *The Criminal Jury Old and New: Jury Power from Early Times to the Present Day.* Winchester, Waterside Press. p. 21.
30. *Ibid.* pp. 21-2.
31. J. H. Langbein. *The Origins of Adversary Criminal Trial. Op. cit.* p. 311.

sarial system is that out of a sharp clash of proofs presented by litigants in a highly structured forensic setting will come the information upon which a neutral and passive decision maker can base a satisfying resolution of the legal dispute."[32] And, in its nature it is based upon a clash which must be rights-based. This was, of course, not the traditional method in England before the eighteenth century when the judge dominated the trial and prisoners' rights were almost non-existent.

Landsman identifies the essence of the modern adversary system when he outlines three elements that are fundamental to it. First, "the decision-maker remains neutral and passive during the trial." Secondly, the parties must produce the evidence and proof. Finally, there must be "an elaborate set of rules to govern the trial and the behaviour of the advocates ..." He adds that, "no one set out to build the adversary system. It was neither part of a grand governmental design nor the scheme of an ingenious legal philosopher."[33] Nor, he might have added, of ingenious judges.

In summing up the advantage of the process Sydney Smith aptly said, "justice is found, experimentally, to be most effectually promoted by the opposite efforts of practiced and ingenious men presenting to the selection of an impartial judge the best arguments for the establishment or explanation of truth."[34]

As to the impact adversary trial made on contemporaries in the eighteenth century, we have the words of the well-known criminal barrister, John Adolphus, who described the excitement aroused by his first experience of it when attending court,

> I cannot describe the effect produced on my mind by the first hearing of an impassioned address, quick taunt, convincing reply, and above all the *viva voce* examination of witnesses and the comments on their evidence.[35]

So different was it from the earlier mode of trial that he added that from that day he became, "early and constant in my attendance"[36] at court.

It must be recognized, however, that there is some questioning of adversary trial. Certain opponents ask if it is a search for the truth or a "game of bluff, suspense and surprise?"[37] They prefer the continental inquisitorial system but, unlike adversary trial, in that system there is no true presumption of innocence and the witnesses are called by the pro-active judge, not by the parties' own lawyers. Defence counsel and juries play a far less prominent role than in the common law system and defendants

32. S. Landsman. `The Rise of the Contentious Spirit: Adversary Procedure in Eighteenth Century England.' *Op. cit.* p. 499.
33. *Ibid.* p. 500.
34. Cited by S. Rogers. (1899) `The Ethics of Advocacy'. 15 *Law Quarterly Review*. London, Stevens & Sons, Limited. p, 259.
35. A. N. May. (2003) *The Bar and the Old Bailey, 1750-1850*. Chapel Hill, University of North Carolina Press. p. 78.
36. *Ibid.*
37. *Time* magazine. (30 September 1966).

are often held in custody before trial for prolonged periods. Nonetheless, adversary trial should not remain unchecked as wealthy defendants have an advantage in often being able to secure the most experienced counsel and a determined counsel, particularly in the United States, can cause endless delays which undermine justice.

Although the English model of criminal justice was adopted in the French Revolution it was largely dismantled by Napoleon in 1808 when he reintroduced the secret, authoritarian inquisitorial system which for nearly two centuries has straddled those parts of the world that were not influenced by the common law. Its impact in twentieth century Europe under the influence of Stalin and Hitler was foreshadowed earlier by a concerted intellectual attack on adversary trial which it was claimed undermined the goal of "social defence". It was promoted by Raffaele Garafalo (1851-1934) - a socialist member of the Italian Parliament and supporter of Mussolini - and Enrico Ferri (1856-1929).

Garafalo called for absolute secrecy in the pre-trial investigation, against members of the Bar who called for complete transparency in trial procedure. The jury was a "grotesque institution", he said, and trials should be held almost entirely *in camera*.[38] For Ferri, criminal procedure should be conducted by the judge to determine the anthropological class of the prisoner. Adversary trial was "grotesque" and the presumption of innocence which had become "mummified and degenerate" should be severely limited. [39]

These ideas of totalitarian, inquisitorial procedure were brought to fruition in Stalin's Russia and Hitler's Germany with their destruction of all aspects of adversariality and due process. The question needs to be asked why much of the former Soviet bloc and communist China today, whilst emphatically retaining political control, are moving towards adversary trial. The answer appears to be that whilst both have embraced a capitalist, market economy this is hamstrung by the power of inquisitorial procurators in a legal system which denies the rule of law and human rights. This was borne out In the year 2000 when Vladimir Putin, on his election as president, declared that judicial reform would be one of his "top priorities" in Russia's transition to a market economy.[40]

In China, its negotiations to join the World Trade Association called into play United State and European assistance in law reform with co-operation in judicial and lawyer training, human rights and legal aid being announced when President Bill Clinton visited Beijing in 1998.[41]

---

38. *Criminology*. (1885) Montclair, Patterson Smith. pp. 344-5 and 365.
39. *Criminal Sociology*. (1884) London, T. F. Fisher Unwin. pp. 148-9.
40. P.H.Solomon. (2002) *Putin's Judicial Reform: Making Judges Accountable as well as Independent*. 11 (1-2) East European Constitutional Review, pp. 117-24.
41. M.C. Stephenson. (2000) "A Trojan Horse Behind Chinese Walls? Problems and Prospects of US-Sponsored 'Rule of Law' Reform Projects in the People's Republic of China". 18 *UCLA Pacific Basin Law Journal*, pp. 64-97.

There has been no rapid change in the old inquisitorial legal culture in Russia or China, however, for two reasons. First, there are powerful procurators who are opposed to changes which undermine their power, and secondly, precisely because of the old legal culture there are few experienced defence lawyers and judges, and training them is a long-term process. Nevertheless, there are clear indications that turning to a market economy, even while retaining tight political control, involves adopting the principle of adversariality.

Torture and oppression have formed part of the history and structure of inquisitorial trial often under the rule of dictators and tyrants. Today, as the above shows, the picture is changing. In the last decade a number of Latin American states have drawn up new codes based on the adversary system. Russia enacted an adversarial procedure code in 2001 and China is proceeding to a similar goal, as are Georgia and the Ukraine. Similarly, there are moves towards adversary trial in France, Spain, Italy and Germany. The impact of such developments is to create a global shift in criminal procedure and due process that makes universal human rights meaningful.

What is apparent is that in England in the eighteenth century a procedural transformation was taking place that was part of the first culture of human rights in the world and it preceded both the Constitution of the United States of 1787, with its right to a speedy and public trial by an impartial jury, and the French Declaration of the Rights of Man and the Citizen of 1789, with its assertion of man's free and equal rights. It also had far-reaching consequences "which would extend beyond criminal trial and impact upon the whole relationship between the state and the individual"[42] as well as the growth of personal freedom, democracy and the rule of law.

In philosophical terms, the theory behind what the English common law was achieving was the assertion of the rights of the individual following John Locke (1632-1704) in his *The Letter for Toleration* in 1689[43] and *Two Treatises of Government* the following year.[44] That such rights were not always acknowledged as self-evident as the American Declaration of Independence proclaimed is shown by the Hegelian Declaration of Rights in Germany in 1848 which spoke not of the rights of man but of the rights of the German people.[45]

The ultimate acceptance of the legal rights of the individual came in Europe with article 6 of the Convention for the Protection of Human Rights and Fundamental Freedoms[46] (agreed at Rome on 4 November 1950 and incorporated into UK domestic law by the Human Rights Act 1998, c.42). In article 6(1) this provides a general right to a fair and public trial by an independent court of law and also sets out certain minimum rights. In particular, article 6(3)(d) states that, "everyone

---

42. R. Vogler. *A World View of Criminal Justice. Op. cit.* p. 51.
43. (1689) London.
44. (1690) London, Awnsham Churchill.
45. M. Cranston. (1962) *Human Rights Today.* London, Ampersand Books. p. 10.
46. www.hri.org/docsECHR50.html

charged with a criminal offence has the following minimum rights … (d) to examine or have examined witnesses against him."

The right to cross-examine witnesses is an intrinsic part of the Anglo-American adversary system of trial and the wonder of it is that it came about not by legislation but by the practical efforts of Garrow and other barristers in their concern not with developing the law (a process which "as establishment men" did not appeal to them) but simply to win cases by the best means available. That they did so in the favourable environment of a growing human rights culture in no way diminishes their achievement.[47]

---

47. Some of these conclusions are worth repeating for public debate and are taken from Hostettler (2006) *Fighting for Justice: The History and Origins of Adversary Trial.* Winchester, Waterside Press.

CHAPTER 6

Government Prosecutor

Garrow soon developed a large and prosperous practice. He extended his career beyond the Old Bailey, into criminal trials outside London, in the service of fee-paying clients, both in defence and prosecution cases.

ASSESSMENT OF GARROW'S EARLY LEGAL CAREER

Near the end of the early part of his career, before he became a law officer of the Crown, a description of Garrow's career to this point was recorded in *Public Characters*, under the title "Mr. Garrow."

> Mr. Garrow does not pretend to be a very deep lawyer, he chiefly shines in personal actions, and scarcely an assault, battery, or breach of the peace, is brought into court, but he is first retained as counsel. His business in the king's-bench, which is exceeded by none but Mr. Erskine's, is chiefly confined to actions of this kind; and at Nisi Prius [a civil action tried in a court of record before a judge and jury], his practice, though not so lucrative, is, perhaps, superior to that of the last-named gentleman.
>
> Mr. Garrow seldom goes further into the country, except upon a special retainer, than Guildford, and he has long monopolized the chief business on the home circuit. It must be confessed that his powers as a pleader are chiefly confined to the humorous, the ridiculous, and the light; no man better understands or better expresses these qualifications; but of the pathos he has, perhaps, less than any other gentleman at the bar. His voice, though not powerful, is clear and melodious, and, while he wisely omits all action, his countenance and expression are nicely adapted to every passion he wishes to excite. No man is heard with more attention by the court, no man gains more upon a jury, or better pleases a common auditor.[1]

The writer of this passage continues, and makes predictions about the future of Garrow's career. He predicts that Garrow would not seek to fill one of the great law offices of state, or become a member of Parliament or judge. In every instance his predictions were wrong. Equally, like all his contemporaries, the author of *Public Characters* failed to see the significance of the emergence of adversary trial yet he does emphasize some memorable qualities of Garrow's early career.

Crown Prosecutions

In February 1793, a few days after the French revolutionaries guillotined the French King, Garrow was appointed King's Counsel to assist in the prosecution of persons

---

1. *Public Characters.* (1799-1809) 4th edn, vol. x. (Microfilm)

accused of treason and sedition against the Crown.[2] The *Morning Chronicle* of 28 January 1793 announced appointments of new King's Counsel. It stated: "Six silk gowns are to be given away in the Court this day; Mr Garrow is to be honoured with one of them." It then was bitter about this appointment because Garrow had once been a protégé of Charles James Fox and had always stood as a friend to the Opposition. The *True Briton* in announcing these appointments, however, described them as the best talent of the age. The reason given for the appointments was to strengthen the Government's ability to defend the Constitution against radicalism inspired by the French Revolution.

Thus, as that revolution was gaining momentum, Garrow's career would endure a major shift in emphasis in response to the perceived threat that the French Revolution would be exported to Great Britain. Indeed, Garrow's career as a government prosecutor was shaped and invested in responding to this threat. His leadership in the Crown side of the King's Bench in the 1790s was seen as reflecting the Tory party's reputation.[3] He had turned from Whig to Tory, his allegiance from Fox to Pitt.

Immediately after "taking silk" Garrow was perpetually engaged in legal contests with the most eminent men of his day: Erskine, Mingay, Law, Gibbs, Park, Topping, Brougham, Scarlett, Denman and Sheridan. He was employed by the government in most of the state trials, including the treason trials, and as he gained seniority, the sole management of many of the cases was entrusted to him. One biographer, writing during this period of Garrow's life, stated "Mr. Garrow's reputation was now so well established, that he was engaged in every cause of importance before the courts. The history of his life, therefore, is upon the files and records of the King's Bench; and his memoirs are best read in the *Term Reports*." [4]

The government suspended habeas corpus in May 1794. This was the law requiring that a prisoner be brought before a court to decide the legality of his detention, a safeguard against illegal imprisonment. In 1795 the Sedition and Treason bills passed in which the Government outlawed all large public meetings. In 1797 the Unlawful Oaths Act was passed which outlawed secret organizations. In 1798 the Newspaper Act passed which established a system of registration that would facilitate the prosecution of printers and publishers believed to be guilty of sedition. And in 1799 the Corresponding Societies Act utterly suppressed and prohibited societies located in England (including Wales), Scotland and Ireland, which were interested in reforming the government, from corresponding with each other and carrying on their own operations.

A story related to Garrow becoming a King's Counsel is a way of introducing

---

2. Garrow's work as Solicitor-General and Attorney-General is dealt with in chapter 8 – "MP and Law Officer".
3. D. Lemmings. (2002) *Professors of the Law: Barristers and English Legal Culture in the Eighteenth Century.* Oxford, Oxford University Press. p. 168.
4. *Public Characters. Op. cit.* (Microfilm frame number 72)

this phase of his service to his government. The record of his quest for this title was published in *The Times* following his death.

> The time arrived, and the extent of his practice required that he should apply for rank; but still his native distrust of himself made him doubtful. He consulted his friend, Mr. Mainwaring, the Chairman of the Middlesex sessions and member of the county, who had observed his progress with friendly interest; and having received from that worthy and honourable magistrate every encouragement, he waited on Lord Kenyon, then Chief Justice of the King's Bench. On his name being announced, his lordship came into the room, and anticipating his business, exclaimed, "So, Mr. Garrow, you want a silk gown, I suppose; I have been expecting your application these two years." A recommendation went immediately to the Lord Chancellor, and, without further solicitation or delay, he obtained that elevation which has been so often withheld or delayed, when applied for by gentlemen of much longer standing than himself, and of undisputed learning and ability.[5]

Immediately, and throughout his service as a state prosecutor, Garrow worked on sedition and treason trials. He prosecuted many other types of cases for the Crown, and continued a prosperous private business on the side, but these state trials continued to be a significant part of his work.

Treason Trials

The Government planned eight hundred arrests, with three hundred warrants made out and signed and ready for execution. To start the prosecution of those charged with High Treason in "compassing the death of the King", the Government made a major effort to convict Thomas Hardy, and then John Horne Tooke.[6] On the eve of the trials it announced the discovery of a huge revolutionary plot and this, together, with the summary suspension of habeas corpus and the other measures mentioned above, caused the eminent Victorian historian, J.R. Green, to describe the government's excesses in prosecution and attacks on freedom at this time as the "English Terror".[7] In similar vein, Lord John Campbell called the frenzied attempts at repression, "a Reign of Terror".[8] The plan was to win convictions in these two cases and then proceed to prosecute the rest of those charged with related acts that the Crown's prosecutors considered treasonable. Garrow played a minor role, although a colourful one, in each of these trials.

Hardy was the first to be tried and was defended by Erskine. The case for the prosecution, but not the evidence, was that the prisoner sought a revolution in England similar to that in France. Erskine presented the defence courageously and,

---

5. "Memoir of Sir William Garrow". *The Times.* 7 November 1840. (From the *Monthly Law Magazine*).
6. For fuller details of these trials see Alan Wharam. (1992) *The Treason Trials, 1794.* Leicester, Leicester University Press, and John Hostettler (1996) *Thomas Erskine and Trial by Jury.* Chichester, Barry Rose Law Publishers.
7. J.R. Green. (1874) *A Short History of the English People.* London, The Folio Society. P. 818.
8. Lord John Campbell. (1847) *Lives of the Lord Chancellors.* London, John Murray. vol. vi. p. 460.

referring to the prosecution allegation about the possibility of meetings leading to disorder, said, "I protest in his [Hardy's] name against all speculations respecting *consequences* when the law commands us to look only to *intentions*. Pointing out that Prime Minister Pitt had once been a franchise reformer, not only like his father before him but also like Hardy, Erskine declared, "It would be the height of injustice and wickedness to torture expressions, and pervert conduct into treason and rebellion which had recently lifted others up to love of the nation, to the confidence of the sovereign and to all the honours of the state."[9]

Hardy was accused of selling copies of *The Rights of Man* by Tom Paine. As one of the prosecuting counsel Garrow cross-examined a witness, Edward Smith, who as a member of one of the corresponding societies was devoted to changing the representation in Parliament. Smith had obtained a copy of *The Rights of Man* from Thomas Hardy. The cross-examination below is quoted from the trial record.

Garrow said "I shall not trouble you with the question the gentleman has repeated several times, whether you are a traitor, and ought to be hanged; I shall not ask you whether you have been guilty of high treason or not". He then did ask:

> Have the goodness to inform a very ignorant man, which I profess myself to be, about all these things . . . what was this plan of the Duke of Richmond's and Mr Pitt's?

Smith: I understood equal representation in Parliament and without it the people would not, as I understood the matter, have their rights.

Garrow: What did you take Mr. Pitt's plan for a more equal representation to be?

Smith: For every man to have his voice.

Garrow: That you took to be Mr. Pitt's plan?

Smith: Yes.

Garrow: So much for the accuracy of your information.

Having established that Smith had read *The Rights of Man*, Garrow proceeded to cross-examine him on its contents.

The trial lasted eight long days instead of the normal one-day state trial and became a precedent. Instead of the jury being held in court for the whole trial, at Erskine's request they were taken each night to a nearby tavern. Despite all the preparation and pressure of the government the jury found Hardy not guilty to the rapturous rejoicing of the crowds outside the court. The tension of the trial so affected the foreman of the jury, a Mr. Buck of Acton, that he delivered the verdict in a whisper and then fainted on the spot.

---

9. J. Hostettler. *Thomas Erskine and Trial by Jury.* Op. cit. p. 114.

Hardy's trial was immediately followed by that of John Horne Tooke. The Garrow connection is this case, as noted by Alan Wharam, is a somewhat humorous footnote-type of event. During the trial Garrow said, "Mr. Horne Tooke said he was a member of the Constitutional Society". But this had not been properly established and Tooke, acting in his own defence, replied, "Mr. Garrow must not slide in upon us anything that has not yet been decided".

Garrow, says Wharam, "regarded this observation as an affront to his professional reputation and rose to justify himself, and at the same time defend himself from the misrepresentations as to his conduct of the case which, he said, were appearing day by day in the press; he had met Horne Tooke on previous occasions; he had no personal animosity against him, and was only doing his duty." Horne Tooke apologised to Garrow and humbly begged his pardon to which Garrow responded, "Mr Tooke has carried his apology much further than I wished."[10]

At the close of arguments, the jury retired, and were back in court within ten minutes. Their verdict was 'Not guilty'. As the result of the Hardy and Tooke verdicts of not guilty, the Government abandoned the other 800 similar treason prosecutions it had scheduled, although other treason trials were undertaken by the government during the time Garrow served as a Crown prosecutor.

Winston Churchill in *A History of the English-Speaking Peoples* wrote about this moment of history:

> In England the Government had been forced to take repressive measures of a sternness unknown for generations. Republican lecturers were swept into prison. The Habeas Corpus Act was suspended. Distinguished writers were put on their trial for treason; but juries could not be prevailed to convict.[11]

History supports the decision of the juries. There is not much evidence that radicals in England were ever planning violent revolution.

Later, after being elevated to Solicitor-General and then Attorney-General of the realm, where he prosecuted cases for the Government, Garrow also had the duty to defend certain types of legal interests of the Government in Parliament, and to introduce and defend legislation in Parliament. His performance of these state duties, and the style with which he spoke in Parliament, are best discussed in *Chapter 8* entitled *Member of Parliament and Law Officer*.

---

10. Alan Wharam. *The Treason Trials.* Op. cit. pp. 200-201.
11. (1957) London, Cassell & Co. vol. iii. p. 249.

CHAPTER 7

The Picton Trials

COLONIAL LAW

Garrow practiced law in the criminal courts during that period of English history when the sugar planters of the West Indies held great power in Parliament. This power helped them maintain a monopoly on the marketing of sugar in England that resulted in huge profits. The industry was possible because of the slave trade, with its various practices to keep the black population subjugated, and the plantations free from the disruptions of the ever present possibilities of rebellion or revolution.

The legal question being struggled with concerned the very practice of slavery and the treatment of slaves and free blacks under English law in the colonies.

Garrow's stand on this issue was clearly described in an article published about him in the *Monthly Law Magazine* and republished in *The Times* shortly after his death. It states:

> With all the zeal which he was ever ready to display in causes confided to him, with all the desire of wealth and honour which could inflame a youthful mind, Garrow was never ready to undertake a case which would oblige him to profess, in a public manner, opinions which were repugnant to his principles. Thus, at an early period of his life, when the question concerning the manner in which Negroes were obtained, and conveyed from Africa to the West Indies, was in agitation, he had formed a most decided judgment on the facts and on the traffic.
>
> One day Mr. Fuller (Jack Fuller, of Rose-hill, as he called himself), a great West India proprietor, meeting him in the street, said, "Well, Mr. Garrow, here is plenty of business, and plenty of money for you; the committee have determined to retain you, and give you the management of all their business in Parliament and elsewhere." He answered, "Sir, if your committee would give me their whole incomes, and all their estates, I would not be seen as the advocate of practices which I abhor, and a system which I detest."[1]

COURT RECORDS

The actual court records are both clear and extensive in describing the proceedings of the Court of King's Bench in the case of Thomas Picton, containing three hundred sixty-seven pages of court records. Garrow was deeply involved in this trial, but a comprehensive look at his involvement is not appropriate in this overview of Garrow's life. However the records of these proceedings do offer a chance to display Garrow's style in a role not previously presented. In this type of state trial, lawyers

---

1. *The Times.* (7 November 1840).

talked directly to the jury, and they made opening and closing statements, in addition to examining witnesses.

Garrow's opening statement to the jury was made on 24 February 1806 and is presented here.[2] It is not merely a random selection from the many recorded trials in which Garrow exercised his skills. It is considered one of Garrow's best speeches. *The Legal Observer*, under the heading of 'Judicial Characters', published at the time of Garrow's retirement from the bench, is considered by some to be in the form of a memoir in which Garrow had a hand in selecting material to be presented. It contains this statement:

> It would be difficult perhaps, on a deliberate exercise of the judgment, to direct attention to the recorded speeches most worthy of notice; but we may merely, from memory, as affording specimens of varied and superior abilities.

A short list of speeches made in court was then presented with the prosecution against Picton as the second item listed.

Garrow's statement is given here in its entirety, not just extracts. It depicts with great clarity Garrow's style of speaking.

Proceedings against Thomas Picton

Mr. Garrow: Gentlemen of the Jury; the task of stating the particulars of this most extraordinary and horrid transaction was originally confided to much greater abilities than those upon which it has now unfortunately devolved. I feel, however, some consolation in reflecting that the present is a case which (addressed to a British jury in a British Court of Justice) requires no embellishment of eloquence, nor any factitious aid, to impress it upon the minds of those who are to hear and to decide upon it. Unless the facts clearly and fully substantiated by proof, force from you a reluctant verdict of GUILTY, I have no hesitation in declaring that the defendant ought not to be convicted; I say "a reluctant verdict of Guilty," because there is no individual present (not excepting even myself, whose duty it is to conduct the prosecution), who would not rejoice if you could justify yourselves to your consciences and your God, in doubting the truth of this accusation.

The indictment, which has been stated to you by my learned friend Mr. Harrison, alleges, that a representative of our sovereign, and Governor of one of our colonial dependencies, who was therefore bound to protect his fellow-subjects, has abused the station to which he was raised, and has disgraced the country to which he belongs, by - what no one in England has heard of without horror and detestation - inflicting torture upon one of his majesty's subjects, without the least pretence of law, without the least moral justification, but solely to gratify his tyrannical disposition, by the oppression of the unfortunate and defenceless victim of his cruelty.

Gentlemen, in the year 1797, the island of Trinidad surrendered to his majesty's forces under the command of the illustrious Sir Ralph Abercrombie, whose name must ever be mentioned by Britons with gratitude and admiration. That great man entered into stipulations by which he conceded to the inhabitants of this Spanish settlement, the continuance of their

---

2. *The Legal Observer.* (18 February 1832) p. 255.

laws and institution; and he appointed a new Governor until his majesty's pleasure should be known, or, in other words, until the sovereign of Great Britain should have, in his paternal kindness towards this new dependence of his empire, extended to it all the privileges and advantages of English laws.

The colony, prior to its surrender to the British arms, had been governed by a code of laws, abating very much of the severity of that of Old Spain; and I have the authority of the defendant himself for stating, that previous to his appointment to the government, the juridical regulations of Trinidad were extremely mild and benignant, and well adapted to the protection of the subject in this remote insular establishment.

The person, whose sufferings form the subject of this day's inquiry, is a young woman of the name of Luisa Calderon. About the age of ten or eleven years, this young person was seduced by a man of the name of Pedro Ruiz, to live with him as his mistress; and although it may to us in this country appear singular, that she should be in such a situation at that tender period of life, yet in that hot climate where the puberty of females is much accelerated, it is common for them to become mothers at the age of twelve; at that early period they either marry or enter into a state of concubinage if they cannot form a more honourable connexion.

Having been seduced by Ruiz, and living with him as his mistress, it appears most clearly (for I have no desire to keep any part of the case a secret), that she was engaged in an intrigue with Carlos Gonzalez, who in the month of December 1801, availing him of the access of the house of Pedro Ruiz, which his connexion with Luisa Calderon afforded, robbed Ruiz of a quantity of dollars which were deposited. Gonzalez was apprehended, and a suspicion arising that she was acquainted with the circumstances of the robbery, if not an accessory to the crime, she also was taken into custody, and examined before an officer of the laws, equivalent to our magistrate or Justice of the Peace.

In the first instance she denied any knowledge of the transaction; the magistrate felt, that according to the laws of Spain, his functions were nearly at an end; she persisted in her denial, and whether her object in so doing was to protect herself or her friend from injurious consequences it is not at all material to inquire. The magistrate or justice felt that he had not authority to adopt any coercive means in order to procure any confession of her own guilt, or any accusation of Gonzalez; and therefore he resorted to the defendant who was invested with the supreme authority of the island, to supply the deficiency; and, gentlemen, I shall produce in the hand writing of General Picton himself, and subscribed with his signature this bloody sentence:

"Inflict the torture upon Luisa Calderon."

You will readily believe that there was no great delay in proceeding to obey this order. The unhappy girl when taken to the gaol was told by the judge, that if she would confess all her life should be saved; but unless she did so, she should be put to the torture; that if she suffered the loss of a limb, or should be deprived of life itself, the consequences would be upon her own head, and that he should be absolved from all blame.

In order to impress this admonition upon her mind, two or three young negresses were brought before her in the room where torture was usually applied who were to undergo the same severities on a charge of sorcery and witchcraft. Here then, we behold a British Governor for the first time introducing torture into a British settlement as a punishment for sorcery and witchcraft, and as the means of extorting confession from a person under accusation.

Notwithstanding all this, the young woman persisted in declaring her innocence, and the punishment was applied which has been improperly called *piqueting*; I say improperly, because piqueting is a known military punishment, but this is properly distinguished by the name of *the torture*; indeed it is a libel upon piqueting to call the torture inflicted upon Luisa Calderon by the same name. True it is that there is some resemblance between the one practice and the other; in both cases the foot is placed upon a sharp wooden point, but in the former that mercy which always attends infliction of punishments in this country; has assigned for the sufferer a means of reposing or raising himself by the interior of his arm (a rope being placed round the body, and passing under the arm, so that when fatigued, he can rest upon it) by which the agony to the foot is diminished.

Not only for the sake of correctness, but for the sake of humanity, I hope this practice will not receive the appellation of *Piqueting*, but that of *Pictoning* that it may be described by the most horrid name by which it can be known, and be shunned as a disgrace to human nature.

I will briefly state to you the particulars of the situation of this unhappy creature during the time she was thus exposed to this exercise of cruelty. While her body was supported by the great toe projected on a sharp piece of wood, the wrist of the hand on the opposite side was drawn up by a pulley, so that her whole weight was sustained by the pulley and the spike; and lest she should afford herself any momentary relief by struggling in such a situation, the other hand and foot which were not concerned in the dreadful operation, were tied together behind her. She complained bitterly and requested to be lowered; she was then told that if she would confess she should be let down, and then she said Gonzalez had certainly stolen Ruiz's dollars. Nothing but the incontestable evidence which I have to produce, could make you believe, that this unhappy creature continued for fifty-three minutes in that dreadful state.

The time was ascertained by a watch which the magistrate had before him, not from any fear that she might suffer too much; but because there was some notion of a supposed law, that the torture could not be inflicted for more than an hour; and had it not been for the watch, the pleasure of inflicting the punishment might have induced the magistrates and the spectators to have continued it for a longer period than the time supposed to be allowed.

She was then lowered, but her confession not being deemed satisfactory, in less than twenty-four hours the torture was again applied. This gentlemen, is a faithful representation of it [producing a drawing in colours], and may give you some notion of the sufferings which a human being in such a situation must have undergone.

It appears to me, that the case which I shall lay before you in support of the prosecution is complete. Our charge is, that Governor Picton, abusing his station, has without reasonable cause or legal justification, inflicted the torture upon this young female. But I understand I am to be told that, although the highest authority in this country could not inflict such a punishment on the meanest individual, yet, that Governor Picton was justified by the laws of Spain as they applied to the island of Trinidad.

Subject to my lord's correction, however, I state with confidence that if it were written in characters which no man could misunderstand, and which he who runs may read, that the laws of Spain as applicable to Trinidad, permitted, in any given circumstances, the infliction of torture, this would afford no justification to a British Governor. Nothing could justify him but the law of imperious necessity, to which we must all submit; he must show that he had no alternative.

What was the duty of a man placed in his honourable and important station? It was his duty in the first moment of his government to have impressed on the minds of the people of this new colony a conviction of the perfect security they would acquire, of the abundant advantages they would derive, from the mild, benign, and equitable spirit of British jurisprudence; and above all, that the moment they were received within the pale of the British government, the torture would be forever banished from the island.

But I moreover assert, that the defendant cannot make out any pretence of a justification, for there is nothing even in the law of Spain as applicable to Trinidad, by which such a pretence can be supported; and I also have no hesitation in declaring, that even if he could establish a right in some cases to inflict the torture, it would not avail him here; he must make out a case of absolute and irresistible necessity, and show that it was his bounded duty to inflict it.

He ought to have remembered, that in England torture is unknown, not because the subject has never been discussed, but because it is so abhorrent to all our feelings, to our regard for personal liberty and the fair administration of justice, that it never has been and never can be tolerated here. What is the language of our legal institutions, as they are explained by a learned and elegant writer adverting to this subject?

"The trial by rack is utterly unknown to the law of England; though once when the Dukes of Exeter and Suffolk, and other ministers of Henry 6th had laid a design to introduce the civil-law into this kingdom as the rule of government, for a beginning thereof they erected a rack for torture; which was called in derision the Duke of Exeter's Daughter, and still remains in the Tower of London, where it was occasionally used as an engine of state, not of law, more than once in the reign of Queen Elizabeth. But when, upon the assassination of Villiers Duke of Buckingham by Felton, it was proposed in the privy council to put the assassin to the rack, in order to discover his accomplices; the judges, being consulted, declared unanimously, to their own honour and the honour of the English law, that no such proceeding was allowable by the laws of England."

General Picton should have carried this with him to Trinidad, he should have borne in mind the folly of supposing that an instrument of torture is an instrument to extract truth. The subject has been reduced by a foreign writer (Beccaria, chap. 16), quoted by Mr. Justice Blackstone into the form of a mathematical problem; "The force of the muscles and the sensibility of the nerves of an innocent person being given, it is required to find the degree of pain necessary to make him confess himself guilty of a given crime."

Nothing indeed can be so absurd and preposterous as the application of this process in the administration of justice. But what are we to say of this man who comes here to defend himself saying, that he has found a law under which he can obtain shelter, when I tell you that it appears by all the volumes sent from Trinidad, that so far from Governor Picton having found torture in daily use under former Governors, so far from his being bound by any circumstances of necessity to inflict it, he has all the merit of the invention. Like the duke of Exeter's daughter, it never had existence until the defendant cursed the island with its introduction.

Gentlemen, that I shall prove this case to you I am most confident, for I have read the depositions, which have been most laboriously collected, and laid before the Court; and if I show that for the first time general Picton, a British Governor, erected this instrument of torture, and that with his own hand he wrote the bloody order for its infliction, I set before you a man without the least shadow of defence.

The date of this transaction is removed at some distance. In the opinion of those who were to advise his majesty as to the manner in which the government of this remote island should be managed, it was deemed expedient that commissioners should be sent over, and among the persons appointed to this important situation was colonel Fullarton. Upon the arrival of those commissioners, this affair was disclosed to colonel Fullarton who felt it to be his duty to put it in a train of inquiry; the result of which is that he has found it necessary to bring this defendant before you, and also to bring before you the unfortunate victim of his tyranny, whom I have this day accidentally seen, in consequence of my being by mistake conducted to a consultation into a room where she was. She will be presented before you, and you will find that she at this moment bears about her the marks of the barbarity of the defendant.

Gentlemen, I shall hear with patience and attention and with as much pleasure as any man what my excellent and learned friend has to offer in behalf of his client; I state the case at present with full confidence in your verdict; I ask nothing from your passions, nothing but justice do I require, and I doubt not, that, at the conclusion of this trial, you will be found to have faithfully discharged your duty.[3]

The trial commenced with all the judicial combat one would expect in such a high profile case, with the issues being debated far more significant to precedents than to the specific case, unless you were General Picton. The case centred on the Spanish law still in effect at the time of the incident. It appeared there was not sufficient information in England to resolve certain issues. At the conclusion of debate the case went to the jury. As the jury returns, the dialogue in the court transcript continues:

> **Foreman of the Jury**: We are of opinion that there was no such law as this [Spanish law authorizing torture] existing at the time of the session.
>
> **Lord Ellenborough**: Then Governor Picton cannot derive any protection from that law. If no law obtained in that island at the time which authorized the severities that were practised upon this young woman, your verdict must be that the defendant is Guilty.

The verdict of guilty was then pronounced by the jury, and recorded.

> **Mr. Dallas** [Picton's lawyer]: Upon the other points I should trouble your lordship hereafter upon a motion for a new trial.
>
> **Lord Ellenborough**: The other points you know will be open to you upon that motion.

A motion for a new trial was made, defended and won for Picton. In the new trial the debate went on and on, without resolution. The judge ordered a recess, and the defendant was free to continue his affairs until the trial could be resumed. But the trial was never resumed.

NATIONAL HERO

Picton went to the continent and became one of Wellington's generals in the war in France against Napoleon's army. He became a military hero and some historians say he played a critical role in the last battle of the war at Waterloo. At a moment when the English and Scottish forces were losing, from a concealed front line position in the hedgerows he apparently yelled the order, "Charge," and waved his sword

---

3. *State Trials.* (1822) pp. 451-456.

over his head as he continued his order, "Rally the Highlanders." These were his last words as a bullet pierced his famous top hat, which he wore to protect his eyes. The bullet struck him on the temple and he fell off his horse stone dead. From this moment the tide of battle turned and the horror of the Napoleonic wars quickly came to a close.

Picton's fame may be due to his choice of an aide-de-camp, a fellow Welshman by the name of Gronow who wrote much read diaries.[4] Gronow told his story of Picton and much else of the Battle of Waterloo. If you are to be appreciated in the history of your nation, it helps to have your own public relations officer. Wellington, however, had his own comments about Picton, as recorded in Elizabeth Longford's *Wellington, The Years of the Sword*.[5] He is quoted as saying that Picton, though a fine soldier, was "a rough foul-mouthed devil as ever lived". As a national hero, Picton's hat with a bullet hole near the junction of crown and brim, is in the National Military Museum, Sandhurst. Picton is buried in the crypt at St. Paul's Cathedral and there is a large statue of him in the north transept of that great cathedral.

MORAL ISSUE OF SLAVERY

Within a year of the Picton trials Parliament passed the Slave Trade Abolition Act of 1807. The statute proved difficult to enforce whilst slave traders continued to enrich themselves from this trade in human beings. Consequently, the first conviction for evasion of the Act took place as long as ten years after its enactment. And, as he made clear to the House of Commons on 28 February 1817, Garrow took pride in securing that conviction.[6] All the available evidence points to the trial being that of John Bean Hannay which took place at the Old Bailey on 19 February 1817.[7] Hannay was charged with kidnapping slaves, men, women and children, and carrying them away from Calabar in what is now Nigeria with intent to sell them. A special jury, sitting with Mr. Justice Holroyd, found Hannay guilty and he was sentenced to transportation for seven years.

The Old Bailey Proceedings report does not give the name of prosecuting counsel but as the trial was by Special Commission it may well have been Garrow who was Attorney-General at the time. Even if he was not personally engaged in the actual conduct of the trial, he would have had overall responsibility for it and, as it was common for the Attorney-General to prosecute, Garrow would have been keen to

4. R.H. Gronow. (1862) *The Reminiscences and Recollections of Captain Gronow, at the close of the Last War with France*. London, Smith Elder.
5. E. Longford. (1969-72) *Wellington, The Years of the Sword*. London, Weidenfeld & Nicolson.
6. R.G. Thorne. (1986) *The History of Parliament: The House of Commoms 1790–1820*. Vol. iv. *Members G–P*. London, Secker & Warburg. p. 7.
7. OBP Online.(www.oldbaileyonline.org) 19 February 1817. Trial of John Bean Hannay. Ref: 18170219-123.

do so in view of his strong views on the moral issue of slavery which he considered an odious and immoral evil. So after many years of effort by William Wilberforce, Henry Brougham and others to secure such a law we must conclude that it was finally implemented by William Garrow. Slavery itself was not legally abolished in the British colonial empire until 1833 with the passing of the Slavery Emancipation Act[8] at the colossal cost of £20,000,000 which was paid in compensation to slave owners. All slaves were to be freed within a year at an average cost of £37.. 10s .. 0d per slave.

---

8.   3 & 4 Will. IV, c. 73.

CHAPTER 8

Member of Parliament and Law Officer

In R.G. Thorne's *The History of Parliament, The House of Commons 1790-1820*, the biographic sketch of William Garrow starts with these words: "Garrow joined the Whig Club, 26 June 1784, and was Fox's 'jaw master general' at the bar of the House on the Westminster election scrutiny." This event is described in some detail later in this chapter and it was in this highly visible role of successfully defending one of the leaders of the Whigs in the House of Commons that Garrow had his start at speaking in that house.

A PROPER PERSON?

The newspapers started to speculate in 1789 that Garrow was about to be sent to Parliament. In *The Times* of 28 December of that year the following notice appeared:

> Some of the papers have been recommending Mr. Garrow as a proper person to sit in the House of Commons; God forbid, says the writer of this, that such an event should ever take place. There are too many lawyers there already, - too many speakers whose bread depends upon letting out their voice to any purchaser, and as lately happened in the King's Bench, to either and to both sides of the question, arguing, that black was white one day, and that the very same white was black the next day. We want men of independence, of honour, and not of oratory and loquaciousness in the House of Commons.

Shortly after, on 5 January 1790, *The Times* reported:

> The Party have some thoughts of bringing Erskine into Parliament in place of Anstruther, who though of superior abilities as a lawyer, yet cannot talk half so fast as Mr. E -. Either he or his chum Garrow, Mr. Fox thinks will be required, as Sheridan is rather dilatory, and Burke cannot command attention.

It was another fifteen years before Garrow became a Member of Parliament. He represented three different boroughs at various times in his career in Parliament sitting for Gatton (1805-1806), Callington (1806-1807) and Eye (1812-1817). These were pocket or rotten boroughs, ancient jurisdictions with very few voters, that retained the right to be represented in Parliament, and were controlled by one family. In each instance Garrow was appointed to the office to represent some specific interest of his patron, an obligation he felt free to avoid on occasions.

HEARSAY IN THE COMMONS

Indeed, Garrow appears to have paid little active attention to his role an as MP, at least until he became a law officer. Although first elected to the House of Commons in April 1805 he did not venture on his maiden speech until a year later, on 22 April 1806. The debate which he then favoured was on a charge against Marquis Wellesley for alleged dereliction of duty in India where he was said to have squandered the property of the East India Company.

Objecting to a proposed adjournment of the debate Garrow said he had not intended to speak, having made a "sort of league and covenant with himself to remain silent." Nevertheless, he felt he must oppose the impeachment of Wellesley as the charge had been brought forward without evidence to support it. "It was for the sake of precedent that he opposed it; it was because he thought the House should not suffer the valuable privilege of impeachment to be in any case, or even for a short time, the instrument of calumny."[1] His remarks appeared to raise no interest and certainly no comment.

He then spoke again in a debate on the affairs of India on 18 June 1806 not out of interest in the sub-continent but on a legal technicality. Lord Teignmouth was being questioned about treaties entered into with native princes when he was Governor-General in India. Garrow showed himself to be out of touch with the nature of proceedings in the Commons when he intervened to say that the opinion of the noble lord should not be sought. "In any other place" he said, "the rules of evidence would not permit an inquiry as to the opinion of the witness."[2]

In response, another member (Dr. Laurence) pointed out that, in proceedings before the House, strict legal evidence was not required "as nothing could be more different than the situation of the House of Commons in search of information and that of a court of law." Garrow immediately withdrew remarking that, "it seemed he had strayed from the courts below to this place, where he found that legal knowledge was totally useless in the examination of witnesses."[3]

Ironically thanking the doctor for his lecture, he continued that "it seemed from his report, that this House had resolved most magnificently to depart from the rules of evidence which had been established by the wisdom of ages for the protection of our lives and liberties." He was decidedly of the opinion, he said, that no hearsay evidence could be received in any British court of justice to advance the conviction of any man, for a conspiracy or otherwise. However, he could not have been unaware that the rule against hearsay evidence, far from being established by the wisdom of ages, had only recently been in the process of being established in criminal courts

---

1. *Parliamentary Debates.* [6] (22 April 1806) cols. 865-6.
2. *Ibid.* [7] (18 June 1806) cols. 748-9.
3. *Ibid.* cols. 749-50.

by the efforts of defence barristers among whom he was in the forefront. Garrow was clearly frustrated on the total lack of a sense of responsibility and honesty in the way the members of Parliament presented hearsay information. In turn, speakers in the House tried to impress upon Garrow that they were not bound by any rules of evidence, and could present anything they wanted.

Garrow was again lectured by the House. Mr. Secretary Wyndham observed upon the tone in which the learned gentleman (Garrow) had spoken, and said that though he had thanked his learned friend for his lecture, he had not profited by it. The question was whether the rules of the courts below applied to parliamentary proceedings? Did the learned gentleman mean to say that they did, where the cases were so very different? If he did not mean to say this, he said nothing at all.

Thereafter he did not intervene in any debate for over six years, until 12 February 1813 when he was a law officer and, speaking in a debate on delays in justice, opposed the transfer of common law judges to relieve the courts of equity.[4]

Garrow did not enjoy his time in Parliament, and as time went on he grew to like it less and less. Apparently he was seldom there unless he had specific business to conduct. However, as he served as Solicitor-General (June 1812-May 1813), and then as Attorney-General (May 1813-May 1817), this work did frequently require his presence in Parliament.

PROTECTING THE REALM

As both Solicitor-General and Attorney-General, the senior prosecutor for the Crown serving during the Napoleonic War, Garrow was responsible not only for managing the prosecution of many of those charged with treason and sedition, he was a leading person for the Crown in getting Parliament to pass laws protecting the realm from revolution. This was a time in England when the Regent and many in his government feared liberal changes to the structure of Parliament, the criminal law, and to long established social policies, such as toward Catholics.

Garrow could be counted upon to support these conservative efforts by the Government, and as such was considered to be "a mere creature of the Regent." The mark he made on history during this phase of his career, as opposed to his earlier modelling of aggressive defence of clients rights, is not that of an innovator who used his talents to bring about much needed changes in these areas. Significant issues were being debated. One concerned how justice and mercy were to be administered in the criminal code. In its simplest form this issue had these dimensions. Traditionally many crimes, even such things as shoplifting, could carry a sentence of death by hanging. In reality, few people were being hanged for these types of

---

4. *Parliamentary History.* [24]

crimes. Even if convicted, the judge or Crown could set aside the sentence, as an act of mercy.

The laws were kept on the books to frighten those inclined to commit such crimes. This system of justice left much power to judges and the Crown to define just punishment in each special instance. Those crusaders demanding change to these laws pointed out that the threat had little power if criminals were convinced the harsh sentence would never be carried out. At the same time many people were reluctant to charge a petty offender with such a crime if they thought the accused could be hanged if found guilty. They claimed the judicial system was not working.

SIR SAMUEL ROMILLY

The following exchange between Garrow and Romilly gives insight into the argument being debated in Parliament. Garrow's interest in preserving traditional processes at this time of national threat is developed in his address to the House of Commons resisting Sir Samuel Romilly's Criminal Law Reform Bills. The exchange between Romilly and Garrow will be quoted in some detail to show opposing views of how the legal system functioned, and the role of judges and the Prince Regent or King in distributing both justice and mercy. Garrow makes the case for the traditional mode and Romilly makes the case for the need to change. By quoting segments of the record of debate in the House of Commons, on 17 February 1813, Romilly's position is described:

> Sir Samuel Romilly hoped, that in again drawing the attention of the House to a part of the general laws of the country, which he had already on a former occasion brought under their notice, he should not be considered guilty of any impropriety ....
>
> (Earlier)...he had proposed to bring in three Bills; one of which was to repeal the act of King William, which rendered it a capital offence to steal property to the amount of five shillings privately in a shop; another to repeal the act of Queen Anne, which pronounced it a capital offence to steal to the value of 40s, in a dwelling-house, and the third, to repeal the act of George II, rendering it a capital offence to steal property to the same amount, from on board a vessel on a navigable river. These Bills were all passed in 1811, by that House, but were rejected by the Lords.
>
> At the present moment he should only move for leave to bring in that one ... considered least objectionable ... stealing property of the value of 5s. in a dwelling-house ....[5]:
>
> This inexpediency was strongly demonstrated by the returns of the criminal courts for London and Middlesex, during the years 1805, 6, 7, 8 and 9 ... During these few years it appeared, that the number of individuals committed for this offence, amounted to 138 of whom 18 only had been convicted. The consequence of the law not being executed ... was that where some punishment was deserved, no punishment was at all inflicted, and the offender escaped altogether with impunity. This was the evil which could not exist if the laws were less

---

5. *Parliamentary Debates.* (17 February 1813). col. 562.

severe, and a certain but mild, although effective punishment, was substituted ... he condemned the retention of a law which was found too cruel for application, and which was, therefore, superseded in almost every instance by a discretionary adoption of that wise and humane principle that no unnecessary suffering, no useless pang ought ever to be inflicted under the sanction of the legislature.[6]

.... The question is, whether in a well-constituted commonwealth it is wise to retain laws not put in force? A penal law not ordinarily executed must be deficient in justice or wisdom, or both. But we are told, that we may trust to the operation of manners to relax the law. On the contrary, the laws ought to be always in unison with the manners, and corroborative of them, otherwise the effect of both will be lessened. Our passions ought not to be right, and our reason, of which law is the organ, wrong.

Who would say that any one for stealing a ribbon or piece of lace above the value of five shillings was deserving of death ... He did not believe that there was a single instance in which the sentence had ever been carried into execution ... There could not be a stronger instance of the general repugnance in men's minds to the carrying of such laws into effect.[7]

The next Bill he proposed to introduce related to the common law punishment in cases of High Treason. The sentence at present, it was well known, was, that the criminal shall be drawn upon a hurdle to the place of execution, that he shall be hanged by the neck, and being alive shall be cut down, that his entrails shall be taken out of his body, and, he living, the same shall be burnt before his eyes, that his head shall be cut off, his body be divided into four quarters, and head and quarters shall be disposed of at the pleasure of the king. In point of fact this horrible sentence was not now executed, the offender being hanged until dead, and his head being then cut off and exhibited to the spectators, a practice to his mind most exceptionable, when it was considered, that it was calculated to excite only disgust in some, compassion in others, and brutal apathy in a third class. ....[8]

Ought then, this punishment to remain to revolt the feelings of mankind, and furnish foreigners with a reproach against our national character? ... Ought the question, whether a man shall perish instantaneously, or by slow, bitter, and protracted torments, to be left to the decision of the executioner?

He was ready to admit, that at latter periods no such horrible exhibitions were exhibited, except by accident, and such instances had occurred; but surely it could never be endured, with any degree of patience, that the unfortunate wretch who was doomed to suffer death should be exposed to the most horrid tortures by the mere inattention or carelessness of an executioner, while the judge had no discretion whatever ... they were bound to pronounce the dreadful sentence of the law, while the mitigation of punishment was left to the care, and the aggravation of the negligence, of the executioner. ....[9]

The Parliamentary Debates record the response by Garrow.

The Solicitor-General (Sir William Garrow) said he did not propose to enter at large into the question in this early stage; but as he was not in parliament when his hon. and learned friend brought his Bills forward, he hoped the House would indulge him while he made some general observations on the principles by which his honourable and learned friend appeared

---

6. *Ibid.* col. 563.
7. *Ibid.* col. 565.
8. *Ibid.*
9. *Ibid.* cols. 566.

to be actuated, although he certainly did not mean to oppose his motion.[10]

He confessed himself totally unprepared to speak on the subject of punishment in cases of high treason, as he had not understood before that this would form a part of the propositions of his honourable and learned friend ....

.... he certainly agreed, that if the obligation of strictly interpreting and literally enforcing the provision of the criminal law were imposed on the judges, no one man would accept an office which would convert the assizes into shambles. But if discretion must be vested somewhere, where could it be so safely reposed as with the judges of the land? Always reserving, too, an appeal to the fountain of mercy - an appeal which, whenever good cause could be shown in support of it, had never been made in vain ....

He had at time been called upon to assist the judges at assizes. In one instance a man had been tried for stealing a piece of timber in the nighttime, and had been convicted. The sentence to be inflicted by the law was transportation for seven years; but if the judge had been compelled to insist on the infliction of that sentence, under the peculiar circumstances of the case, it must have made his situation miserable indeed.

The prisoner was a poor but industrious tailor; everybody bore testimony to his good character, even the prosecutor himself was constrained to say that he believed him to be the most industrious, and excellent creature living. When called on for his defence, and to state why he had committed the theft, the poor man said, "It is true that I stole the piece of timber as I was returning home from my club; and I intended to make stools of it for my poor, sick children." Such was the feeling on the judge, after having heard all the heart-rending circumstances, that he instantly and rapidly said to the prisoner - 'I hope your appearance here will be of no detriment to you hereafter - it ought not to be - you have suffered much already - go hence, and bless the laws which have enabled the judge to exercise some discretion on your case: - Gaoler, discharge the prisoner!'

What would have been the situation of the judge had there been any written scale of law which must be applied to such a case? Would not any further punishment that this poor man had already received have been too much? This case applied to ninety-nine out of every hundred; yet there were instances in which it was advisable for the security of society to exert the utmost rigour of the law. ... He admitted that it would be most horrible if the letter of our penal code were to be abided by in every instance, for there were many cases where to inflict the punishments prescribed by the statutes for the offence would be little short of the most barbarous cruelty.[11]

Garrow then stated:

No man had a higher veneration for the trial by jury then he had, and for those who composed the juries of this country. Few men had seen more of the proceedings in criminal courts than he had; but after thirty years' experience, he had not known six instances where, had he been of the jury, he should not have felt himself bound to determine precisely as the jury had determined. But after they had brought in their verdict, they were, like other men, accessible to pity. The doors of the jurymen might afterwards be crowded by the daughters, the sons, or the mothers of those who had been convicted, praying their interference. They would admit the justice of the conviction - they would acknowledge the offence of their relatives; but they would add - '*you cannot wish them to expiate their crimes with their lives - you cannot desire that they should be hanged; think, then, on our feelings for those who, we believe, may be saved if you*

10. *Ibid.* cols. 567-8.
11. *Ibid.* cols. 571-2.

will petition the Prince Regent. You will not refuse to sign this paper – life is valuable to the meanest being that crawls!' Thank God! Few Englishmen could withstand such an appeal as this! The Petition was signed under those circumstances, and was forwarded to the fountain of mercy, where it would always have due effect if a fair case were made out.

While assisting the judges at assize, it was once unfortunately his duty to pass sentence of death on six individuals, some of whom he could not leave for execution, and of course no such order was left. But such feeling towards the unhappy individuals could not be communicated to them. The consequence was, when he was about to leave the town the carriage wheels were beset; and there were loud prayers, calling on him "for God's sake not to leave the criminals for execution!" It was ascertained that those who were offering up the petitions so fervently, were actually the prosecutors; and they admitted the offence, and the justice of the sentence, but said that the poor men's lives ought to be spared – for life was valuable.

Such has ever been the case, and if the judges were not so to run a race of humanity with the prosecutors, their carriage wheels would be so obstructed that they would be unable to move. It had the happiest effects, it communicated mercy to those who merited it, while the law was to be called into action against greater offenders. The severity of the law was not too much for some cases; for the utmost rigour was sometimes called for out of mercy to society.[12]

.... he had addressed (Parliament) for the sole purpose of doing away that prejudicial impression which might be made on the public mind, had the statement gone forth to the world without some observations being made upon it.

Mr. Frankland spoke to the effect that foreigners often viewed the criminal code as barbaric, but observed these opinions were formed from a knowledge of the criminal code without knowing how it was administered. He added that had they seen the manner in which those laws were administered they would have never expressed such opinions.

Sir Samuel Romilly replied:

(He) expressed his hope that he had not been so misunderstood by the House in general, as he was sorry to observe he had been by his two honourable and learned friends, who had attributed to him many propositions which were by no means his, but which he considered to be as mischievous as they considered them. He wished particularly that his honourable and learned friend, the Solicitor-General, would take the trouble of informing himself more correctly as to his opinions, and he would find that they were as opposite as night and day to those which he had ascribed to him.[13]

Years later, Parliament passed laws institutionalizing the position promoted by Romilly and those of similar conviction.

---

12. *Ibid.* col. 571.
13. *Ibid.* col. 572.

Attacks by Romilly

Garrow was opposed to both political and law reform and clashed more than once with the reforming zeal of Romilly who led the nineteenth century movement to mitigate the rigours of the penal law, which may well account for Romilly's attacks upon him. On 5 April 1813 Romilly's Bill on attainder of treason and felony was before the Commons. Its purpose was to take away in cases of treason and felony the feudal doctrine of "corruption of the blood" by which a person found guilty could not hold or inherit land or, more importantly since the penalty for these offences was frequently death, transmit a title by descent.[14] As Solicitor-General, Garrow declared that the Bill would remove one of the safeguards of the Constitution.[15] When the question was debated again a few days later he repeated the remark and drew from Mr. Ponsonby the response that he was astonished at the assertion that the mode of execution for high treason was one of the safeguards of the Constitution.

According to Sir Leon Radzinowicz, Garrow maintained that he would never have voted for the old law if it were then to be enacted, but since it had the sanction of centuries, he was against changing it.[16] There can be no doubt that despite his revolutionary approach to advocacy, Garrow remained at heart a traditionalist. When the Bill was defeated Romilly wrote in his *Memoirs* that, "the Ministers have the glory of having preserved the British law, by which it is ordained that the heart and the bowels of a man convicted of treason shall be torn out of his body while he is yet alive."[17] This "safeguard of the Constitution" was not abolished until the Forfeiture Act 1870[18] - over half a century later.

As we shall see, in 1814 Garrow was appointed Chief Justice of Chester.[19] This led to a protest in the House of Commons by Romilly who opposed his taking the judgeship on the ground that the offices of judge and Attorney-General were incompatible. He considered that the appointment as chief justice was "objectionable in its nature" as the Attorney-General was proposing to hold the two offices together. "To appoint a gentleman," he declared, "holding a lucrative office at the sole pleasure of the Crown (and removable from that office the very moment that he might give dissatisfaction to the Crown) to a high judicial situation, was extremely inconsistent with that independence of the judicial character which it was so important to preserve inviolate."[20] In some cases persons would be tried by an individual who had advised and directed their prosecution. Could, he asked, such a person be

---

14. *Ibid.*
15. *Ibid.* col. 764.
16. Sir. L. Radzinowicz. (1948) *A History of English Criminal Law and its Administration from 1750: The Movement for Reform.* London, Steve ns & Sons Limited, vol. i, p. 519.
17. Sir S. Romilly. (1840) *Memoirs of the Life of Samuel Romilly, Written by Himself.* London, John Murray. vol. iii. p. 100.
18. 33 & 34 Vict. c. 23.
19. 17 *Parliamentary Debates.* (1810) col. 1207.
20. *Hansard.* (1 March 1814) vol. xxvii. col. 330.

considered as an independent judge?[21]

To a large extent however, Romilly undermined his position by indicating, without giving any reason, that he did not propose to make a motion on the matter, and Garrow was left free to proceed in both posts. Apparently, Garrow had absented himself when the attack was made and next day wrote to thank Romilly for his compliments![22]

In his *Memoirs,* Romilly also complained that Garrow, as Attorney-General, had dealt with a matter about which, Romilly claimed, he knew little. He objected that,

> He appeared at the Bar of the House of Lords with a written argument, the whole of which he very deliberately read, without venturing to add a single observation or expression of his own. In the Stafford peerage, which stood for the same day, he did exactly the same thing. He merely read an argument which somebody had composed for him.

And, he continued:

> Two days afterwards, in the Court of Chancery ... I said that it would be difficult for a counsel to do his duty in that court by writing arguments and sending them to some person to read them for him. The Lord Chancellor interrupted me by saying, "In this court or in any other?" And after the Court rose, he said to me, "You knew, I suppose, what I alluded to? It was Garrow's written argument in the House of Lords." So little respect has his Lordship for an Attorney-General, whom he himself appointed because he was agreeable to the Prince.[23]

The Times of 18 April 1815 records another of these confrontations. Romilly tried to get the House of Commons to petition the Prince Regent on behalf of a man convicted of bigamy. His punishment was transportation, and Romilly was attempting to get the House to ask the Prince Regent to rescind this punishment. *The Times* reports the following action before the House.

> Sir S. Romilly, pursuant to his notice, moved for an address to the Prince Regent, requesting he would order to be laid before the House a copy of the Report of the Recorder of London of the judgment passed on Robert Lathrop Murphy who was tried for bigamy at the Old Bailey in January last. He said that this case was one which required the greatest publicity, as it was a case of great hardship, and the punishment most peculiarly severe.
>
> It was one of the slightest cases of bigamy he had ever heard of and yet had received a sentence of the highest punishment the law would allow. Since the act had been passed which attached the punishment of transportation to this offence (now eight years) not one in four had suffered this sentence. Out of 104 cases, only 23 persons had been transported for the offence, and in general the punishment was only one year's imprisonment, or a small fine. The second wife knew perfectly well of the first marriage before she married the prisoner, and ... the prisoner ... was convinced the first marriage was illegal.....

21. *Ibid.* cols. 331-2.
22. R.G. Thorne (ed) *The History of Parliament. The House of Commons. Op. cit.* p. 6.
23. Romilly. *Memoirs of the Life of Samuel Romilly, Written by Himself. Op. cit.* vol. iii. Pp. 127-8.

The Attorney-General (Garrow) said the crime of bigamy had been found so common and so much on the increase, that an act had been passed, giving the judges a power of sentencing persons who committed this crime to transportation for 7 years. He differed with the honourable and learned gentleman who made the motion so far as to deem this case instead of the slightest to be one of the greatest offences of the kind.

The person found guilty of this crime had married a most respectable young lady in Ireland; and after living with her several years as her husband, he came to England, and married a second wife, who had a fortune of £10,000 on her marriage and was entitled to £70,000 more on the death of her mother. If she had consented, the guardians and mother had been imposed on; for he had married by licence, by which he had sworn he was a single man, and they had added perjury to bigamy. He had, also, greatly injured the first wife, whom he had reduced to a state of widowhood, without the power of marrying the most honourable and desirable man that should offer so long as the prisoner was alive. From the prisoner's own statement, he had no hesitation in advising that the sentence should be carried into execution, and as such he must oppose the motion.

The House refused the request to petition the Prince Regent on this man's behalf. Garrow carried the day.

CORN LAWS

Another highly contentious issue, that came before the House from time to time in the early nineteenth century was the prospect of repealing the Corn Laws. Landed gentry, a major force in Parliament, sought to maintain tariffs on imported grains, and other food stuffs to artificially maintain a high price for the products of their agriculture-based estates. Imports would have lowered prices. Therefore, the common people in cities and elsewhere wanted the Corn Laws repealed. No issue was so violently controversial and so dangerous politically, as the Corn Laws.

As a footnote to Garrow's career in Parliament, during the debate on repealing the Corn Laws during 1815, his speech to Parliament concerning his relationship with the common people made *The Times*. The 7 May issue of that newspaper carried the following story:

Mr. Garrow He had been the last member to enter the House from without. To avoid passing through the throng, he drove to the entrance gate of Westminster Hall. When his carriage arrived there, the door was opened, and he was asked who he was by numbers, who also insisted on knowing how he meant to vote on the Corn Bill . . . He was aware that for years past he had been too well-known in Westminster to be able to disguise himself. He was never ashamed of his name, nor could he conceal it. And many, probably, knew him well enough. He said to the people, "I won't deceive you, nor will I state what my vote will be. I shall certainly act accordingly to the dictates of my conscience, after hearing this measure fully discussed. Unless you pursue a different conduct you and all of you may yet regret your present attempt to over awe members in parliament, and if my life were in danger, I would sacrifice it in such a case as this."

Some of the mob said he had always been a friend of the people. He thought that among so many, all might not think of him so handsomely. Some, however, formed an escort for him through the hall to the steps ascending to the lobby. There again he found an immense number, not to be resisted by mere peace officers. There again they called upon him for a pledge, they urged the sufferings of the poor during a long war and desired not to be offered up to the interests of the Irish. He told them there, that he had no objection to state his sentiments, that parliament would certainly do its duty, but that if something were not done, they might have soon to depend for their existence on foreign bread.

Garrow also sponsored legislation to control the practice of surgery throughout the United Kingdom of Great Britain and Ireland. One provision of the Bill would assign midwifery to the surgeons, and make it unlawful for physicians to assist in the delivery of babies. *A Letter to Sir William Garrow, His Majesty's Attorney-General,* written by James Hamilton, M.D. and Professor of Midwifery in the University of Edinburgh, attacked the merits of this proposal. Many libraries around the world hold this widely published letter lobbying against this practice. It is one of the most widely available references to Garrow.[24] The Bill did not pass into law.

ANIMAL RIGHTS

In the early 1800s appalling cruelty to many kinds of animals was widespread. William Hogarth had earlier drawn studies revealing four stages of cruelty in order to show that brutality to animals leads to brutality to humans. Jeremy Bentham, for his part, insisted that cruelty to animals should be made a crime punishable by law.[25] But, in general, the public remained unmoved. Then, in 1809, Erskine introduced into the House of Lords a Bill for the prevention of "malicious and wanton cruelty" to animals. "Extending humanity to them", he exclaimed, would have a most powerful effect on men's moral sense and upon their feelings and sympathies for each other."[26] His speech was published as a pamphlet and the Lords found no difficulty in accepting the Bill. In the Commons, however, William Windham sneered that for Erskine to be the first who stood up as the champion of the rights of brutes was, indeed, a marked distinction, and the Bill was defeated.

As we have seen, in 1816, Garrow, when he was Attorney-General, was to introduce his own Bill, known as the "Stage Coach Bill." This sought to increase the penalties for overriding horses, which often ended in their death, but it too had been defeated. Here Garrow was siding with Bentham and the Utilitarians and in respect of cruelty to animals, both lawyers were in advance of their time. However, a few years later they must have felt vindicated when, in 1820, another Bill drafted

---

24. A letter to Sir William Garrow from James Hamilton, M.D. Fellow of the Royal College of Physicians of Edinburgh and Professor of Midwifery in the University of Edinburgh. 2nd edition, London, 1818.

25. Internet. www.rspca-act.org.au/default.asp?dsx=history

26. 14 *Parliamentary Debates.* (1809) col. 553.

by Erskine was introduced into the Commons where, with Windham no longer present, it was accepted and, after passing through the Lords, was enacted.[27]

Concerning Garrow's role in state trials held during the time he served as Solicitor-General and Attorney-General, the author of the article on Garrow in *The Legal Observer* had this analysis:

> The manner in which Sir William Garrow acquitted himself in discharging the general duties of these high state offices; (universally admitted to be most unpopular and yet responsible) the directing and conducting of state prosecutions was carried into execution during the time that he was Attorney-General, with singular forbearance and propriety.
>
> Convinced, by long experience and observation of the dangerous effects of failure in proceedings of this nature, caution and deliberation seem to have characterized his resolutions, and to have dictated the advice he was called upon to offer to the government upon such subjects. Hence it may be seen that, although during his official responsibility, the number of state prosecutions were few in comparison with those instituted by some of his predecessors, rarely can there be found an instance in which an acquittal added to the evil intended to be suppressed ... [or] encouraged a repetition of the offence.
>
> Well may it, therefore ... be remarked, that in this respect at least, Sir William Garrow's discreet and vigilant exercise of the powers entrusted to him as a public law officer, entitles him to no mean commendation.

GOVERNMENT SERVICE

Looking back to the beginning of his entrance into his professional career, it is clear Garrow was being drawn into a practice that was a combination of law, politics and government service. When Parliament was dissolved in 1784, he was an assessor to Alderman Plomer, an active supporter of Charles James Fox and the Whig party at the Hertford election. Plomer said to Garrow, "Pray, Sir, shall you have any objection to be engaged for Mr. Fox at the approaching election for Westminster?" Garrow answered that he should consider it a high honour. "Then, Sir," said the alderman, "you may consider this conversation as a retainer."

When asked why he chose Garrow, Plomer answered that he had read Garrow's argument in "The King and Aikles," which convinced him that the man who could produce that argument was equal to any task in his profession. Garrow proved himself worthy of this confidence. During the election the polling was both contentious and protracted, lasting forty days. The voters were subjected to every technique the contending parties could devise; intimidation, bribery and corruption, even murder, as well as noisy processions and riots to keep feelings high and tempers hot. On the lighter side, one butcher thought a kiss was an appropriate price for a vote, and the Countess of Salisbury, a supporter of Fox, was reported to have obliged, although it was probably the countess's sister who delivered the kiss.

---

27. 3 Geo. IV. c. 71.

After being behind for much of the forty days, Fox pulled ahead at the last and earned one of the two seats for Westminster. Then the high bailiff granted a scrutiny, a challenge to the results. Defeated candidates often avenged themselves for their failure at the polls by unseating a victorious rival on charges of bribery or corruption, or the manufacture of illegal votes, or the use of intimidation. Keeping Fox, the leader of the Whigs, from representing Westminster was such an attractive possibility, that the Tory government of William Pitt tried again to unseat him. The scrutiny, which lasted two sessions of Parliament, was finally stopped by a vote of the House of Commons and Fox finally obtained his seat.

During this election and scrutiny Garrow distinguished himself by great firmness, activity, and ingenuity. Not only did the legal manoeuvring apply pressure on Garrow, the opposition newspapers daily assailed him with abuse and ridicule. But in this situation, Garrow acquired new strength and flourished.

Perhaps the best way to understand the drama of this event is with Garrow's own words as he described one event in this legal battle, or as the record states "not exactly perhaps in his own words, but strictly according to his narrative." Concerning the retainer to represent Mr. Fox, Garrow's narrative continues:

I thought no more of the matter, but on the following morning, when I was in court at the Old Bailey, I was told that a gentleman wished to speak with me; I went into the Lord Mayor's parlour (a room to which in those days counsel used to retire to consult, to refresh themselves, or to see their friends or clients) and there I found Mr. Fox. 'Oh, Mr. Garrow,' he said, 'my petition is to be heard at 4 o'clock, and I shall depend on your assistance to support it.' I said I could not do it; I had no time for preparation, nor any instructions. "Instructions! pooh pooh!" said Mr. Fox, 'you know the business better than anybody; and if instructions were required, we should look to you to give, not to receive them. We shall expect you - I won't detain you from your other business--good morning!' and so he bowed himself out of the room.

I went to the House, and Mr. Douglas (Lord Glenbervie) was first heard on the petition. I make my speech, determined to suppress no portion of my opinion, unless compelled by authority.

Of this speech no trace or record remains. Unfortunately, and by some unaccountable means, the notes of the short-hand writer were lost or purloined, and no copy preserved; but of the effort of the speech a truly remarkable evidence may be given. Sir Lloyd Kenyon (then Master of the Rolls) had shown himself, during the election and after it closed, a strenuous partisan of the interest opposed to Fox. When Mr. Garrow had concluded, he rushed to the bar, and seizing him by both hands, exclaimed - "Young man, I congratulate you! You have made your fortune, young man!"[28]

The *Parliamentary History* shows Garrow spoke for nearly two hours but gives us none of his words. It does say, however, that, "although Mr. Garrow had been

---

28. *The Times.* (7 November 1840).

but newly called to the Bar, and never pleaded before the Commons of England till that night, he acquitted himself in a manner equally tending to the advantage of his clients and to his own honour and credit."[29]

Although Garrow was able to take silk because of his formidable success as a barrister, it was widely believed that his political views were crucial to the appointment and that he, and others, were engaged to defend the government against the radical challenges to the unreformed parliamentary franchise. Certainly, his leadership in the Crown side of the King's Bench in the 1790s was seen as reflecting the Tory party's reputation.[30] As a consequence, Garrow had turned from Whig to Tory, his allegiance from Fox to Pitt, and newspapers claimed he was given silk to help defend the Constitution in the courts against the radicals.[31] In fact, he did become an important government prosecutor in state trials in the early 1790s[32] having previously acted mainly for defendants at the Old Bailey.[33]

In the Hilary term a year later, by Erskine's influence, he became a legal adviser to the Prince of Wales. At that time, 1805, Erskine, as the Prince's Attorney -General and legal adviser, arranged for Garrow to be his assistant as Solicitor-General to the Prince. Later, in February 1806, Garrow succeeded Erskine as the Prince's Attorney-General.

The letter Garrow wrote accepting this position as the Prince's Attorney-General is included in *The Correspondence of George, Prince of Wales, 1770-1812*. It is a good example of the way Garrow expressed himself. With this letter we have Garrow's own words, not someone's dictated notes on what Garrow said or someone's recollections years after the event. This letter acknowledged his dependence on the Prince's friendship but reserved the right to show his gratitude for Pitt (a prime minister who had recently died) and Lord Melville if questions concerning them arose in Parliament. Garrow wrote to William Adam on 7 February 1806:

> Nothing could have been more agreeable to me than the communication which you have been directed to make to me, nor could it have been conveyed through any channel more agreeable to me. The gracious unsolicited offer from his Royal Highness the Prince of Wales of the distinguished honour of being appointed Attorney-General to that illustrious personage leaves me no choice. I accept it with the highest satisfaction. The value of this favour is much enhanced by the very kind and obliging manner in which you represent that his Royal Highness has had the goodness to express himself upon the occasion adding by a condescension peculiar to himself to the value of the benefit conferred.

29. *Parliamentary History*. (1794) London, Longman and Others. vol. xxiv, cols. 857-8.
30. D. Lemmings. *Professors of the Law: Barristers and English Legal Culture in the Eighteenth Century. Op. cit.* p. 168.
31. J.M. Beattie. (1991) "Scales of Justice: Defence Counsel and the English Criminal Trial in the Eighteenth and Nineteenth Centuries". 9(2) *Law and History Review*, University of Illinois Press.
32. E.Foss. (1864) *The Judges of England: with Sketches of their Lives and Miscellaneous Notices Connected with the Courts at Westminster from the Time of the Conquest.* Vol. ix. London, John Murray.
33. OBP Online. (www.oldbaileyonline.org).

It is a great satisfaction to me that in availing myself of the opportunity offered to me of engaging my humble efforts in the service of his Royal Highness I make no sacrifice of principle nor am guilty of any desertion of friends to whom I had been long attached or with whom I had been engaged in established habits of political intercourse, but that on the contrary it brings me nearer to the great man to whom I have always looked with gratitude as my earliest friend, the founder of all my prosperity.

I hope that it will not be thought improper that I avail myself of this opportunity of explaining myself upon a matter which appears not wholly unimportant. You know that my introduction to Parliament was an act of great personal kindness from Mr. Pitt, that I felt much bound to him and must always entertain an affectionate regard for his memory and grateful recollection of his friendship. You are likewise well acquainted with the numberless instances of interesting kindness which I have at all times experienced from my friend Lord Melville and his incomparable Lady. What I should request then is that you would, if you see no impropriety, suggest for me a hope that if any question of a personal nature affecting either the honour or memory of my illustrious deceased friend or the interests of Lord Melville should be agitated, I shall not incur the displeasure of his Royal Highness if I should follow the impulses of gratitude and friendship and should not concur in measures which may be approved by the friends of his Royal Highness. These occasions will not probably occur but I wished to guard against the possibility.

To you, my dear friend, I entirely confide myself on this most interesting and important occasion and hope that you will do for me what I feel myself unequal to accomplish to my own satisfaction, by expressing in a proper manner to his Royal Highness my unbounded gratitude for the high honour which he has in so gracious a manner been pleased to confer on me.[34]

There is a story reported in *The Farington Diary* concerning the relationship between the Prince and Garrow and is related to the Prince calling Garrow to be his personal Attorney-General. While it is told to illuminate how the Prince jealously maintained his inherited rights, it also shows something of the relationship of these two persons. It reads:

Wm. Offley related a trait of the Prince of Wales shewing His Royal Highness to be jealous of all His rights which belong to Him in his high situation. He said he had been told Mr. Garrow, the King's Council, had mentioned it as having happened to Cornwall (sic) Garrow, who had often been with the Prince, expressed his acknowledgment by calling at Carleton House and leaving His Card: but it was signified to him that would not do; that He must go to Carleton House full dressed, & make a formal acknowledgment for the favour done him.

This Mr. Garrow did, & the Prince recd, Him and accepted His thanks ceremoniously, which being done, the Prince then said "Now Mr. Garrow we are friends (meaning now we may talk with equality) but nothing that properly belongs to my situation shall be given up by me".

It is not clear to what extent Garrow supported the Prince with legal advice in his tangled legal struggles with the King, Parliament, his wife and those to whom he owed large sums of money. However, a letter Lord Erskine wrote concerning a peti-

34. A. Aspinall. (1971) *The Correspondence of George, Prince of Wales 1770-1812.* New York, Oxford University Press Inc., p. 335.

tion on behalf of a Mr. Foster, who was pleading for his life, suggests one type of consulting Garrow performed for the Prince Regent, and also shows Lord Erskine's opinion of Garrow as a source of legal advice in the field of criminal law.

Lord Erskine to Lord [.....]
Saturday evening, 9 March 1811

> I forwarded to Colonel McMahon a petition in favour of the unfortunate Foster who is now under sentence of death for forgery, & he has explained to me the difficulties which attend his case for there being two other persons convicted of the same crime whose cases are not distinguishable . . . I understand from your Lordship that the Prince was to see Garrow & I am glad of it, as he knows more of the real justice and policy of everything connected with the criminal law than any man I am acquainted with, and I am confident he will deliver a sound opinion on the subject.[35]

The Prince must have agreed with this evaluation of Garrow's understanding of the criminal law, and, on 17 July 1812, he knighted Garrow in a ceremony at Carlton House and Garrow became Sir William Garrow.[36]

Solicitor-General
In the 1812 general election he was returned for Eye in the interest of the Marquess of Cornwallis and became Solicitor-General in the ministry of Lord Liverpool, as a friend of the Tory government. The appointment aroused some rancour. James Scarlett (a formidable lawyer and later Lord Abinger) described Garrow as:

> An eloquent scolder with a fine voice and most distinct articulation, a great flow of words, considerable quickness in catching the meaning of a witness, and great abilities in addressing juries in ordinary cases, [who] without education, without taste and without law, acquired and maintained a high reputation with the public, but none in the profession. He was not much known in private life ... but I believe he was kindhearted, generous and humane.[37]

Such partisan and partially inaccurate remarks may stem from a distaste for Garrow's lowly background but they are too common to ignore. Furthermore, they give credit for the very attributes that not only made him such a powerful defence lawyer but also had an ineradicable effect on the establishment of adversary trial.

Attorney-General
With Liverpool still in the early years of his long premiership, Garrow became Attorney-General on 4 May 1813, succeeding Sir Thomas Plumer. A little-known MP, Joseph Jekyll, suggested that, "Garrow's vanity on his new office is the joke of

---

35. *Ibid.* p. 268.
36. G.F.R. Barker. (1975) Dictionary of National Biography. Oxford, Oxford University Press.
37. R.G. Thorne. (ed) (1986) *The History of Parliament. The House of Commons, 1790-1820.* London, Secker & Warburg, p. 6.

the bar. As a vulgar man he wonders to find himself at ministers' dinners and talks of nothing else."[38] But again one questions how reliable such remarks are.

We have already noticed something of Garrow as Attorney-General in the House of Commons. But, of course, the office also involved him in prosecuting on behalf of the Crown. Few of Garrow's cases whilst Attorney-General have, in fact, been reported but one was *Dixon v. Bell*[39] in April 1816. Here the defendant had left a loaded gun at his lodgings and sent his servant, a young girl aged about thirteen, to collect it, asking the landlord to remove the priming and give it to her. Later, the girl injured the plaintiff's small son when she drew the trigger. The jury found for the plaintiff (the landlord) on the ground that the defendant had negligently entrusted the young girl with the gun. As Attorney-General, Garrow moved for a new trial but his motion was dismissed by Lord Ellenborough and Mr Justice Bayley who said it was incumbent on the defendant to render the gun safe and innocuous.

In September 1816 Garrow, again as Attorney-General, prosecuted two senior police officers, George Vaughan, and his agent, John Dannelly. Although both men were charged with burglary, they were found guilty only of stealing in a dwelling-House and Dannelly's conviction was overturned on a technicality. The case, and other similar cases, had, however, aroused serious public disquiet and Garrow had shown no hesitation in bringing the prosecutions.

Whilst Attorney-General Garrow, chastened by his earlier experiences in debates, generally spoke only briefly in the Commons on legal questions although he intervened on a number of occasions in the summer of 1816. First, he defended Lord Ellenborough from attack on 30 April 1816.[40] He then made a defence of an Aliens Bill, which was considered by its opponents to be illiberal, on 10 May[41] and he also moved, on 10 June, a bill to impose speed limits on, and prevent inconsiderate driving of, stage coaches. In doing so he referred to enormous abuses of stage coach drivers which put at risk lives and limbs of passengers and others, and proposed that magistrates should have the power to imprison for three months in atrocious cases.[42]

In one of these more frequent interventions in the House of Commons, he told members on 30 April 1816 that, as he had himself done, counsel should not fear to point out to a judge, even in a trial of the meanest individual, that the judge had erred in law. He should do so, "treating the noble and learned judge with all the respect due to his high character and situation, without fear of his displeasure, or without thinking of courting his approbation by a different line of conduct."[43] An example of his having done so is to be found in Garrow's altercation with Mr. Justice

38. R.G. Thorne. *Ibid.*
39. 5 M. & S. p. 198.
40. *Parliamentary Debates.* (April-July 1816) First series, cols. 121-7.
41. *Ibid.* col. 463.
42. *Ibid.* col. 1040-41.
43. *Ibid.* col. 126.

Heath in the trial of William Bartlett at the Old Bailey on 11 January 1786 which is cited earlier.[44]

On 8 May in the same year Brougham had introduced in the Commons a Bill entitled, "For securing the Liberty of the Press". In introducing the Bill he stated that in all cases of criminal libel prosecuted by information *ex officio* the Crown "never went to trial without a special jury." He added that, "all other crimes and misdemeanours, felony, and even the highest crime known to the law, high treason, were always tried before a common jury. He saw no reason for giving to the Crown, in the instance of libel, a right of selection which it did not possess in any other case"[45] Garrow opposed Brougham and argued that, in trials of libel prosecuted by the Crown, it was the defendant who could choose to be tried by a special jury.[46] This seems an odd claim, however, since, apart from Brougham's claim that in libel cases the Crown always had a special jury, such a jury, made up of men of higher social standing than those on a petty jury, was not generally favoured by prisoners.

According to Garrow a special jury was formed by the sheriff attending the master of the Crown office, with an agent for each party to the case, and selecting forty-eight names of prospective jurors. Each party was then allowed to strike out the names of twelve of them so that it was impossible for any man to say which twelve out of the remaining twenty-four would form the jury on the trial."[47] The resulting jury became known as a "struck jury." Although, to an extent, this allowed the parties to pick the jury there can be little doubt that special handpicking went on, a court official collaborating with the Crown Solicitor for the purpose.[48]

LEAVING THE COMMONS

When Garrow resigned from the Attorney-General post, to become one of the Barons of the Court of Exchequer in May 1817, he resigned his seat in the House of Commons. A William Wellesley Pole had this to say about Garrow leaving the halls of the House of Commons: "It will be a great relief to government to get him out of the House of Commons. He did not succeed there. I believe he had good taste enough to detest it." Another author stated this observation more directly. In the *Law Review and Quarterly* (November 1844-February 1845) in an article on Garrow, and concerning Parliament, it states: "Indeed he cordially hated the place, and was with difficulty induced to enter it, or having entered, to address it. Speak, however, he did...."

It is indisputable that Garrow did not shine as a Member of Parliament.

44. *Ante*, page 60.
45. *Hansard.* [34] (April-July 1816). First series, col. 393.
46. *Ibid.* col. 394.
47. *Ibid.* col. 395.
48. W.R. Cornish. (1968) *The Jury.* London, Allen Lane. The Penguin Press. p. 131.

Although there have been many successful barristers in Parliament, for some the skills of oratory required there are different from those that are successful before a jury in a court of law. Lawyers like Pitt were politicians first and generally gave up work at the Bar. And, a barrister used to weighing arguments in detail and treating all causes with equal gravity could easily bore the commons or treat its members as if they were an undiscerning jury.[49]

Garrow's critics and his friends will use different criteria in evaluating his performance. The role that history and his position in government thrust upon him during this phase of his career was not that of innovator and champion of human rights, but that of defending the status quo. It was what he thought the times demanded. England, he believed, was at war abroad and at home against the revolutionary forces of France.

---

49. R.Stewart. (1986) *Henry Brougham 1778-1868. His Public Career.* London, The Bodley Head, p. 63.

CHAPTER 9

Garrow vs. Brougham

At the time we are dealing with, the early 1800s, two Scottish lawyers shone at the English Bar. They were known for their skill in advocacy and defence of clients.

ENLIGHTENMENT LAWYERS

These Enlightenment lawyers were firstly Thomas Erskine, later Lord Chancellor and one of the greatest barristers of all time. He was a friend of Garrow's and they appeared with, and against, each other in court on a number of occasions. Indeed Erskine had a significant impact on Garrow's career. *The Times* referred to Garrow as Erskine's chum.[1] As we saw in *Chapter 8*, it was Erskine who brought Garrow into the service of the Prince of Wales when Erskine, serving as the Prince's Attorney-General, had Garrow appointed as his assistant, the Prince's Solicitor-General. And then when Erskine moved on, it was Garrow who became the Prince's Attorney-General.

When a picturesque coloured view of Pegwell Bay with Garrow's house was drawn, etched and sold by Amelia Noel in 1797, Erskine's name appeared on the subscribers' list - a sure sign of their friendship.[2]

The second Enlightenment lawyer was Henry Brougham, also later Lord Chancellor. He made his name for himself by his defence of John Hunt and John Leigh Hunt in two prosecutions for seditious libel in their newspaper, *The Examiner.* The first trial, on 22 January 1811, arose from an article opposing flogging in the army. Brougham secured an acquittal and the presiding judge, Lord Ellenborough, said his speech was remarkable for "great ability, eloquence, and manliness." However, at the second trial in 1812, when Garrow prosecuted and Brougham unsuccessfully defended the Hunts against the Prince Regent, Lord Ellenborough said that Brougham was "inculcated with all the poison of the libel".[3]

It should be remembered that Brougham's defence of Sir Henry Mildmay, as described in this chapter, took place in 1814. This was thirty years after Garrow established his reputation as the leading defence attorney. Also it was six years before Brougham defended Queen Caroline (1820) on the charge of adultery before the House of Lords, and protected her from the charges levied by her husband, King

---

1. *The Times.* (5 January 1790) within a notice: "The Party".
2. *Proposals for Publishing by Subscription Twenty-Four Picturesque Views,… drawn, etched and sold by Amelia Noel* (including the drawing Pegwell-Bay) "Subscribers' Names under the patronage of Her Royal Highness the Princess of Wirtemberg." Both Thomas Erskine and William Garrow were subscribers.
3. *The Law Magazine.* vol. 52. pp. 21-22.

George IV to obtain a divorce. It was in his role of defender of Queen Caroline that Brougham made the often quoted statement describing the role of defence counsel:

> An advocate, by the sacred duty which he owes his client, knows, in the discharge of that office, but one person in the world, that client and none other. To save that client by all expedient means - to protect that client at all hazards and costs to all others, and among other to himself, - is the highest and most unquestioned of his duties; and he must not regard the alarm, the suffering, the torment, the destruction which he may bring upon any other. Nay, separating even the duties of a patriot from those of an advocate, and casting them, if need by, to the wind, he must go on reckless of the consequences, if his fate it should unhappily be, to involve his country in confusion for his client's position.[4]

He was to back-track on this shortly afterwards saying the speech was, "anything rather than a deliberate and well-considered opinion on the general question of an advocate's duties."[5]

Brougham on Garrow

Clearly, in the early stages of his career Garrow was associated with the ideas of these Enlightenment lawyers, but any description of William Garrow's career invariably includes Henry Brougham's description of Garrow's lack of an academic legal education along with his mastery of courtroom-based forensic skills. Four years after Garrow's death Brougham's description of Garrow appeared in his Memoir, *"Mr. Baron Garrow"* published in the 1 *Law Review* (1844-1845) and states:

> There have probably been few more ignorant men in the profession than this celebrated leader. To law, or anything like law, he made no pretence… With so slender a provision of law, his ignorance of all beside, of all that constitutes science, or learning, or indeed general information, nay even ordinary information, was perfect.

In this same article Brougham readily acknowledged Garrow's skill in examining witnesses, and referred to his remarkable ability to acquire, seemingly without effort, a perfect knowledge of the facts and, through skilful questioning, to elicit a clear story that carefully steered away from any potentially damaging information. He states:

> With all these great deficiencies, with this confessedly slender stock in trade, Mr. Garrow was a great, a very great advocate. To describe him as merely quick, clear-seeing, wary, prompt, nimble, bold, in very sense of the large word, skilful, would be too general, though it would be quite correct if each of these phrases were extended to the superlative degree.

Only a few biographical type articles were written about Garrow during, or shortly

---

4. *Speeches of Lord Brougham.* (1838) Edinburgh, vol. i. p. 105.
5. W. Forsyth. (1849) *Hortensius: the Advocate.* p. 389. Cited by D.J.A. Cairns. (1998) *Advocacy and the Making of the Adversarial Criminal Trial.* Oxford, Clarendon Press. p. 139.

after, his lifetime. Brougham's is the most quoted of these articles and did much to form his public image following his death. Even today, with all the careful research being done on Garrow's role in the emergence of the adversarial type criminal trial, Brougham's work is still being extensively quoted and has a significant influence on how Garrow is remembered. Therefore it seems appropriate at the beginning of this chapter describing a courtroom contest between Garrow and Brougham to put Brougham's Memoir, "Mr. Baron Garrow" into a context in which his words might be better interpreted. His entire article on Garrow is available in *Appendix 3*.

Brougham's interest in, and knowledge of, literature and science was deep and he was always a whole-hearted supporter of the causes of education, law reform, anti-slavery, Catholic emancipation, parliamentary reform and a free press. He was a great orator, debater and organizer. On the other hand, he was often impulsive, excitable, wayward and capricious. As a consequence, he was widely distrusted and one of the nicknames coined for him was "Wicked Shifts". His brilliance often led him to patronize those whom he saw as lesser mortals and, for the same reason, although he was a fearless and energetic advocate, he was not very successful with juries. These latter traits have to be borne in mind when considering the comments of this high-born gentleman on the relatively more humble Garrow - and even Erskine.

In this context, the following trial has special interest, in that it describes William Garrow and Henry Brougham engaged in legal combat.

TRIAL BETWEEN LORD ROSEBERRY AND SIR HENRY MILDMAY FOR CRIMINAL CONVERSATION

On Saturday, 10 December 1814, William Garrow represented Lord Roseberry in the prosecution of Sir Henry Mildmay for "criminal conversation" with Lady Roseberry, the plaintiff's wife. This case is of general interest, not only because of the nature of "criminal conversation," or because a large sum of money (£30,000) was at stake, but also because a short-hand record of the proceedings was published. Adultery seemed to be a business for the courts, and Garrow is known to have pursued "criminal conversation" as a source of legal business.

Criminal conversation was a polite term for adultery, but with a special twist. It concerned equity, damage to the value of property, a theme of special interest in English law. When a man committed adultery he could be sued for the financial loss sustained by the injured husband, and for damages to his family's well-being. A money value would also be set for "exemplary damage," a financial penalty intended to discourage potential adulterers from acting on their impulses.

The report of the prosecution of Sir Henry Mildmay for criminal conversation appears in *Crim Con!!, Damages Fifteen Thousand Pounds!* This forty-eight page book was published immediately after the trial and sold for one shilling.[6]

Sir Henry Mildmay had pleaded guilty, so trial by jury concerned one issue, damages to be paid by Mildmay to Lord Roseberry. Recorded here are some of the highlights of the trial, with the goal of illustrating the exchange between Garrow and Brougham. Although Garrow was at this time the Attorney-General, in this case he was serving as an independent advocate.

Garrow made the opening statement - a long and detailed account of the affair which, presumably, evidence presented by witnesses would support. He stated that:

> ... in the whole course of his life, he had never felt anything approaching the difficulty, distress, and embarrassment, he now experienced. He had endeavoured, as his duty to the plaintiff, and his duty to the Jury whom he had the honour of addressing ... to put his thoughts into something like formal arrangement; but he found that absolutely impossible, the circumstances of this case differing so much from every thing he had ever seen, read, or heard of before, differing from all others in the extraordinary atrocity by which it was peculiarly distinguished. This had placed him in a situation of being obliged, as well as he was able, to state the circumstances to the Jury just as they presented themselves to his memory. He had felt a degree of disgust by the perusal of the details of the case, which rendered it impossible for him to do any more than trust the moment for such expressions as might occur to him.

If what followed was indeed presented from memory, without notes, and without his taking time to organize his thoughts to achieve his goal, then his native ability and years of experience before the bar was adequate to the task. He further stated:

> The first thing he had to state was who these parties were - who they were individually, and as members of the community; and to add to the melancholy and afflicting task of telling ... who they were as related to each other.
>
> The plaintiff was a nobleman of ancient creation in the northern part of his Majesty's dominions ... Not having known him, he could only speak from the information of others ... His honoured and learned friend (the Solicitor-General) had well characterized him: he had said of him: 'Oh, my friend, he was such a man that if any person of the highest rank had a daughter most dear to him and of marriageable age, he could not have found a fitter husband for her than Lord Roseberry, and having united her with him, he might have considered all his cares about her happiness as entirely at an end.'
>
> He was a most affectionate, indulgent, and tender husband, watching every opportunity of gratifying his wife, not by those frivolities described as constituting the agreeable part of life, but by everything by which there was a rational hope of conducing to the happiness of her who was the object of his attention.
>
> He married this lady (Lady Rosebery) in the year 1808; she was then of the age of eighteen, in the possession of every charm that could captivate, of every ornament and accomplishment that could constitute the happiness of a married life. She was the daughter of a man whose name must be known to the Jury, because men like them could not be unacquainted with one of the greatest philanthropists of the age: they could not but have heard of the Honourable Mr. Bouverie, known as the brother of the Earl of Randor ... This lady was one of his daughters....

---

6. Crim Con!! Damages Fifteen Thousand Pounds! Trial Between Lord Rosebery and Sir Henry Mildmay for Criminal Conversation with the Plaintiff's Wife. (1814) London, John Fairburn.

Who were the others?

The defendant, Sir Henry Mildmay, had married one of the others. The defendant's wife had borne him a son, and he had the misfortune to become a widower; he lost his lady in 1810.

It was another part of this melancholy history that the brother of the defendant was married to another of Mr. Bouverie's daughters; so that this case presented, not a case of adultery alone, not a case of seduction alone, not a case in which it was imputed to the defendant that he had violated all the ties of friendship, and broken down all that belonged to the laws of hospitality; but that he had added to those crimes the additional one of multiplied incest.

After the death of Lady Mildmay, at a period when it seemed, and it was to be feared when it only seemed, that Sir Henry Mildmay felt as an affectionate husband might be expected to feel upon that greatest of all possible calamities, the loss of an affectionate wife, the mother of an infant son, where was he so likely to look for consolation as in the highly respectable society of the relatives of his deceased wife? ....

Garrow then makes the case that Sir Henry Mildmay should be there to defend his own case so that the jury could judge him by his own language and sentiments. He reminded them that Mildmay was not there and assured the jury that when they had heard the evidence of the case, unparalleled in its atrocity, they would come in with a verdict recording the full extent of the damages charged on the record.

He then outlined the evidence they would hear from witnesses.

The father of the Lord Roseberry had taken ill at his seat in Scotland, and it became necessary for Lord Roseberry to visit his father and to be present in case of "that calamity, which eventually did happen." At the time of Lord Roseberry's departure, Lady Roseberry, attended by the Countess Dowager, left London for their seat in Norfolk. Sir Henry Mildmay was constantly their visitor. Garrow believed the jury would have no difficulty in persuading themselves most convincingly, that Sir Henry Mildmay availed himself of opportunities to ingratiate himself with this lady, to alienate her affections, to seduce her mind, and debauch her person.

Upon his return, "Lord Roseberry found it necessary to remonstrate with the defendant upon his too marked attention to Lady Roseberry!" The Honourable Mr. Bouverie, father of Lady Roseberry, also spoke with Sir Henry Mildmay, in which he warned him that he was "bringing ruin on all that was valuable within the circle of domestic happiness."

At this time Sir Henry Mildmay was writing letters to Lady Roseberry, and as Garrow said: "in terms which any man of honour should be ashamed of; telling her that he would roam the world with her." He was pressing her at once to leave her husband and family, and to take him as a partner for life. Because of his wife's altered conduct, Lord Roseberry found it necessary to take his wife to his seat in Edinburgh. Sir Henry Mildmay chose to also go to Edinburgh. However because he was not allowed to enter the Roseberry home, he chose to travel in an assumed name as Colonel de Grey of the Foot Guards. He then assumed a new identity as a sailor, and grew a beard. Garrow continues to describe what he plans to present as evidence, as the climax of this series of events.

> The habit of Lord Roseberry's family was to dine about six o'clock; the ladies retired to the drawing-room about seven, the gentlemen remaining together till about nine, when they joined the ladies. During the period which was marked by the arrival of the defendant in disguise, it was observed that Lady Roseberry, after dinner, did not continue long in the society of her mother, but, that as soon as she left the dining room, she retired to her own bed-chamber; this led to a suspicion that something was going on which was not well. It was conjectured, it could be accounted for by no cause except for Sir Henry Mildmay being in the neighbourhood.
>
> This led an honourable person, Mr. Primrose, the brother of Lord Roseberry, to observe her, on a particular day, after she had left the room; he tried the door of the bed-chamber, which he found fast locked, though, under ordinary circumstances, it would not have been so; he then endeavoured to break it open, when the door was opened by Lady Roseberry, and in that room was Sir Henry Mildmay, in the disguise of a common sailor, armed with a brace of loaded pistols.

Garrow said he would not attempt to describe the scene that followed, but that it ended when Mr. Primrose ordered Mildmay to leave the room the same way he came in - clandestinely through the window. The next morning Lady Roseberry took her departure, but instead of repairing as she had requested, and had been advised, to the house of her father, Mr. Bouverie, she followed the defendant, to become his partner for life, on the Continent. Indeed, this is what transpired.

Lady Roseberry's desk was opened and letters addressed to her were found. The letters were from Sir Henry Mildmay. Much of the rest of Garrow's presentation to the jury was to read and discuss these letters. The short-hand notes of the trial record the following:

> The first of these letters began by stating, that the ambition of the defendant induced him to attempt everything that could make a man notorious and respectable - notorious enough he was, said the Attorney-General (Garrow), whether he would ever again be respected in society was a question that was not doubtful; the defendant added, that his pride of family was exceeded by none, that his views were bounded by nothing in the power of man to obtain; but he assured Lady Roseberry, that he would give up all for her, - that, blest with her society, he would retire from the world, alike forgetting and forgot, - that he would leave his home; his friends and all, if she would accompany him, - that he would roam the world with her, and bless the hour when for her sake he had quitted his friends and connections....
>
> The jury would say how such a man ought to be dealt with - a man, the object of whose ambition was to debauch the wife of his friend, the sister of his deceased wife, and the sister of the wife of his own brother. ....
>
> It would be found in the letters that he had a difficult task in accomplishing the destruction of this ill-fated lady. It would be found that the seeds of virtue implanted in her mind had made her long resist his attempt to debauch her. In the character he had given of himself, it would be seen that his ambition to be notorious was only to be gratified by his obtaining the possession of her, whom he ought to have protected against the approach of any person who was contemplating her with the eye of lust. How ought such a man to be dealt with after he had accomplished his object?

Letter by letter he then proceeded to present and discuss the series of letters. Garrow then expressed the following:

> Would to God that those women of rank and character, such as Lady Roseberry had been, would, when first addressed by such men as the defendant, take a view of those abodes the most miserable that could be imagined, where the wife, having abandoned her family, was found with no consolatory association, no friends or relatives to cheer her - no attendants but remorse and despair. If anything could enable a woman to resist such seduction as had been practiced by the defendant, it would be the giving her a slight opportunity of seeing the horror of such a situation.
>
> The defendant's letters proceeded to state the misery he should suffer if he inhaled her breath no more, if he had taken the farewell kiss ....
>
> Hypocrisy, base and detestable! This man was talking of love in terms that would disgrace the obscene books exposed for sale at the Palais Royal ....

Garrow then plants the seed of an idea that Sir Henry Mildmay was considering challenging Lord Roseberry to a duel.

> It would be found, that he had intimated to her that he meant to make Lord Roseberry call him out- - not that he had any intention of shooting Lord Roseberry, - no; his object was only to deprive him of his wife; observing that he had given his Lordship satisfaction, by allowing him to fire at him, and firing his own pistol in the air; Lord Roseberry would then, according to the etiquette among men of honour, be obliged to bow to him and notice him in the street.

With the following words Garrow moves to close his summary of the case to the jury. He states "With the eloquence of a devil, he urged her to cast off her husband, to abandon her duties as a mother and wife, and to sell herself to perdition." And then with a few words Garrow talks to the jury about the Learned Gentleman, who would defend Sir Henry Mildmay's interests. They would be addressed by a gentleman of great eloquence - but he defied the Learned Gentleman to remove his claim for exemplary damages.

He reminded the jury of Lady Roseberry's words when she was found out ... "Oh! Mildmay, you found me innocent; Oh! Remember what I was." He then told the jury that it would be an idle waste of their time to detain them with a longer presentation. He observed that Lord Roseberry had been widowed by this defendant, who knew what the loss of such a wife was, and was sensible of the deprivation he had committed upon the happiness of his friend.

> The jury would be able to appreciate the loss a man must sustain, by having the affectionate partner of his life, the mother who was to cherish and educate his children, thus cruelly torn from him, by a man who had no incentive but the gratification of his sensual passions. They were to tell British society upon what terms they were to live for the future; and they would

answer that question well or ill, by giving the whole of or less then the thirty thousands pounds damages claimed on this record.

Garrow then proceeded to call witnesses to establish the charges he had described ... and indeed the witnesses tended to establish these facts, even under cross-examination. The major witness was Mr. Primrose, brother to Lord Roseberry. He described in detail his confrontation of Mildmay in Lady Roseberry's room and Mildmay leaving through the window, as he had come.

Brougham For Sir Henry Mildmay

However, for our purposes we will jump to the record of Brougham's statement to the jury to see how he countered Garrow's oratory. He quickly acknowledged that his client had pleaded guilty, and that it had become his painful duty to finish the proceedings of the day by offering his humble assistance to the Jury in choosing a remedy for the injury sustained by Lord Roseberry. He urged them to find an "adequate remedy - one, that while it consulted Lord Roseberry's honour, should not carry with it the utter ruin to the defendant." He then established his relationship with all the parties in this present case.

> He had the happiness, if at that moment he might call it a happiness, to be acquainted not with one only of the three noble houses whose character, and feelings, and interests were mingled in the present cause, but with all; he might boast the honour of a close intimacy with all of them, and he was proud to acknowledge the profound esteem he felt for all: indeed he now found himself in the distracting predicament, that he knew not for which of them his esteem and his attachment were the greatest ....
>
> And most happy he should deem himself, if, in executing the task ... if in assisting to pour the healing balm into wounds which were no sooner inflicted than mourned, he could succeed in obtaining from them such damages as might satisfy the ends of justice, vindicate the honour of the noble plaintiff, and assert the cause of public morals, without striking the defendant into irremediable ruin.
>
> But if they guided themselves by all that had fallen from his Learned Friend, the Attorney-General, if they simply trusted to his inflamed and exaggerated statements, heightened by all those powers of eloquence which he so well knew how to employ, they would not render that service to all the branches of the three noble houses which was sought for, nor would they render that service to the noble client of his Learned Friend, which he knew was alone desirous to obtain.
>
> It became, therefore, a binding duty upon him (Mr. Brougham) not to allow them to deliberate upon the case fresh from the influence which must have been produced by the unmeasured statements of his Learned Friend, without endeavouring to place before them the real, the unmagnified features of the case in their plain and undistorted size and colour.

Mr. Brougham then attempted to make the case that Sir Henry Mildmay wanted nothing in the proceeding to injure or degrade Lord Roseberry. Notice again how he refers to Henry as Harry, the more familiar form of the name. He states how he has been restricted in the conduct of the case:

With regard to that Noble Plaintiff, his instructions bound up his hands, and he was forbidden to utter a word, to breath a single syllable which might be construed into the slightest allusion to the conduct of Lord Roseberry ... It was the anxious wish of Sir Harry Mildmay that not one word should be said which might tend to irritate the feelings, not only of the Noble Lord, but of any other branch of his family ....

That forbearance, however, was no reason why exaggerated statements should be permitted to pass unnoticed, and he was accordingly obliged to call their attention to one or two most serious charges against the defendant, which, he lamented to say, were not only unsupported, but absolutely contradicted by the evidence.

Brougham then challenged Garrow's presentation and interpretation of the facts in a critical moment in the events that transpired when the brother of Lord Roseberry discovered Sir Harry Mildmay in Lady Roseberry's room. Brougham continues:

The Attorney-General had told them, (faithfully pursuing, no doubt, the instructions he had received,) abruptly and nakedly told them, without once adverting to all those intermediate scenes that took place on the fatal Saturday, that, upon Sir Harry Mildmay being discovered in Lady Roseberry's room by the brother of Lord Roseberry, he, the witness, peremptorily ordered him to quit the house by the way he had entered it, namely the window, and that he immediately obeyed.

In their circle honour was a critically important attribute of an English gentleman, and Brougham charged that Garrow had presented the facts in such a way as to cloud the sense of honour of a man, even Sir Harry Mildmay in the situation he was in. Brougham attempted to give another version of the story:

.... that which was imputed to him by the Attorney-General was worse than all ... a man could sooner stand up in the world against any accusation than the degrading, the humiliating one, which his Learned Friend had leveled at the head of the defendant. At his head did he say? No, it was at his breast, at his heart, that he directed the foul charge.

It affected his courage, and placed it under such imputation, that he could not have lived one hour longer, had the facts been as stated by his Learned Friend.

But how was the case, as delivered by Mr. Primrose himself, an impartial, an honourable witness, and one, whose minute and laboured accuracy they all know. He had told them that, instead of a peremptory summons, it was a request, urgently solicited; instead of the degrading order, 'go as you came - out the window with you,' it was, 'pray go; you had much better - -it will be more convenient for all parties - it will save unnecessary exposure - you may retreat gently and unperceived.' Such was the proceeding. There was no insult in the manner - no rudeness in the expressions ....

But he was really astonished how his Learned Friend had contrived in other parts of his statement to confound differences by passing over some things, and noticing others, and then dwelling upon what he selected with that exaggerated eloquence which perplexed and confused things in themselves perfectly plain and intelligible.

....nothing was more common than for an advocate to fall into the error of portraying a present case, merely because it was a present one, as the most atrocious, the most dreadful, the most horrible, the most abominable that had ever before been known. Such indiscriminate appeals were most injurious, not only to the general but even to the individual interests of justice; and in the present case, the exaggeration was most obvious.....

He begged he might not be misunderstood. He did not mean to deny, that because there were none of those aggravations, that therefore there was no guilt; he did not mean to deny that a crime was committed; the record proved the contrary;...But he would say, that when his Learned Friend extended to the offence of the defendant that extremity of censure which he had applied, and called for that severity of punishment, he performed the very worst service he could to the general cause of justice and morality ....

Brougham then attacks Garrow's understanding and use of the charge of "multiplied incest" challenging Garrow's technical or legal and apparently archaic use of the term instead of present day usage:

The Attorney-General ... characterized the crime of the defendant by the epithet of 'multiplied incest,' because Sir Harry Mildmay had been married to a sister of Lady Roseberry, while another sister was married to a brother of the defendant. How his Learned Friend, with his accustomed accuracy, came to make such an assertion he knew not, but it did so happen there was no multiplied incest at al ... Men's feelings were not so repugnant to that species of relationship as to justify his Leaned Friend's expression, whatever technical and precise distinctions prevailed in the law with respect to it, by which, marriages so contracted, became null and void.

Brougham then attempts to use the tactic of telling the jury that if only he could use information he had, but was sworn not to use, he could put a more human face on the predicament faced by his client:

.... if he were permitted, he could produce numberless letters, and numerous witnesses which would prove the agony, the sorrow, the wretchedness, which the conviction of their transgressions had excited in their minds ... He knew but one person in the world who could effectually have done so (interceded early as the problem was developing) but his hands were tied up, and he could not tell the Jury who that person was, because he was enjoined not to breathe even a whisper which might affect the conduct of the plaintiff.

In closing his statement to the jury, Brougham gets to the heart of the decision the jury must make, determining the size of damages that Sir Harry Mildmay must pay to Lord Roseberry for his adultery with Lady Roseberry, and for convincing Lady Roseberry to leave Lord Roseberry and to join with him as a life partner. Speaking to the jury he says:

He should only entreat them once more, as men of plain and ordinary understandings, not to separate without looking at the case calmly, dispassionately, and impartially; they would then be prepared to give such damages as would amply vindicate the character of Lord Roseberry, and that was all they had to consider, as men were in the habit of saying, or pretending to say, that in such cases it was not pecuniary damages they required, it was not their wife's dishonour which they wished to coin into money, but their own honour which they sought to justify ... [and he recommended] a verdict of such moderate damages as would satisfy the ends of justice and, at the same time, the honour of the noble plaintiff.

The jury after considering the case for about an hour and a half, pronounced a verdict for Lord Roseberry - damages of fifteen thousand pounds.

The nature of legal combat

Professor John Beattie recently reviewed the record of this case and this discussion. From his perspective as an historian of the development of English criminal law, he had some additional observations and ideas to emphasize, on the legal combat undertaken by these two brilliant barristers as they positioned themselves to represent their clients and appeal most effectively to the jury on the issue at hand. In closing the discussion on this case, some of Beattie's comments are appended here:

> (Their strategies) came down to the employment of rhetorical language and rhetorical devices - and no doubt theatrical gestures - to work on the jurors' emotions. The facts were not in dispute. The game was for Garrow to spin the facts in ways that would lead the jurors to feel outrage and compassion for the husband, and for Brougham to play down the reprehensible character of the offence, not to justify it, but to diminish the emotion and heightened colouring that Garrow's speech created. So Garrow's saying that he found impossible to prepare properly because the case was so unusual and distressing and caused him to feel such a degree of disgust ... is all part of the game. Of course he prepared fully and skilfully. His speech is full of emotional language and creates vivid pictures for the jury of the devoted and tender husband, the beautiful, charming, vulnerable wife, the horror of the world she allowed herself to be drawn into by giving in to Mildmay's blandishments ... rhetoric that Brougham points to when he says it is his duty to counter Garrow's "unmeasured statements" by (of course) rhetorical devices of his own.[7]

John Beattie then noted that lawyers who could engage in these verbal battles most successfully - including Garrow - became well-known because such trials were widely read. Indeed, both Garrow and Brougham became well-known, in part because of their use of rhetorical techniques which made legal proceedings entertaining, a forerunner of today's celebrity trials.

---

7. Personal correspondence with John Beattie.

Coat of Arms of Sir William Garrow

CHAPTER 10

Judge

BARON OF THE EXCHEQUER

On 6 May 1817, Garrow was promoted to be a Baron of the Exchequer in which office he remained until he retired in 1832. During this last phase of his professional career he served as one of four Barons of the Exchequer, judges in one of the highest courts in the land. This ancient court was set up to settle revenue disputes, especially when the Crown had an interest, but as it evolved it also handled other issues of interest to the Crown. By the late seventeenth century the Exchequer had become the third court for hearing a wide range of issues as in the other higher courts, the Common Pleas and the King's Bench. In Garrow's day (at least until the later years of his tenure) it was located in Westminster Hall, just a few hundred yards from his home on Great George Street.

He was generally considered to be an undistinguished judge, mainly, it was said, because his knowledge of the finer points of law was rather weak.[11] Indeed, Campbell, whose views on lawyers were not always reliable, claimed that, "he had never read anything except a brief and a newspaper."[22] But this alleged weak knowledge of the law, in so far as it was true, may well have worked to Garrow's advantage in the development of criminal advocacy. Although he sometimes argued points of law when pleading at the Old Bailey, his main focus was directed to the art of advocacy and understanding the people before him in the courtroom. On the other hand, it may have resulted in his being strict as a judge.

It should be noted that in addition to serving on the Exchequer court dealing with issues that demanded an in-depth knowledge of the complex issues in the broad field of commercial law, Garrow spent much of his time on the Assizes circuits as an itinerant judge. This court system was devoted especially to criminal matters as experienced by the common man, and in Garrow's case, typically dealt with matters involving life or death for the accused. Issues included murder, manslaughter, arson, theft, riot, rebellion, treason, manufacturing counterfeit coins, and sheep stealing. And in dealing with these felony issues, Garrow was the expert on the law.

---

1. Lord Brougham. (1844-5), "Mr. Baron Garrow", *The Law Review and Quarterly Journal of the British and Foreign Jurisprudence,* vol. i. pp. 319 and 327.

2. M. S. Hardcastle. (ed) (1881) *Life of John, Lord Campbell. Lord High Chancellor of Great Britain; consisting of a selection from his autobiography, diary and letters.* London, Murray, vol. i. p.198.

ASSIZE TRIALS

It is in the Assize circuits, with Garrow now sitting as a judge, that the new practice of what would become known as adversary trial was being played out in the everyday criminal trials of the era. A new generation of defence and prosecution barristers were working under the watchful eyes of Garrow, and other judges. These barristers had learnt the art of examination and cross-examination by observing Garrow's skills in these areas. Now, as a judge, Garrow was administering the rules of evidence which he had helped to evolve. While the criminal trial remained in transition, the changes recently achieved were being institutionalized, and a new generation of junior barristers, learning their craft in the Assize circuits, were being tutored in this school of on-the-job training by the master of their craft, Judge Garrow. Much of the generally available information in the public record on Garrow as a judge comes from his serving on the Assize circuits.

At this time in history, judges travelled from one county town to the next trying, with a jury, all the people bought up before the Assizes who had been charged with more serious criminal offences. The Assizes were normally held twice a year in Lent and Summer. In some counties the Assize was an annual event and therefore people could spend many months in prison awaiting trial.

For a detailed picture of the drama and procedure of the Assize trials, one is best referred to John Beattie's book, *Crime and the Courts in England 1660-1800, Chapter 7*, "The Criminal Trial". While Garrow served as a judge immediately following this period, Beattie's description of the trial by 1800 is thought to represent Garrow's experience, or at least the traditions that led to the practices in the period of 1817-1832. The following general observations are taken from that source, and touch only some of the highlights thought to be of general interest from Beattie's detailed description.[3]

Beattie describes the Assize courts as striving, not always successfully, to create an atmosphere of dignity and solemnity in which the trials would take place. This ceremony started as the two judges assigned to the specific session reached the border of the county. They would be met there and escorted to the Assize town with a truly triumphal entrance accompanied by leading families of the county. Beattie quotes a French visitor, Cottu, who described the scene and reported that in 1820 at their approach to the Assize town the judges "are received by the sheriff, and often by a great part of the wealthiest inhabitants of the county; the latter came in person to greet him, or send their carriages, with their richest liveries, to serve as an escort, and increase the splendour of the occasion. They enter the town with bells ringing and trumpets playing, preceded by the sheriff's men, to the number of twelve or twenty,

---

3. J.M. Beattie. (1986) *Crime and the Courts in England. 1600-1800.* Oxford, Clarendon Press. p. 314.

in full dress, armed with javelins".[4]

The ritual for the court session continued with the judges in their scarlet robes going to the local parish church where the sheriff's chaplain preached the Assize sermon to the judges and the community. Thus reassured, the company moved to the courtroom where the first business was immediately enacted; the opening and reading of the judges' commissions conferring upon the Assize judges the unlimited jurisdiction that enabled them to deal with all the criminal cases pending. They normally adjourned at that point until the next morning. They retired to their lodgings or perhaps to the house of a local worthy for some of the entertainment that made the Assizes a social occasion for those on the right side of the law.

The next morning the clerk for the criminal (not civil) proceedings would call the names of the members of the commission of the peace for the county, noting those present, and also the mayors, coroners, stewards, bailiffs, and constables.

Next the grand jury would be called, and the judge would give them directions, and swear them in. Soon after their swearing-in they would retire to a separate room to receive the bills of accusation and listen to the evidence against each prisoner presented verbally by the prosecutor and his witnesses. The accused was not present or represented. On the basis of prosecution evidence, the jury would decide if the case should be tried. They recorded their verdict on the back of the bill, finding either a "true bill" which sent the accused on to trial on the charge alleged, or "no true bill" in which case the prisoner would be discharged.

While this is a general description of the ceremonies at the start of an Assize, a newspaper account of the commencement of the Assize in Reading appeared in a 1827 issue of the *Windsor & Eton Express*. Judge Garrow was one of the two judges in this court session.

The Assizes for this county commenced yesterday at Reading. Thomas Duffield, Esq. High Sheriff, arrived at the Bear Inn, on Thursday afternoon, from his seat at Marcham, and yesterday morning, at about half past eight, proceeded, escorted by his halberdiers [along the] Maidenhead-road, to meet Baron Garrow and Baron Vaughan, his Majesty's Judges of the circuit. A long train of carriages and upwards of 400 horsemen escorted their lordships and the Sheriff into the town. About ten o'clock the cavalcade with the judges, returned, and their lordships immediately proceeded to the Town-hall, where the ceremony of opening the commission took place. The Judges, with their legal officers, and the officers of the county, heard divine service in St. Lawrence's church, where an appropriate sermon was preached by the Rev. G .Evans. A sumptuous public breakfast was given by the Sheriff, at the Bear, the George, the Angel, and the Upper and Lower Ships, and the Black Horse inns. Immediately after leaving church, the business of the court was entered into. After the gentlemen of the grand inquest had been sworn in, Mr. Justice Vaughan delivered the charge to the grand jury.[5]

4. *Ibid.* p. 317.
5. *Windsor & Eton Express*. (3 March 1827).

Beattie observed, "The meetings of the assizes and quarter sessions did not make a festive season for the men and women who waited in their chains for the moment when the grand jury adjourned to their room to begin considering the bills and to hear the evidence brought forward by the prosecutors. For them, the serious business of the session was about to begin."[6]

GARROW'S STYLE

The trial format was different from today's trial. The prosecutor, usually the victim of the offence, would tell his story to the jury. He or she would be followed by the witnesses for the prosecution. These could include a constable who might testify about the circumstances of the prisoner's apprehension - what he said, what was found. Prosecution witnesses gave their evidence under oath, and risked being prosecuted for perjury if they were found to have lied.

Historically the judge was very much in charge. During the time Garrow was a judge, the role of the judge was changing, in response to the gradual shift from a trial in which the accused, if he were able, conducted his own defence, to a trial that was beginning to be a conflict between lawyers. So Garrow not only played a central role in changing the trial into a contest between lawyers, he also, as a judge, was a part of the changing scene in terms of the role of the judge, although in this instance, sometimes a reluctant participant. During that period in history where prisoners were defending themselves, the judges were accustomed to joining in the cross-examination of witnesses if this seemed necessary to get at the facts of the case. The change taking place was described by Beattie in the words of Cottu. As a visitor to the English courts in 1820 Cottu, reporting on provincial assizes, observed that "the judge remained almost a stranger to what is going on during the trial."[7] This would be very different from previous years when, in the absence of a credible defence being conducted by the prisoner, and with significant issues unexplored, judges would conduct their own examination.

There is evidence that, even with a defence counsel appearing, Judge Garrow would revert to the older style and conduct his own examination of the witnesses if he thought it necessary to get at required facts. Garrow's style of being a judge was described by Henry Brougham in his biographical sketch of Garrow published five years after Garrow's death. It states:

> After the counsel on both sides had exhausted their questions, it was his custom to luxuriate in an examination of his own, and here he often evinced his perfection in the art of which he was an admitted master. Nor did he shrink at times from, as it seemed, lowering his dignity,

6. J.M. Beattie. *Crime and the Courts in England., 1600-1800. Op. cit.* p. 331.
7. *Ibid.* p. 376.

by the most lavish display of that peculiar knowledge which can only be acquired at the school in which he had studied ....

There was no term of the art in the vocabulary of crime with which he was not familiar. At times the effect produced by him was most amusing. None who were present will forget the impression thus made upon an unhappy coiner, tried before him on the Oxford circuit. This man conducted his own defense, and did so with much skill and more effrontery. The judge seemed quite absorbed in admiration of the prisoner's ingenuity, and contrived to fill him with the delusion that he was so - a delusion from which there was soon to be a fearful waking. 'My Lord,' he vociferated, 'there were only two bad half-crowns found upon me. If I was making a trade of it, it stands to reason I'd have had more' and he looked up to the bench quite confident of its sympathy. Garrow's white eyes glared upon the culprit, and in a tone which assured him all their secrets were in common, playfully replied, 'Perhaps, sir, the WALLOP was exhausted.' The word, and the tone of its enunciation, at once unnerved the prisoner--he felt he had before him a professor of his craft, whom it was quite useless to attempt to mystify, and he resigned himself to his fate. 'Gentlemen, (said Garrow blandly to the jury, who shared in the ignorance of all around them,) a WALLOP is a term of free-masonry amongst coiners. It means the hidden heap of counterfeits to which they resort for a supply when the exigencies of the profession may require one.'[8]

Brougham noted that as a judge, especially in the criminal courts where Garrow found himself at home, he occasionally ventured on "very perilous oratorical experiments." Once when serving as a judge on the Oxford circuit he passed judgment on an unhappy sheep-stealer. He sentenced the man to death, and then talked at some length of the heinousness of the offence. He assured the offender that all hope of a pardon was an illusion. He then added:

> I have, however, one precious consolation- - this is not the final trial which awaits you - you will ere long appear before another and all-merciful Judge, who will hear with patience all you have to say, and should he feel a doubt, will give in to your favour.[9]

Concerning this incident, Garrow did recommend a mitigation of the sentence, as indeed was his custom when he felt that the character of the person and crime would allow him to do so. Brougham notes, "It was ... by no means unusual with him, perhaps by way of admonition to the by-standers, to excite apprehensions which he never intended to realize."

As a trial judge in the court of the Exchequer, and on the Assize circuits and at the Old Bailey, Garrow presided over a wide variety of legal proceedings - crimes committed by lords and ladies, organized crime syndicates, as well as the crimes of common people. His friends and adversaries alike considered him to be in his element when the issue was as one critic stated "horse issues." The notes on the following case show judge Garrow actively cross-examining a Mr. Warburton, the father of a person accused of practicing as an apothecary without a license. It

8. Lord Brougham. *Mr. Baron Garrow. The Times. Op. cit.*
9. *Ibid.*

concerned a "common people" type of crime. It also provides an example of Garrow summing up the evidence for the jury and directing them concerning the evidence and the law.

THE CASE OF THE LEARNED APOTHECARY[10]

In an Act of Parliament made in 1815, entitled "An Act for the better regulating the practice of Apothecaries," there is a very salutary clause, which enacts, "that from and after the first day of August, 1815, it shall not be lawful for any person (except persons already in practice as such) to practice as an apothecary in any part of England or Wales, unless he or they shall have been examined by the Court of Examiners of the Apothecaries' Company, and shall have received a certificate as such."

The first conviction under this Act took place at the Staffordshire Lent Assize of 1819, before Sir William Garrow, when the Apothecaries' Company brought an action against a man of the name of Warburton, for having practiced as an apothecary without being duly qualified. The defendant it appeared was the son of a man, who in the early part of his life had been a gardener, but afterwards set up as a cow leech. The facts were stated by Mr. Dauncey for the prosecution, and supported by evidence.

Mr. Jervis, for the defence, called the father of the defendant, Arnold Warburton, to prove that he had practised as an apothecary before the passing of the Act.

Cross-examined by Mr. Dauncey.

Mr. Dauncey. Mr. Warburton, have you always been a surgeon?

Witness asked the judge whether this was a proper answer.

The Judge. I have not heard any answer; Mr. Dauncey has put a question.

Witness. Must I answer it?

Judge. Yes: why do you object?

Witness. I don't think it a proper answer.

Judge. I presume you mean question, and I differ from you in opinion.

The witness not answering, Mr. Dauncey repeated - Have you always been a surgeon?

Witness. I am a surjent.

10. R. Percy. (1868) *The Percy Anecdotes*. vol. i. "Anecdotes of the Bar". *Learned* Apothecary. London, Frederick Warne & Co.

Mr. Dauncey. Can you spell the word you have mentioned?

Witness. My lord, is that a fair answer?

Judge. I think it a fair question.

Witness. 'S y u r g u n t.'

Mr. Dauncey. I am unfortunately hard of hearing; have the goodness to repeat what you have said, sir.

Witness. ' S u r g e n d.'

Mr. Dauncey. S-, what did you say next to S, sir?

Witness. 'S y u r g u n d.'

Mr. Dauncey. Very well, sir, I am perfectly satisfied.

Judge. As I take down the word sur-, please to favour me with it once more.

Witness. ' S u r g u n t.'

Judge. How, sir?

Witness. 'S e r g u n d.'

Judge. Very well.

Mr. Dauncey. Sir, have you always been what you say? that word, I mean, which you have just spelt? (A long pause.)

Mr. Dauncey. I am afraid, sir, you do not often take so much time to study the cases which come before you, as you do to answer my question - 'I do not, sir.' 'Well, sir, will you please to answer it?' (A long pause, but no reply.) - Well, what were you originally, Doctor Warburton?'

Witness. 'Syurgend.'

'When you first took to business, what was that business? Were you a gardener, Doctor Warburton?'

'Surgent.'

'I do not ask you to spell that word again; but before you were of, that profession, what were you? - 'S e r g u n t.'

Mr. Dauncey. My lord, I fear I have thrown a shell over this poor man, which he cannot get rid of.

Judge. Attend, witness; you are now to answer the questions put to you. You need not spell that word any more.

Mr. Dauncey. When was you a gardener?

Witness. I never was. The witness then stated, that he never employed himself in gardening; he first was a farmer, his father was a farmer. He (witness) ceased to be a farmer fifteen or sixteen years ago; he ceased because he had then learnt that business which he now is.

'Who did you learn it of?'

'Is that a proper question, my lord?'

'I see no objection to it'.

'Then I will answer it; I learnt of Dr. Hulme, my brother-in law; he practised the same as the Whitworth Doctors, and they were regular physicians.

Mr. Dauncey. Where did they take their degrees?

Witness. I don't believe they ever took a degree.

'Then were they regular physicians?'

No! I believe they were not, they were only doctors.'

'Only doctors! Were they doctors in law, physic, or divinity?'

'They doctored cows, and other things, and humans as well.'

'Doubtless, as well: and you, I doubt not have doctored brute animals as well as human creatures ?'

'I have.'

Judge to Witness. 'Did you ever make up any medicine by the prescription of a physician?'

'I never did.'

'Do you understand the characters they use for ounces, scruples, and drachms?'

'I do not.'

'Then you cannot make up their prescriptions from reading them?'

'I cannot, but I can make up as good medicines in my way, as they can in theirs.'

'What proportion does an ounce bear to a pound? - [A pause]

'There are 16 ounces to the pound, but we do not go by any regular weight, we mix ours by the hand.'

'Do you bleed?'

'Yes.'

'With a fleam or with a lancet?'

'With a lancet.'

'Do you bleed from the vein or from the artery?'

'From the vein.'

'There is an artery somewhere about the temples; what is the name of that artery?'

'I do not pretend to have so much learning as some have.'

'Can you tell me the name of that artery?'

'I do not know which you mean.'

'Suppose, then, I was to direct you to bleed my servant: or my horse (which God forbid) in a vein, say for instance in the jugular vein, where should you bleed him?'

'In the neck, to be sure.'

Judge. I would take everything as favourably, for the young man as I properly can, but here we have ignorance greater perhaps than ever appeared in a court before, as the only medium of education which this defendant can possibly have received in his profession.

Several other witnesses were the examined for the defence. Baron Garrow, in summing up, observed, that this was a question of considerable importance to the defendant in the cause, on whose future prospects it must necessarily have great influence, and it was of great importance to the public. Garrow commented strongly on the ignorance of the defendant's father, a man, he said, more ignorant than the most ignorant that they had ever before heard examined in any court. Was this man qualified for professing any science, particularly one in which the health and even the lives of the public were involved? Yet through such an impure medium alone had the defendant received his knowledge of this profession. There was not the least proof of the defendant having for a single minute been in a situation to receive instruction from any one really acting as an apothecary. If the jury thought that the defendant had acted as an apothecary before the time mentioned in the Act, they would find a verdict for him; but otherwise they would find for the plaintiffs in one penalty. The jury almost instantly returned a verdict for the plaintiffs.

TRIALS BEFORE GARROW

Additional historic information that may be of some interest is displayed in *Appendix 2*.[11] It lists the results of the Lincolnshire Lent Assize for March 1818 in which Garrow was judge. Of the twenty-two who were brought to trial, ten were sentenced

---

11. "A Snapshot of Crime and Punishment in the 1800s"

to death. It appears as a very harsh example of the "Bloody Code" of capital offences in English criminal law. We should note the crimes charged, and the outcomes of the trials. However, before being carried out, Judge Garrow would have written a letter to the King recommending mercy in certain cases. As a result, by the King's prerogative the sentence might be commuted, often to transportation to Australia. One historian observed that in 1818 there were 1,170 capital convictions in England of which 103 were executed, ninety percent being reprieved.

At the Old Bailey and in the Assize circuits Garrow sat as a judge in scores of trials from May 1817 to April 1831. In some of them his close attention was shown by his asking questions of witnesses but questions of law do not appear to have been raised or noted in the records and, unfortunately, his summings-up to the jury are not recorded so that it is impossible to assess his attitude to the offences and offenders before him. The cases were remarkably similar to those in which he had earlier appeared as counsel and the sentences were frequently death or transportation with judge, prosecution or jury recommendations for mercy, usually on the grounds of the prisoners' youth or distress.

When the Bloody Code was being debated in Parliament, and Samuel Romilly and Garrow were taking different sides on the issues, it was Romilly speaking for reform, and Garrow supporting the existing system that depended on petitioning the King for his mercy. Garrow observed that the daughters and sons and mothers of those convicted would at the close of the trials immediately crowd around the judge asking that he seek to save the life of the person under death sentence and substitute some lesser punishment. Sometimes they would resort to even blocking the wheels of the judge's carriage to get his attention and make their emotional plea understood.[12]

Sometimes Judge Garrow would directly intercede to administer mercy to the prisoners during a trial. During a city Assizes in Norfolk on 29 November 1831, shortly before Garrow retired, a group of men and boys were brought to trial before him on the charges of "unlawfully, riotously, and tumultuously assembled ..." With force they had pulled down and destroyed a saw mill and set it on fire. Certainly, according to the bloody code, these were serious crimes. Soldiers were called in to apprehend those in the act of destroying the mill, and as the soldiers were attempting to take their prisoners through the city streets to the magistrates, a mob ripe for any mischief, vented their fury on the soldiers, including throwing stones that severely bruised some of the party. Excitement in the city was high. Then after being charged and on their way to the city goal, an additional escort of mounted Dragoons was thought necessary, in that it was doubtful that a small number of soldiers on foot would have been successful in getting their prisoners to the gaol. During the trial, lawyers for the accused convinced them to change their first plea and plead guilty.

---

12. *Parliamentary Debates*. [24] (17 February 1813) Sir Samuel Romilly's Criminal Law Bills. col. 571.

In pronouncing sentence the court reporter described Garrow's words:

> Mr. Baron Garrow addressed the prisoners observing that their Counsel had very kindly advised
> them as to the course they had adopted - whether they could have satisfied the Jury that they, the
> prisoners, were not so assembled it was impossible for him to say, but if, after hearing the case,
> the Jury had felt bound to give a verdict of guilty against them, it would have been impossible
> for him, sitting in that situation to administer justice, to have passed over the offence without
> serious punishment. After strongly advising them to keep henceforth out of such assemblies, his
> Lordship said he should adopt a course with respect to them which he would not press from
> them unless from their future conduct; the sentence he should pass would be that they should
> enter onto an obligation of £20 each to keep the peace and appear if called upon.[13]

In other words, Garrow sentenced them to provide a bond, and keep out of trouble,
with the threat that he didn't want to see them in court again.

In July 1817, two solders, John Hall, aged 22, and Patrick Morrison, aged 25,
were charged, on the evidence of a thief-taker, with assault in a drunken brawl at
a public house. The man assaulted was Jack Read, an unemployed vagabond in his
early fifties, from whom it was alleged the solders stole a shilling and a bad penny.
Writing a history of his family from 1742 to 1998, Nicholas Mander outlines the
trial and states that Garrow was "a hanging judge ... and the soldiers were allowed
no counsel,"[14] which, if correct, reveals a different Garrow from the robust defence
counsel of the Old Bailey. Hall and Morrison were found guilty of robbery and
sentenced to be hanged. However, they were generally considered to be innocent
and public outcry secured a reprieve from the home secretary, Viscount Sidmouth,
and a subsequent free pardon which was supported by Garrow.[15]

In 1824 Baron Garrow dealt with a case in which death was caused by collision
with a cart driven at an unusually rapid pace. He ruled that it was the "duty of every
man who drives any carriage, to drive it with such care and caution as to prevent,
as far as in his power, any accident or injury that may occur."[16] For some reason, in
medical cases he accepted a lower standard of care. In the case of *R. v. Long*,[17] he set a
subjective standard of care as the same for the presidents of the College of Physicians
as for the "humblest bone-setter of the village", namely, to "perform as well as he
can." He distinguished cases of driving by saying, "Why is it that we convict in cases
of death by driving carriages?" "Because", he replied, "the parties are bound to have,
skill, care and caution" - qualities he did not require of medical men.

---

13. This story is taken from the Norfolk Mills website www.norfolkmills.co.uk which reports articles taken
    from the *Norfolk Chronicle* for 4 and 11 December 1830 and 30 July 1831.
14. N. Mander. (1998) *Varnished Leaves: a biography of the Mander family of Wolverhampton, 1742-1998.*
    Internet. http://www.localhistory.scit.wlv.ac.uk/genealogy/Mander/The%20Book/CharlesMander.
15. *Ibid.*
16. *R. V. Walker.* (1824) 1 Carrington & Payne Reports. 320, 171 English Reports, 1213.
17. (1834) C & P 398. ER 756.

PRECEDENTS

Are any of Garrow's cases being cited as precedents in contemporary common law based criminal trials? The answer is, Yes. The Supreme Court of Canada's decision in *Vetrovec* vs. *The Queen* [1982] cited a passage in "Trial of William Davidson and Richard Tidd for High Treason" (1820) conducted in the Old Bailey, in which Baron Garrow instructed the jury on how to treat the corroborative testimony of accomplices.[18] Also in July, 2006, the Irish Court of Criminal Appeal quoted Garrow in its review of the 1982 conviction of Brian Meehan for the murder of journalist Veronica Guerin.[19] Again the court called attention to Garrow's instruction to the jury in the Trial of William Davidson and Richard Tidd for High Treason in establishing the usefulness of testimony of accomplices. The quoted words were:

> … you are to look to the circumstances, to see whether there are such a number of important facts confirmed as to give you reason to be persuaded that the main body of the story is correct … you are, each of you, to ask yourselves this question … Do I, upon the whole, feel convinced in my conscience, that this evidence is true, and such as I may safely act upon?[20]

What makes this especially interesting is that Davidson and Tidd were being tried as a part of the Cato Street Conspiracy in which the plan was to murder all of the British cabinet ministers, including the Prime Minister, Lord Liverpool. Davidson, Tidd and the other conspirators were alleged to be attempting not only to assassinate the cabinet ministers, but also to overthrow the government, and to oversee a radical revolution like that in France. It was a poorly planned affair, instigated by the Home Office which was able to infiltrate the group and set the plotters up for their capture. While a total failure as a revolution, the plot captured an unforgettable place in English folklore.[21] Some of the collaborators testified in great detail, in exchange for dropping charges against them. This is the context in which Garrow charged the jury with his now quoted statement concerning the use of evidence given by accomplices.

While the use of corroborative testimony remains a complex legal issue, Garrow had considerable experience with evaluating this type of testimony, along with other rules of evidence that he had helped introduce. With fifty years of criminal trials as a barrister and then judge, Garrow's expertise in examining witnesses apparently helped to establish practical guidelines in dealing with issues concerning evidence. It is interesting to note that while the trial of William Davidson and Richard Tidd for high reason is reported in great detail in the *Old Bailey Proceedings*, the record

18. *Vetrovec v. The Queen.* (1982) Can. L II 20 16348 16349.
19. Court of Criminal Appeal of Ireland. Record number 177/99 dated 24/07/2006.
20. 33 Howell's *State Trials.* p. 1338.
21. See John Hostettler. (1993) *Thomas Wakley: An Improbable Radical.* Chichester, Barry Rose Law Publishers. pp. 22-30.

does not contain Garrow's instructions to the jury, an example of one of the failings of that source to give a full account of the events in these early trials.[22] One must go to the formal state trial reports to find this information.

On the lighter side of Garrow's career as a judge, as he travelled the Assize circuits, apparently he had a phobia about catching smallpox. This was remembered by a copy writer for the 2 December 1840 issue of *The Times*.

The late Sir William Garrow, during his lifetime, entertained a fearful apprehension of catching the natural smallpox; for although he had undergone the operation of inoculation on many repeated occasions, as a preventive against the disease, yet strange to observe, it never produced any viable effects on his system. When he travelled upon the circuit, the first question he invariably put to those parties who might be the foremost to accost him in the town where the assizes were held, was "Has the smallpox manifested itself in this place recently?" He could only account for his never having received the above malady from the singular circumstance of his mother having been grievously afflicted with it while she was pregnant with him.

The press enjoyed repeating such stories about Garrow, even after his death.

LINCOLN'S INN

In later life Garrow was elected a Bencher of the Honourable Society of Lincoln's Inn. The published records of the Inn, commonly known as the Black Books, have a few references to him which show that he was an active member of the Inn's governing body. He held all five major offices of the Inn culminating in 1801 as Treasurer.[23] The other great offices he held were Master of the Walks, 1799; Keeper of the Black Books, 1800; Master of the Library, 1802 and Dean of the Chapel, 1803.

In 1798 he proposed a motion (which was passed) that the Inn should donate £1,000 to the Bank of England as a voluntary contribution "towards the exigencies of the country."[24] This was no doubt meant to assist the prosecution of the war against Napoleon and 1798 was the year in which Pitt introduced income tax. He also served on the committee that was set up in 1814 to deal with the building of a new court within the Inn.[25] He left Lincoln's Inn on becoming a Serjeant-at-Law in May 1817 when his arms were ordered to be painted in the Hall and he was given by the Inn £10 .. 10s .. 0d (and £1 .. 8s .. 0d for a silver net purse).[26] The Inn has an oil painting of Garrow by George Henry Harlow which was presented by an anonymous donor in 1904.[27]

---

22. OBP Online. (www.oldbaileyonline.org).
23. Black Books of Lincoln's Inn. vol. iv. p. 90.
24. *Ibid.* p. 73.
25. *Ibid.* pp. 134-6.
26. *Ibid.* p. 147.
27. Information about Garrow at Lincoln's Inn supplied by Mrs. F. Bellis, Librarian.

CONCLUSION

Although an opponent of both political and penal reform it is paradoxical that Garrow helped to produce a revolution in criminal trial procedure that has had global repercussions for the human rights of prisoners. But it is significant that at the time of his death in 1840, three-quarters of a century after his great successes at the Old Bailey and after the enactment of the Prisoners' Counsel Act, no mention was made in the law journals or *The Times* of his, or any other lawyer's, contribution to the establishment of adversary trial. The same applied four years later when *The Law Review* wrote in a belated obituary that Garrow had, "reached the lead of the Old Bailey practice and domineered without a competitor at the bar." [28] Not a word about adversary trial - the real significance of Garrow's advocacy being hidden then and for a long time to come.

As is so often the case, contemporaries are blind to what is happening and even an upheaval as overwhelming as the Industrial Revolution was not seen for what it was for many years.

As indeed was the case with adversary trial for Garrow himself. He could not have been at all conscious that he was one of the prime architects of the adversary system of trial in the criminal courts. No mention of such a system passed his lips or those of any contemporary lawyers. Equally, it is clear from his remarks in court that he would have been only dimly aware that with his advocacy he also played a prominent part in securing the rules of evidence for criminal trials.

In the event, adversariality and the rules of evidence soon travelled to, and became rooted in, many parts of the globe which suggests that society was ready for them. As a contributing factor in the establishment of a culture of human rights, adversariality has had a large and lasting impact on world-wide jurisprudence. For the crucial part played in the drama of the birth of criminal advocacy by this intrepid lawyer from a humble background, his name shines forth like a beacon.

---

28. 1 *The Law Review. Op. cit.* p. 318.

CHAPTER 11

Garrow's Homes

Insight into Garrow's lifestyle may be acquired by knowing something about the places he called home. As previously described, his childhood home was in his father's school, which was held in The Priory in the parish of Monken Hadley in Middlesex. As a student learning the business of law he would have lived near the office he attended on Milk Street, Cheapside, not far from St. Paul's Cathedral. As soon as his career was underway, he moved to Exeter Court and then to Bedford Row near the Inns of Court, where he and Sarah raised their family. During this time he built Pegwell Cottage on Pegwell Bay just south of Ramsgate. It was the family retreat away from his busy life in London.

Sometime after Sarah died, he moved to Great George Street, near Westminster Hall and was near his business both in Parliament and the Exchequer Court. Upon his retirement he moved his permanent residence to Pegwell Cottage, where he spent his remaining years. He is buried in the churchyard of St. Lawrence, Thanet, not far from Pegwell Cottage.

Each of the places which Garrow called home are described in greater detail below in order to provide snapshots of lifestyles that he enjoyed from time-to-time. The chapter also contains a number of related images.

CHILDHOOD HOME

As previously noted, The Priory, where William Garrow spent his childhood, was a large and attractive neo-gothic structure which, with its grounds of about nine acres, served both as the family home of the Reverend David Garrow and as his school for young gentlemen. It was the largest house on the road leading from Hadley Green to the church. Located in the parish of Monken Hadley, often referred to as Hadley, in Middlesex, The Priory was just north of London, adjacent to the larger parish of Enfield. Hadley was also adjacent to the parish of East Barnet where Dr. William Garrow, Sir William Garrow's uncle, had his medical practice, and to Totteridge, the site of other family activities. The Priory was away from the crowded hustle and bustle of London. His family's home as well as his school were all in one place.

EARLY HOMES IN LONDON

For at least five years, as a student in the service of the eminent attorney, Thomas Southhouse, William Garrow would have lived near his office on Milk Street.

This is directly between the Guildhall and St. Paul's Cathedral. The area had all the charm and inconveniences of ancient city patterns. When this area was rebuilt after the fires of 1666 the old style of small winding streets, and earlier cityscapes were restored, unlike the wide boulevards of the western side of the city. Sir Joshua Reynolds suggested, "The forms and turnings of the streets of London, and other old towns, are produced by accident, without any original plan or design; but they are not always the less pleasant to the walker or spectator, on that account".[1] It was in this old style of London that Garrow studied. And it was in this area that some of the debating societies were located that he frequented.

As a young successful lawyer at the Old Bailey, and with the resulting income, Garrow lived first on Exeter Court and then moved to 25 Bedford Row. This is on the corner of Bedford Row and Theobald's Road, a very short walk from both Lincoln's Inn and Gray's Inn, two of the major law societies in England. In this home Garrow lived with Sarah and it is where they raised their family.

The Garrow home on the corner of Bedford Row
and Theobald's Road still exists. It has served
as law offices and was renovated in the spring of 2002.

1. J.M. Crook. "Metropolitan Improvements: John Nash and the Picturesque". *London-World City 1800–1840.* (1992) Celina Fox, editor. New Haven & London. Yale University Press. p. 76. It is a quote from Sir Joshua Reynolds' thirteenth *Discourse.*

IN PEGWELL

On 6 July 1790 *The Times* announced: "Mr. Garrow has purchased the delightful situation near Ramsgate, called Pegwell Bay, for the purpose of securing an agreeable retreat during the Old Bailey recess."

During 1796, Amelia Noel drew and etched a piece of art depicting Garrow's "delightful situation." Amelia was the drawing Mistress to the daughters of King George III. She published sets of drawing, and gave carefully bound volumes of them as special gifts to the princesses. These sets of drawings, including the one of Garrow's home which she called "Seat of William Garrow Esq., at Pegwell Bay," were also sold to subscribers in 1797. Garrow's name appears on the subscriber's list, as does that of Thomas Erskine.[2]

Amelia Noel's depiction of Garrow's Pegwell home.

Garrow owned this property for fifty years. He and his family and extended family members must have spent quality time there. It would be his retirement home from 1832 until his death in 1840. A few quotations from the record concerning the Pegwell Bay "Cottage," however, will give additional glimpses of the role of this home in the family life of the Garrows.

One account by J. Wilson, in his *A Biographical Index to the Present House of Commons, to April, 1807,* states:

---

2. Announcement of the series of the set of published pictures reads: Proposals for Publishing by Subscription twenty-four Picturesque Views, Etched and Coloured as High-Finished Drawings ... [list of views including Pegwell Bay] Drawn, Etched and Sold by Amelia Noel. Published 1ˢᵗ June 1791 by Mrs. Amelia Noel, 189, Piccadilly, Opposite York House.

After this (receiving the silk gown) he went on the home circuit only, except on very extraordinary occasions; and was accustomed to spend the long vacations at a charming villa, situated in the immediate vicinity of Ramsgate, within sight of the coast of France.

A.W. Bonner, in 1831, published a note on Garrow's Pegwell home, in his book, *The Picturesque Pocket Companion to Margate, Ramsgate & Broadstairs with Places Adjacent.* It includes a drawing of Pegwell Cottage at that time.

Under the heading "Sir W. Garrow's Villa," it states:

> Returning from Pegwell, on the road towards Ramsgate, we arrive at the residence of Sir William Garrow, one of the Barons of the Exchequer, who built this house as a summer retreat from the bodily fatigue and mental exertion consequent upon his high judicial station: here the worthy Baronet, during his short sojourn, recruits his health and strength, and then invigorated by the salubrious air of Pegwell, returns to execute the important duties of the Bench, which he has so long adorned.[3]

A painting depicting Regatta Day in 1828 shows the village of Pegwell and the chalk cliffs on which stands Garrow's property. His home was just behind the buildings on the right part of the village.

Pegwell Bay during Regatta Day, 1828

---

3. A.W. Bonner. *The Picturesque Pocket Companion Margate, Ramsgate & Broadstairs.* (1831) p. 174.

GREAT GEORGE STREET IN LONDON

As Garrow's career moved more towards serving the government, in 1810 he moved to a home next to the seat of government. That address was 27 Great George Street. This was located across a large intersection from Westminster Hall where Parliament met, and about the same distance from Westminster Abbey. (Today, Big Ben, is a few hundred yards or so from where his home was located.)

This location served Garrow well for the next twenty-two years as he continued in Parliament, became Attorney-General, then a Baron of the Exchequer with offices, at least initially, in Westminster Hall. Garrow's London home and his professional life were right in the middle of the highly competitive struggles and pomp of government service where he served at near the highest levels.

Photo taken from the sidewalk on Great George Street
where William Garrow's home once stood.
It looked like the home beyond the nearest London bus.

Garrow moved to Great George Street some time after his wife died when his children were married adults. As it happened, his daughter lived there before him. The record observes that Eliza Sophia, after marrying Samuel Fothergill Lettsom, lived in the house at 27 Great George Street for four years before moving out in 1810, at which time William Garrow moved in. Later, when Eliza Sophia's husband became bankrupt and fled to France to avoid debtor's prison, it appears that Eliza Sophia moved back in with her father and may have continued to raise her family there.

William Garrow lived at his home on Great George Street, as his major residence, until his retirement in 1832. When the houses on the north side of Great George Street were demolished for new construction, the London County Council made a survey of the properties and published photographs and descriptions of noteworthy features of both the interiors and exteriors of the homes. We therefore have the exact location of No. 27, a photograph showing how it appeared outside, the floor plan inside, its history and the note: "The interior was plain and contained no features of interest." The neighbours' homes, however, had grand details worthy to be recorded for posterity. Today, across the street from where No. 27 once stood, one home still exists and appears to be identical to those that were destroyed.[4]

IN PEGWELL AGAIN

Garrow's eight years of retirement, as previously noted, were spent at his home on Pegwell Bay. By now people were using more elegant words to describe this property, such as Garrow's Marine Villa.

Garrow's Pegwell home as it appears today is little different from that of Garrow's time. The underground kitchen that was on the left has been removed, and the solarium is of more modern design. A small room on the right has been added.

The home itself has some distinguishing features. While it appears to be a brick structure, actually the outside walls are surfaced with glazed tile. There is an impres-

---

4. M.H. Cox & P. Norman. (1926) *Survey of London, Volume X, The Parish of St. Margaret, Westminster. – Part 1.* London, published for the London County Council by B.T. Batsford, Ltd., pp. 42-3 with plates 14 and 46.

sive sight as you enter the house. You enter a large open room, where a stairway leads to the second floor. A walkway goes all around this open space and you enter each of the rooms from this walkway. The centre of the structure is open from floor to the tower on the roof. Inside this circular tower is a bas-relief and some small windows that allow light to fall onto it.

Upon entering the home, the large open area
contains a staircase and a walkway
around the second level.

Bas-relief in the cupola high above the entrance way.

There was a large conservatory, which today we would call a solarium, which covered the entire east and south exposures of the house. While this solarium has been updated, the purpose and effect remains the same as in Garrow's day. While Garrow owned many parcels of land in the area, the part immediately around the home is of special interest. The drawing of the grounds shows that the lawn went right to the edge of the cliff with an orchard close by.

Of special interest is the walled garden. While walking the area today, one can observe that major parts of the wall have been removed; however, enough remains to show the size of the plot and the height and construction of the wall.

These walled gardens, which were a part of major estates in England of this and earlier periods, were the source of much of the food for proprietors and staff of these estates. Their design and care were a carefully developed industry at the time. For those interested in this area, there is a fascinating resource, *The English Gardener* by William Cobbett, first published in 1829 and reprinted today as a Bloomsbury Gardening Classic. It was the definitive guide to gardening in Garrow's day and Sir William would have owned a copy. Included are directions for the design and construction of a walled garden, preparation of the soil, seeds and propagation techniques, kitchen-garden plants to be cultivated, fruit trees and berry plants and their care, diseases and vermin control and directions for cultivating a wide variety of flowers. The guide ends with a calendar of work to be performed month by month. It is interesting to imagine Garrow, as a country gentleman, supervising the care of such a garden.

At Garrow's death, the firm entrusted with the sale of this Pegwell property described it with the following words in an advertisement in the *Kentish Observer* on 19 November 1840.

> The late Right Honorable Sir William Garrow's very beautiful Marine Villa at Pegwell Bay for its delightful situation, aspect, tasteful arrangement, in perfect order, unrivaled on the Coast; also other valuable FREEHOLD ESTATES contiguous at Ramsgate.
>
> Messrs. Daniel Smith and Son are commissioned by the Trustees under a settlement by the late Sir William Garrow to bring to Public Sale, early in the Spring (unless acceptable offers should be previously made by private contract) the singularly beautiful and most comfortable freehold villa, at Pegwell, for many years the envied retreat of that eminent Judge, with its range of elegant conservatories, (forming a tasteful pavilion, connected with and screening a whole suite of rooms) excellent salt and fresh water baths, ornamental cottages, good stabling, and various out offices (most abundantly supplied with superior spring and salt water), walled gardens, and well dressed secluded lawns, bounded by the bold chalk cliff and opening with a full south aspect to all the grandeur of the magnificent bay.

In a subsequent advertisement published on 31 December, the description was generally repeated with these additional phrases:

… various small detached properties in the Village, and a small farm, comprising sundry enclosures of rich pasturage and arable land, part close to Ramsgate, commanding invaluable sites for breeding, with extensive frontages both to the road and cliff, amid embracing splendid sea views. The villa cannot be viewed without an especial order.

William Dyce made a painting of the cliffs of Pegwell in 1858-1860, shortly after Garrow's death. He called it "Pegwell Bay, A Recollection of October 5th, 1858,"and it commemorated the arrival of a comet which can be seen only upon close inspection of the original in the Tate Gallery.[5] The cliffs were those of Garrow's estate, and the roof of Garrow's home can be seen in the painting, again only upon close inspection of the original. Laure Meyer states in her *Masters of English Landscape* that this was one of the most popular landscape paintings in England at the end of the 19th century.[6]

As part of the loving care being given by today's owner of Garrow's seaside villa, Mrs. Alma Beaty is attempting to restore it to its original attractiveness. The structure had seen hard times. During World War Two it served as a searchlight station, and then after the war it was left derelict. It is now classified as an historic property and all restoration work must conform to the standards established to preserve the original character.

Even today this estate has a delightful setting, and is the only home in the area located right on the edge of the cliff. On a clear day one can see the coast of France from the upstairs bedroom window. Indeed, William Garrow had a "delightful situation" for a retreat during his extensive legal career and in his retirement years.

---

5. This is unmistakably Donati's Comet, one of the brightest and most visible of the nineteenth century; as discovered by Giovanni Donati on June 2, 1858, just a few months before the picture was painted.
6. L. Meyer. (1993) *Masters of English Landscape*. Paris, Finest S.A./ Editions Pierre Terrail. p. 176.

CHAPTER 12

Sarah

IRREGULAR RELATIONSHIP

Mystery and intrigue surround Sarah Dore. Research has uncovered hints of a high-birth Irish family background that shuffled her into a relationship with Arthur Hill (Viscount Fairford), who would become one of the wealthiest men in Ireland and England. Her life then becomes a mosaic of time gaps and glimpses of events linking her permanently with William Garrow and the Garrow family story. In *The Farington Diary* it was noted to be "a connection Garrow formed somewhat irregularly".[1]

Waddesdon, the Rothschild Collection (The National Trust)
Photograph © Waddesdon and the Photographic Survey,
Courtauld Institute of Art.

---

1. J. Farington. Edited by James Greig (1922) *The Farington Diary*. Hutchinson. Entry for October 20, 1811.

Thomas Hague, in his letter to William Garrow, created a colourful innuendo in which Garrow 's relationship with an Irish lady of high birth moved from cook or maid to mistress to wife. However, on page 43 in the same letter he writes, " ... you married under the most auspicious and honourable circumstances, to a lady of high birth, elegant accomplishments, softness, delicacy and sweetness of temper".[2] What is one to believe?

This idea of an irregularly formed relationship is reinforced by the dates of the births of their children, and the date of Sarah and William's marriage. The first child, David William, was born on 15 April 1781, and the second child, Eliza Sophia, was born three years later on 18 June 1784. Then Eliza Sophia was baptized at St. Andrews, Holborn, on 30 September 1784. A week later David William was baptized in the same church on 5 October 1784. William Garrow and Sarah Dore afterwards married at St. George the Martyr, Queen Square, Holborn, on 17 March 1793, when the children were almost twelve and nine years old. Certainly it appears everything was done out of order.

Mementos of Sarah and William Arthur Hill
passed down through the Dorehill generations.

2. T. Hague. (1808) *A Letter to William Garrow, Esq., In which the Conduct of Counsel in the Crossexamination of Witnesses and Commenting on their Testimony is fully discussed and the Licentiousness of the bar exposed.* London, Printed by R. McDonald for J. Parsons. p. 37.

And then there is the story of Sarah's previous marriage, if indeed it was a marriage. Based on tradition in the Dorehill family, Sarah Dore had some form of marriage to Arthur William Moyses Hill (Viscount Fairford), who later became the 2nd Marquis of Downshire. She had a son in this relationship, William Arthur, born in 1778. By this time, the father had earned a Master of Arts (9 July 1773) from Magdalen College, Oxford University, and was serving as an MP for Lostwithiel in Cornwall (1774-80) and later for Malmsbury (1780-84). Sarah, indeed, was keeping interesting company. It is the family tradition that the Hill family disapproved of the "marriage" because Sarah did not bring adequate wealth to the union, and had it annulled. To establish his parentage, William Arthur was given the surname of Dore Hill, Dore from his mother and Hill from his father, the source of the name Dorehill used today.

FINANCIAL SUPPORT

Recently discovered letters between the 3rd Marquis of Downshire and William Arthur Dorehill paint a clearer picture of this relationship. They confirm some of the family traditions with details of the relationship. Indeed William Arthur Dorehill received lifetime financial support from the Downshires, and they considered him in a family way. Although these letters concern the financial support being given to William Arthur Dorehill, they also contain a friendly exchange of information on family matters. William Arthur Dorehill was clearly accepted in a special way as a member of the Hill family. These letters also suggest that the financial support for William Arthur, provided by the Downshires to Sarah as William Arthur's mother, may have also provided early financial support to Sarah and William Garrow as they started their own family. This would have been while William Garrow was a struggling student and then a new member of the Bar. This is inferred in one of these letters written by William Arthur Dorehill, now an adult, to his half-brother, Lord Downshire, the 3rd Marquis of Downshire, after the death of Sir William Garrow. He remembered an obligation or debt of gratitude that Garrow owed to the Marquis of Downshire, and it is the financial nature of this obligation that is of interest here. His letter states: "I well remember the time, when in early life, he (Garrow) was for many years under the greatest pecuniary obligation to your Lordship's much lamented, and revered father, my generous Benefactor, and kind patron;"[3] It would appear that young William Garrow was living with Sarah and young William Arthur Dorehill along with his newborn David William and Eliza Sophia on money provided by the Downshires.

---

3. Letter sent by Arthur Dorehill to Lord Downshire, (29 December 1840)

After his relationship with Sarah, Arthur William Moyses Hill married Mary Sandys (1786), a "notable heiress." Then, upon the death of the Marquis of Downshire, Arthur William Moyses Hill became the 2nd Marquis of Downshire with one of the largest land holdings in Ireland and England, a very wealthy man. He died early, and his will may have been somewhat of a shock to his widow. His will charged her and their children with responsibilities to his son, William Arthur, to treat him "as one of the family." The will also supported two other children he had sired out of wedlock. Concerning William Arthur Dorehill, the will established that he was indeed the son of Sarah and Arthur William Moyses Hill.

This will also established that this Sarah was the same Sarah that married William Garrow. It stated that "Mrs. Garrow, wife of counselor Garrow, has had the care of and has (been) paid the Care of a Mother to him". It also stated that Mr. Garrow be paid the cost of his schooling. William Arthur Dorehill floated freely between his Hill and Garrow families. Evidence indicates this relationship lasted for thirty years. Lady Downshire gave the grandchild, Sarah Ann Dalton (nee Dorehill) a trousseau and a necklace on the occasion of her marriage.

There is a letter written by the wife of the grandson of Sarah Dore to her son Lewis dated 11 February 1880. In this letter she states: "Baron Garrow lived at Pegwell near Ramsgate. He married . . . your dear father's grandmother, a lovely woman. Your grandfather was her only child by 1st marriage, she had one son and a daughter by Baron Garrow - who were your father's 'Uncle Garrow' and 'Aunt Lettsom.'"[4] In another family journal by Lewis Dorehill it is written, "Sarah Garrow was a great horsewoman and used to ride from Ramsgate to London. Sir William Garrow had two houses, one at Pegwell near Ramsgate, the other the Corner House of Great George Street, Westminster (now pulled down). She was from all accounts a very handsome woman and her pictures bear evidence of her good looks."[5] Certainly Sarah's portrait by the famous pastel artist John Russell proves this point. One slight correction needs to be made to this account. The second house in Sarah's time was a corner house on Bedford Row and Theobald Road near Lincoln's Inn, not the house on Great George Street which Sir William moved into after her death.

There is an interesting story told of Sarah Garrow that has been passed down through the Dorehill family. It seems that Sarah and her granddaughter, Sarah Ann, were travelling by coach from Ramsgate to London when highwaymen stopped the coach and robbed everyone of all their valuables. The coach then proceeded along the road, and the same highwaymen stopped the coach again. This time they gave back to Sarah Garrow all the things they had stolen from her, and the little necklace taken from the granddaughter, keeping all they had stolen from others in the coach. And they apologized to Sarah for taking her property. Apparently there is honour

---

4. Correspondence record held by Jan Dalton.
5. Journal record held by Jan Dalton.

among thieves. When learning they had stolen from their protector in the Old Bailey, they found it in their interest to return her property.

SARAH'S CHARACTER

A few authors commented on the character and bearing of Mrs. Garrow. Thomas Hague, in his letter to William Garrow, expressed very positive memories of Mrs. Garrow, in contradiction to the descriptions he gave in the feigned case attacking Garrow's courtroom behaviour. Concerning the feigned case he added, "… the facts and points upon which I have taken the liberty of examining you, are ideal, absolutely unfounded ….". Addressing William Garrow, he then wrote about Sarah:

> I had once the honour of being introduced to her, which is the more marked in my memory, because at that time, such were her condescension and diffidence, that she expressed it an honour to be introduced to me. It was before you arrived at the dignity of a silk-gown; and I am not certain whether Mrs. Garrow had then displayed the elegance of a silk petticoat; … However, it is in your gown and Mrs. Garrow's petticoats only, that a change appears … Mrs. Garrow retains the soft melody of her voice, with all those delicate and feminine qualities .[6]

Thomas Hague, in this same letter, suggested that while William Garrow was busy with the affairs of the courts, Sarah was often elsewhere. In the feigned interrogation he asked the question: "Do they live happily together?" And the answer was: "If I may judge from their being so much apart, they cannot be long unhappy together."[7] It is unfortunate that one of the major records on the relationship of Sarah and William is the Hague letter, which by intent was to slander William Garrow through the use of exaggeration and innuendo. The Hague letter was published a few months before Sarah's death, during the time of her declining health.

However, if Sarah spent much of her time in their Pegwell home, she lived in comfortable and interesting surroundings. She is remembered in various books on the history of the Ramsgate area. Typical is the record in *Memoranda of the Cliffs*:

> Pegwell Cottage has also a part in the reminiscences of the past. It was originally built by Mr. Garrow, a member of the Bar, who took an active part in the affairs of the day … He and his family identified themselves with the various institutions of the parish; and it has often been my lot to hear from the old inhabitants, fathers and grandfathers of the present race of the active interests which Lady Garrow took in the schools of St. Laurence in that day. It was her custom to have a certain number of the boys and girls of the school, in turn, home to dinner every Sunday throughout the year, after morning service, the children calling at the village bake house for the joint and carrying it to Pegwell. Sufficient still remains of the house and grounds to tell of the care with which everything was arranged.[8]

---

6. T. Hague. *A Letter to William Garrow etc. Op. cit.* p. 37.
7. *Ibid.* p. 38.
8. C.T. Richardson. (1885) "Memoranda of the Cliffs". *Fragments of History.*

Pegwell Cottage in the earliest photograph, shortly after William Garrow 's death.

While this gives an interesting glimpse of the Sunday routine, Sarah Garrow's elevation to the title of "Lady" was a little premature. William Garrow was knighted about four years after Sarah's death. Sarah died on 30 June 1808. The *Gentleman's Magazine* had this to say under the heading of death notices: "In Bedford Row, after a long and painful illness, which she endured in a most exemplary manner, Mrs. Garrow, wife of William G. esq." [9]

MYSTERIES

She was buried at St. Margaret's Church, a beautiful old country church outside the village of Darenth in Kent a few miles southeast of London. Her tomb is a table vault with an iron fence around it located near the wall of the church. Buried next to her are the remains of Margaret (1714-1801) and George Dore (1745-1805). Why was she laid to rest in this churchyard and next to these people named Dore? Could it be that they are Sarah's mother and brother?

Her gravestone reads that she was fifty-six at the time of her death. Sarah's relationship with William Garrow had lasted twenty-eight years. At the time of her death her husband was forty-eight years old, and their son, David was twenty-seven, married and was a graduate of Christ Church, Oxford. He had been called to the Bar by Lincoln's Inn (although he was destined to spend his life as a minister). Their

9. *The Gentleman's Magazine and Historical Chronicle.* (July 1805) p. 682.

daughter, Eliza Sophia, had also married, and a most curious marriage it turned out to be. Sarah's first son, William Arthur Dorehill, was married and had left the home many years before. Sarah was a grandmother. By this time William Arthur had given her three grandchildren, and Eliza Sophia had given her two more. Her son, David, may have given her a granddaughter. It should also be remembered that it was during Sarah's life with William Garrow that he would achieve those accomplishments in his professional career for which he would be most remembered in the evolving history of English criminal law - establishing the practice of providing an aggressive defence for those accused of felonies.

Sarah's tomb by St. Margaret's Church, near Darenth, Kent.

Mysteries remain. Who were Sarah's parents and what was her family heritage? What were the details of her relationship with Arthur William Moyes Hill? What were the detailed circumstances of Sarah's early association with William Garrow? Under what circumstances were the children born? How and where did she raise her three children before she formally married William Garrow? Was she Catholic? If events seemed to have unfolded in an unusual order, what were the causes of these irregularities? Whatever the replies might be, it all ended well with a vigorous family life and healthy children who all became accomplished adults.

CHAPTER 13

Garrow's Will And Trust[1]

Concerning Garrow's wealth, a series of interesting questions can be proposed. At the end of his life did Garrow have a large or meagre estate? How much money and property had he acquired? What happened to this wealth? What did Garrow attempt to accomplish with his wealth through wills and other legal instruments? In the vernacular, who got the money? In Garrow's case, these are questions that can, in part, be answered.

HOW WEALTHY WAS SIR WILLIAM GARROW?

Two years before his retirement as a judge, and ten years before his eventual death, Garrow wrote and signed two legal instruments that determined how his wealth would be managed during the remainder of his life and how it would be distributed after his death. The first was his will, and the second was an indenture or trust.

The will was terse and had two demands. First that he desired "to be buried at Hadley [the place of his nativity] as near the remains of my late Uncle Doctor William Garrow as convenient without parade or unnecessary expense." And the second was to set up his trust. The will states: "I give devise and bequeath all my real and personal estate whatsoever and wheresoever and of what nature and kind soever to my said ... executors upon the trusts and for the uses, interests and purposes declared in and by the ... Deed of Conveyance." While the will was simple and straight forward, the indenture or trust was sixteen handwritten pages of convoluted legal language that in places is almost impossible to interpret, both by a layman, and even by a member of the legal profession.

While some details may appear clouded, the general thrust of what Garrow chose to do with his wealth is clear. He wanted professional help in managing his estate, he wanted to take care of succeeding generations of his family, and he wanted to avoid death duties. How wealthy was Garrow? His trust lists properties and also money invested in the Bank of England, insurance policies in his name and other equities. Concerning properties the trust lists:

1. Messuages (dwelling houses with outbuildings and adjacent lands) farms, lands in Kent, Hertford, Middlesex, and Glamorgan.
2. Messuages or tenements, lands, and other hereditaments within the Manor of Barnet.

---

1. A copy of the Will is in the possession of the authors.

3. Leased meadows, closes, pieces or parcels of land, tinworks, mills, messuages tenament or dwelling house and other premises in the Parish of Cadoxton near Neath in the County of Glamorgan.

In a draft of this trust held in the Heritage Collection at the Ramsgate Library, Garrow is more specific in listing his properties. This list includes:

1. Pegwell properties.
2. Barnet properties including those obtained by the will of his uncle, Dr. William Garrow, including the Two Brewers.
3. Enfield property near the obelisk in the Great North Road.
4. Property at or near Rowley Green near Barnet. (will of uncle)
5. Messuages, farms and land called Aberdulais and mills and forges called Aberdulais Mills.
6. Messuages, farms and land called Winualt and Bryhioheeth or Bernwith and Maer Llerwellyn.
7. Woods, woodlands, mines and minerals in Parish of Lantwill by Neath in County of Glamorgan.
8. Properties in counties of Kent, Hertford, Middlesex and Glamorgan.

The Glamorgan properties are in the Neath area just outside Swansea in South Wales. It is interesting to speculate that the Glamorgan properties held by Garrow at his death were obtained when his son-in-law, Fothergill Lettsom, became bankrupt. Garrow was a major investor in his son-in-law's business adventure in tin works in Wales, and Garrow may have obtained the properties in partial payment for money extended. And concerning money, insurance and other equities, the value of the trust was £22,000. This included:

1. £12,000 3 ½ % interest in Bank of England
2. £5,000 secured by mortgage; and
3. £5,000 in three insurance policies.

TRUSTEES

When Garrow reached the age of seventy he turned the detailed management of his assets over to the executors of his trust. These men were Leonard Smith of the City of London, a merchant, Edward Lowth Badeley, of Paper Buildings, Temple, Esquire, and William Nanson Lettsom of Grays Inn, Esquire. William Nanson Lettsom was the cousin to the husband of Garrow's daughter. These men had the authority to buy and sell assets as needed to manage the investments and meet the obligations of the trust. During Garrow's lifetime this was to be done only with his consent.

The trustees were appointed for life. They were to appoint their successors and give them the same authority. This was necessary because the trust was designed so that it could last, if not forever, at least for an extended number of years.

The following people were to receive money from the trust upon the death of Garrow. Joseph Garrow, the son of William Garrow's brother by an Indian lady, was to receive £1000 pounds, or if Joseph Garrow was not alive at William Garrow's death, then the money was for his daughter Theodosia. The trust was to provide £200 each to three of Jane Monk's children, Jane being William Garrow's sister. The Jane Monk children mentioned were Eliza Eleanora Elwin, Selina Augusta Blanc, and Charles Edward Monk. Jane Monk was to receive the interest, dividends and annual product of £2000 for the rest of her life, and on her death this income was to be transferred to another of Jane's daughters, Myra Charlotte Monk. (Jane received this inheritance for one year and died, passing the inheritance to Myra Charlotte.)

The remainder of the estate was to be divided into two parts or "moieties", one part to support Sir William Garrow's son's widow, Charlotte Caroline, and her posterity. The other part was to support Sir William Garrow's daughter, Eliza Sophia Lettsom, and her posterity. How this was to be accomplished is of special interest.

Charlotte Caroline was to receive £300 a year for the rest of her life from interest from her side of the family's money. The corpus of this money was to be divided equally among her children. Her male children would get their share when twenty-one years old. Female children could only receive the interest from their share, specifically "to receive the dividends, interest and income…during her life for her sole and separate use and without any power to anticipate, change or encumber" this money. After the death of a daughter, the money was to be divided among that daughter's children. Again, male children were to receive their share at age twenty-one, and female children were, again, to receive only the interest and again without the authority to encumber the money. Apparently, through the female line, this strategy would continue indefinitely.

Eliza Sophia Lettsom, Sir William Garrow's daughter, was also to receive £300 a year for the rest of her life, but in this case the conditions were spelled out in great detail. The Trust document states in part that she was to receive: "yearly income of £300" and to "pay the dividends, interest and annual income thereof into the proper hands of the said Eliza Sophia Lettsom, wife of the said Samuel Fothergill Lettsom, to and for her separate use and benefit apart from and independent of her said present husband or any future husband to whom she from time to time may be married and free from the control, debts and engagements of her said present or any future husband . . . Eliza Sophia Lettsom shall not anticipate, charge, assign or in any manner encumber or dispose of the said dividends, interest and annual income respectively before the same shall become actually due and payable ...". There was also a complex provision for an additional £200 a year, if required, to be divided in any proportion between Eliza Sophia and her husband, who, as the document stated, "now live separate and apart from each other on account of the pecuniary circumstances of the said Samuel Fothergill Lettsom." This may have been the source of funds that supported Samuel Fothergill Lettsom as he lived out his life in Boulogne, France, avoiding debtors prison in England. The children of Eliza Sophia were to participate in the trust in the same manner as the children of her brother, David William Garrow.

There was one additional provision apparently made for the "children, grand-children or issue" and that is that money could be drawn for maintenance, education and advancement, but such money would be drawn from that person's share of the trust. The trust document also spells out how to handle every conceivable contingency in the life of the trust or in the lives of the people touched by the trust over an extended span of time. This specifying how to deal with all these contingencies makes the document an exceedingly complex affair.

NO DEATH DUTIES

Garrow structured his affairs in such a way that his estate paid no death duties. He knew the rules better than most. And with this knowledge he may have structured one of the first tax shelters. Upon his death, Garrow's will along with a detailed account of his assets went to probate. The Commissioner of Stamps attempted to collect the death duty. The worksheets used to calculate his duty show a significant effort to arrive at the duty. Apparently a review of this effort was requested, and this review went all the way to the Attorney-General's Office. The result of the review was documented on the worksheets. The record states:

> Boards Minute, 3rd April 1843. Read report of the Assistant Solicitor that he has submitted a note to (from) the Attorney & Solicitor-General on the will of the late Sir William Garrow whose opinion is as follows: "We are of opinion that no Legacy Duty is payable on the property comprised in the passing of the Deed of Settlement made by Sir William Garrow and that it will not be proper for the Commissioners of Stamps to insist upon any." He ordered that the Comptroller of Legacy Duty be instructed accordingly.

WOMEN

We know from the wills of Garrow's granddaughters that the trust was a significant part of their assets, even though females could only draw the interest earned on the funds they inherited. Garrow had six granddaughters. Of these only three married, and of these, two married late in life. Only one married at the usual age when young ladies found husbands. It would appear that when they could afford it, the grand-daughters lived off granddad's money and remained independent. For instance, Anna Maria Garrow, spinster, died in Canterbury at about forty years of age, leaving almost £3000 to her sister Georgina Laetitia, also a spinster at the time.

There were only three great grand children born to Sir William Garrow, and two of these were girls. And only one of these girls had children. Carolina Georgina Philips Hacker had four children, two girls and two boys. Of the two girls born to this generation, only one had children - Edith Elizabeth Hacker Snead, great great granddaughter of Sir William Garrow, who had three girls and two boys.[2]

Shortly after his retirement, Garrow added an attachment to his will. In this he ordered that "Mrs. Sarah Young, widow (and his housekeeper) should receive his bed, bedstead, mattresses, bolsters, pillows and other things as I now use, the same together with two complete changes of the best linen of all sorts for the same, and also the wardrobe glasses, tables and chairs and all other things in and about or which are used in my bedchamber."

After Garrow's death, Mrs. Sarah Young continued to live at Pegwell Cottage. The *Kentish Observer* recorded the following death notice on 19 November 1840. It seems that Mrs. Young lived less than two months after Garrow's death.

> Suddenly, at Pegwell Cottage, the residence of the late Sir William Garrow, in whose family she had been many years, Mrs. Young, Widow of the late W. Young, esq. Surgeon, age 69.

FUNERAL

There is one last observation. Wills do not guarantee desired ends. Garrow was not buried at Hadley near the remains of his beloved uncle, as he requested. He was buried in the churchyard of the parish church, St. Lawrence, Ramsgate, Thanet near his home. Also his table vault tomb may have been more expensive than he specified. It was his request that his funeral be "without parade." Again the record, in this instance the *Kent Herald* of 15 October 1840, describes the funeral including the "parade." It states: The funeral of Sir William Garrow, Knt. took place on Sunday's night. It was the wish of the deceased that he should be buried on a Sunday. As a mark of respect a great many of the inhabitants and tradesmen of Ramsgate followed his remains to the grave. A funeral sermon was afterwards preached by Rev. Mr. Sicklemore from 1st Corinthians, 15th chapter, 51, 52, 53 verses.

---

2. Edith Elizabeth was the grandmother of the author, Richard Braby.

Behold, I shew you a mystery; We shall not all sleep, but we shall all be changed, in a moment, in the twinkling of an eye, at the last trump; for the trumpet shall sound, and the dead shall be raised incorruptible, and we shall be changed. For this corruptible must put on incorruption, and this mortal must put on immortality.

Located not far from the door to the church, the tomb is surrounded with an iron fence, and covered with ivy. The inscription is difficult or impossible to read, however records indicate these are the words that were cut into the stone.

Sir William GARROW, of Pegwell Cottage, third son of David Garrow of Hadley, County Hereford. Born 13ᵗʰ April 1760, and in 1793 was appointed by King George III one of His Majesty's Counsel. In 1806 he was made Attorney General to his Royal Highness George, Prince of Wales. In 1812 he was promoted to the office of Solicitor General, and in 1813 to that of Attorney General to King George III. In 1814 he was constituted Chief Justice to the County Palatine of Chester. In 1817 he was raised to the dignity of Baron of the Court of Exchequer, and having discharged with uprightness and ability the duties of that office during a period of nearly 15 years, he retired from it in February 1832 and was immediately afterwards appointed by King William IVᵗʰ one of His Majesty's most honourable Privy Council. He died at Pegwell, beloved and honoured, 21ˢᵗ September 1840, aged 80 years.

Sir William Garrow's tomb today.

CHAPTER 14

Garrow's Extended Family

William Garrow is remembered as having supported a vibrant family life. A contemporary of Garrow, writing in *Public Characters, 1799-1809*, observed that he was a family man, much loved and esteemed in private life and further observed that no one lived more orderly and temperately.[1]

AN INTRODUCTION TO GARROW'S FAMILY

To appreciate William Garrow, one needs to understand something of the composition of his immediate and extended family, the people he knew intimately and cared for. Indeed, his life was imbedded in the life events he experienced within this large and colourful family group.

This chapter is intended for two types of reader. For the student of the history of the adversarial trial attempting to better understand William Garrow's role in the legal scene, this chapter will give background material to add depth to his character, qualities lacking in all other accounts of his life. Information on the major players in the Garrow family will be helpful in understanding the rich family environment in which William Garrow moved, and found special meaning. For the genealogist, interested in the family story, this chapter will introduce a range of characters that make up this extended family.

From a genealogist's perspective, at least twelve generations have passed since Dr. William and Rev. David Garrow moved from Scotland to England, resulting over the years in a population of people dispersed around the world that in some ways are connected to this Garrow story. This account will help them connect to their roots and to celebrate their connections to Sir William Garrow. Generations after his death, certain of his posterity would recall family gatherings at his homes on Great George Street in Westminster, and at his Pegwell cottage by the sea near Ramsgate. In addition, in his will and trust, he took great care in acknowledging his extended family and in organizing his estate in such a way that three or more generations of the children that followed him were provided financial assistance in their maintenance, education and advancement, prior to their receiving their share of their inheritance when they became of age or at the death of their parents.

One such remembrance of a family gathering was in a letter sent by Mrs. M. Dorehill, dated 11 February 1890 to her son Lewis. It states:

---

1. "Mr. Garrow," *Public Characters, 1799-1809.* 4th edition. Various editions were published and are available through The British Library.

Your father (Sarah's grandson William John Dorehill) used to spend his holidays with the Garrows, either at Great George Street or Pegwell, had a happy pleasant life of it and the Garrow boys and two Lettsom sons were fond of him.[2]

Based on this letter and other family records, it is possible to reconstruct such a holiday. If such a gathering took place in 1823 the children specifically mentioned would be:

William John Dorehill (age 8)
William Garrow Lettsom (age 18)
Samuel Lettsom (age 16)
David William Garrow (age 14)
Edward William Garrow (age 8)
George William Garrow (age 5)

This large family gathering of Dorehills, Lettsoms and Garrows would have included Sir William Garrow, but by now his wife Sarah had been dead for 15 years. Certainly there would have been William Garrow's daughter, Eliza Sophia Lettsom, with her 3 children, ranging in age from 10 to 18 years. She is thought to be living at this time in the Garrow home raising her family there. Her husband, having become bankrupt, was now living in France to avoid debtor's prison. William Garrow's son David and his wife Charlotte Caroline would have been there with their eight children, ranging in ages from 5 to 15 years. William Arthur Dorehill, Sarah's son by Arthur Hill, now 44, would have been there with his wife Mary Mair, with their son William John (mentioned in the Dorehill letter) and their other 5 children ranging in age from 1 to 21 years of age. Joseph Garrow, who grew up in the Garrow home, could have been there with his wife, Theodosia, who would soon become pregnant with their daughter Theodosia.

Garrow's seaside cottage, or as it later was called, his marine villa, would have been an ideal setting for such a gathering. The house and conservatory opened onto carefully cared for lawns above the chalk cliffs at the sea's edge, and on a clear day one could see France from the upstairs windows. Family members without rooms in the main house could stay in what were called ornamental cottages. The estate had walled gardens, high stoned enclosures where the food for the family was grown, and an orchard that supplied fruit. There were stables and pastures, and fresh and salt water baths as well as the sea. At low tide shell fish could easily be gathered on the salt flats exposed by the receding water. It must have been a wonderful place to be a child, and for adults to gather. Adjacent to the estate was the village of Pegwell with small shops and places to eat, and a cave-like tunnel

---

2. Unpublished correspondence held by Jan Dalton, a descendent of Sarah Garrow and Mrs. M. Dorehill who wrote the letter.

leading to the water's edge. Little wonder that it was known by many in later years as the envied retreat of the eminent Judge Garrow.

These children and youths that were a part of such a family gathering would grow up to make their mark on English history in various ways. William John Dorehill would become a Major General in the Army serving in India, Australia, and Ireland. Joseph Garrow, who would live in Florence, Italy and would translate Dante's "Vita Nuova" into English and become friends with the Brownings and W.S. Landor. And his daughter, who was specifically called out in Garrow's trust, would grow up to marry Thomas Trollope and become a part of the Trollope literary family. As an author she would be celebrated as a heroine of the Italian Revolution, for her work in reporting that revolution. Garrow's son David had earned the Degree of Doctor of Divinity from Oxford University and was serving as the Rector of the parish in East Barnet and was also serving as a Chaplain-in-Ordinary to the Royal Family. His son Edward would become the Rector of Bilsthrope, in Nottinghamshire and like his father, and great grandfather devote his life to the Church. And a grandson, William Garrow Lettsom, after a long career in government foreign affairs, would serve as a Consul-General in the foreign service.

Another person who may have on occasions attended these family gatherings was William Nanson Lettsom, who in 1823 had just graduated from Cambridge with a Master of Arts and would become a distinguished Shakespearian scholar.[3] He would play a major role in Garrow's caring for this extended family and their descendents as an administrator of his trust. Many others in this extended family would lead successful yet less public lives, in part with William Garrow's wealth and William Nanson Lettsom's administration of that wealth.

Indeed, if William Garrow's brothers and sister and their children were to be included on occasions in this family celebration, it would be a most colourful collection of people, many of whom made fortunes in India, and brought into the Garrow family the merging of English and Indian blood lines. Some of these Anglo-Indian Garrows returned to England, and others remained in India to perpetuate the Garrow bloodline in that country.

With a few exceptions, to study Garrow's extended family it is necessary to delve into genealogical type records. His family life has not been described in books or newspaper accounts, such as has been his professional life. Only formal notices of births, marriages and deaths of members of Garrow's family appeared in the press. Wills of family members present some significant information. The stories presented here were retrieved by individuals with the skills and determination to search through the endless musty records of Regency and Victorian England, and to

---

3. J.A. Venn (1940-1954) "Garrow, Joseph," Alumni Cantabrigiensis; Part 2. A biographical list of all known students, graduates and holders of office at the University of Cambridge from the earliest of times to 1900.

organize bits of significant information into meaningful life stories. We will attempt to give credit where credit is due, although genealogists tend to borrow from each other making it difficult to determine who first located a specific piece of data, and who merely copied it from someone else 's account.

First, stories about his son and the son's family will be presented. Then stories about his daughter and her family will follow. Stories from the life of Sarah's son William Arthur will then be added. These in turn will be followed by stories of his brothers and sisters and their families. We will assume that these were the people who knew and cared for each other, who corresponded and who would gather together on occasions, when possible, during the lifetime of Sir William Garrow and in his presence. If indeed this happened, it would have been a most interesting family reunion. These were the people Sir William Garrow knew and cared for as he went about his business of being a barrister and a judge.

SON DAVID AND FAMILY

David William Garrow (1781-1827) Educated at Christ Church College, Oxford University, David earned the degree of Doctor of Divinity (D.D.), and he served as the Rector of the East Barnet and Chipping Barnet parish, north of London. He also served as one of the Chaplains in ordinary to the Prince of Wales. With his wife Charlotte Caroline they had eight children.[4]

Sir William Garrow's only son was born on 15 April 1781. This was while Garrow, the father, was still a student under Mr. Crompton and over two years before he would be called to the Bar. The boy's sister would be born almost three years later. Presumably he grew up on Bedford Row in London near the Inns of Court while his father was quickly becoming one of the best known criminal lawyers. He was educated at Charterhouse; then on 1 July 1799, he enrolled at Trinity, but a year later migrated to Christ Church College, Oxford University. There he earned a Bachelor of Arts (1804). Interspersed with this study he was admitted by Lincoln's Inn to study law during 1799 and was called to the Bar in 1806.

David William Garrow married Charlotte Caroline Proby at Stratford St. Mary in Suffolk on 5 November 1805. His bride was the daughter of Reverend Narcissus Charles Proby, the Rector of Stratford St. Mary.

It was in the ministry, not law, that David Garrow would find his life's work. He returned to Christ Church, Oxford University, where he earned a Master of Arts (1807), a Bachelor of Divinity - (1814) and then a Doctor of Divinity (1818). Also in 1818 he published the book *The History & Antiquities of Croydon* that may have

---

4. Frederick Charles Cass (1885) *The Parish of East Barnet*, Westminster . Nichols & Sons. p. 237.

met part of the requirements for his Doctor of Divinity degree.[5] He was ordained a deacon in 1810 and became the Parish Clerk of Tidmarsh, Berkshire. During 1811 he became a Chaplain-in-Ordinary to the Prince Regent.

He became the Rector of the parish in East Barnet, Hertfordshire on 7 November 1815, and set about making a major revision to the church building. He was elected Governor of Barnet Grammar School on 21 December 1815.

In 1820 David published a four hundred and twenty-three page book containing twenty of his sermons, *Sermons Comprising Various Matters of Doctrine and Practice*, including a sermon he preached in St. Paul's Cathedral.[6] This sermon was given during the Festival of the Sons of the Clergy on 21 May 1818. It was entitled "The Importance of the Sacerdotal Office," and was for the purpose of raising funds to support the widows and children of deceased clergy. Accompanying the sermon there were nine pages of notes providing the theological justifications for the statements made, and presented in English, Latin, or Greek, as appropriate. It was a carefully crafted statement, and appeared to have some of the eloquence that would be expected from the son of Sir William Garrow. A short passage from the sermon will illustrate this point.

> What, then, are the occupations of the parish Priest? Not alone the ministry in the presence of the congregation, which was required by the Mosaic law; not alone the administration of the important rite of Baptism, by which he initiates the infant members of his flock in the blessed covenant of Christ; not alone the solemn and interesting ceremonial by which he afterwards unites them in the sacred engagement of conjugal alliance; not alone the awful, melancholy office, which finally constrains him to consign them to their native dust. Not to these momentous callings are the employments of the parochial Minister confined.
>
> While he fulfills the ministrations of the Church, he is mindful that the requisitions of his duty are not satisfied if he forgets the cottage. He visits, therefore, exhorts, encourages, expostulates, reproves; by his approbation he distinguishes the worthy; by his displeasure he marks the hardy and the forward; he induces them by his demeanour to consider him as the person whose good regard they must obtain, and thus in his humble, but honourable sphere, he teaches them the inestimable value of character.
>
> But his attentions, his cares, his labours, end not here. Full many an instance may be mentioned in which the poor man, uninformed, but anxious as to his worldly affairs, can find no one to be consulted but the Minister of his parish; to him he makes known his difficulty; from him he receives information and advice, whether it be as to the application of some small pittance during life, or as to the disposition of it after death.
>
> For the religious education of children, too, the parochial Clergy are most laudably concerned; this great object they promote by every method which they can command; by their pecuniary contributions, by the application of their time, by their superintendence and authority.

5. D.W. Garrow. (1818) *The History & Antiquities of Croydon, with a variety of other interesting matter; to which is added a sketch of the life of The Most Reverend Father in God John Whitgift, Lord Archbishop of Canterbury.* Croydon, printed for W. Annan, High-Street: and sold by Geo. Cowie & Co. Poultry, London.
6. D.W. Garrow. (1820) *Sermons Comprising Various Matters of Doctrine and Practice.* London, F.C. & J. Rivington.

Again, contemplate the parish Minister in the last affecting stage of intercourse with those committed to his charge; see him in the rude hut, bending over the homely pallet, gently infusing the balm of Gospel truth, into the heart of some poor decaying brother, who in a few short hours must resign 'his spirit unto God who gave it.' There view the Minister of Christ - see him with most kind concern watching each movement of the feeble sufferer - hear the calm, pious accent of exhortation which he breathes - his holy precept - his admonition respecting penitence and faith - his devout prayer when he supplicates for the weak languishing mortal, that the Father of spirits may "send him help from his holy place, and evermore mightily defend him;" that 'enemy may have no advantage of him, nor the wicked approach to hurt him.'

If, in the course of such truly Christian occupations, the Preacher of the Gospel shall have assisted in preserving one individual from the danger of eternal perdition, if he shall have placed but one soul in the avenue to happy immortality - how much must he in such a case have done for a fellow-creature, how much must he have accomplished for himself!

Such are the faithful endeavours, the conscientious labours of our parochial Priests - profoundly beneficial to man, highly acceptable, we must believe, in the sight of heaven.[7]

His title as one of the Chaplains-in-Ordinary to the Prince of Wales requires additional comment. When the Prince of Wales became acting King in 1811 as a result of the mental illness of his father, King George III, David's father William Garrow had been serving as the Attorney-General to the Prince of Wales. William Garrow probably used his influence to obtain this volunteer position for his son. There were fifty-two ministers with the title Chaplain-in-Ordinary to the royal family, each serving one week a year. However, having some responsibility for the moral and spiritual behaviour of this royal personage would have given any conscientious man of the cloth a high level of concern.

During these same years of school and service to the Crown and to the "Father in Heaven," the Reverend David Garrow had been busy in other ways. He sired eight children. According to the recorded or estimated dates of birth they were: Charlotte Mary Ann (1808), David William (1809), Arabella (1811), Georgina Laetitia (1812), Anna Maria (1813), Katherine Caroline (1814), Edward William (1816) and George William (1818). All of these children lived to adulthood, and all three of David's sons were named William.

The Reverend David Garrow died suddenly on 11 April 1827 at East Barnet Rectory. The parish record indicates that he dined the previous evening at Everley Lodge, and was found dead in his bed in the morning. It is interesting to note that in his will the first person mentioned is his brother William Arthur Dorehill, and that he pays respect to his father by giving him any of his books he may select "as the last trifling mark of my respect and gratitude".

There is a monumental inscription to him on the wall of the East Barnet church. He was survived by his father who was still serving as a judge, his wife (forty-nine)

7. *Ibid.* p. 404.

and their eight children ranging in age from nine to nineteen. His wife Charlotte Caroline lived another fourteen years dying on 3 June 1841 at the Garrow family home, the Priory. His sermon, preached in St. Paul's Cathedral to raise funds for the widows and the families of deceased clergy, may have been a premonition to his own life story in that at his death he left a wife and large family.

A brief description of the lives lived by each of the children is presented next, followed by a more in depth discussion, to the extent that information is available.

Charlotte Mary Ann (1808-) Little information is available. She was thirty-three and was with her sisters at the Priory at the death of her mother in 1841. When her father died she was nineteen, and when her grandfather Sir William Garrow died she was thirty-two.

David William (1809-1845) Almost eighteen when his father died, he joined the Madras Army at that time, spending his life in India. He died five years after his grandfather Sir William Garrow's death. There is no record of a marriage.

Arabella (1811-1868) She was unmarried and twenty-nine at the time her grandfather, Sir William Garrow died. At thirty-six she married Waldo Hicks Philips, a gentleman and son of a minister. They had one child, Caroline Georgina.

Georgina Laetitia (1812-1888) She was unmarried and twenty-eight at the time that her grandfather Sir William Garrow died. She lived as a single lady (spinster) until she was forty-six when she married her cousin, Robert Crawford. They had no children.

Anna Maria (1813-1853) Little is known of Anna Maria's life. She was twenty-seven when her grandfather Sir William Garrow died, and fourteen when her father died. She died at Canterbury, Kent at the age of forty.

Katherine Caroline (1814-1904) She married William Bradstreet two years before her grandfather Sir William Garrow died, and together they had two children: William Carolus, and Caroline Anna. William Bradstreet was a minister.

Edward William (1815-1896) When his grandfather died, Edward was twenty-five and had recently graduated with a Bachelor of Arts from Oxford University, and was ordained as a deacon. With more education at Oxford, he served as the Rector of Bilsthorpe, Nottinghamshire until his death at eighty. Edward married his cousin, Harriet Elliot. There were no children.

George William (1818-1847) When his grandfather died George was a student at Oxford University. He served as a clergyman in a small rural parish before becoming a Royal Naval Chaplain, dying in Jamaica eleven days before his twenty-ninth birthday.

More detailed accounts of the children of the Reverend David Garrow, D.D., and his wife Charlotte Caroline Proby are given below. The extent of the information presented is limited by the lack of family data. All the information comes from public records.

Charlotte Mary Ann (1808-) Baptized privately into the church on 6 May 1808 at Stratford St. Mary in the Bloomsbury district of London by Rev. Thomas Cautley who was the husband to Charlotte Caroline's mother's sister. Little information is available on the life of Charlotte. She was present at the Priory in Totteridge, Hertfordshire on 6 June during the 1841 census, along with three of her sisters, which was taken three days after her mother's death. Apparently the family had gathered for Charlotte Caroline's passing. There is no record of Charlotte Mary Ann ever marrying.

David William (1809-1845) Born on 17 July 1809, he was baptized on 23 April 1810 at St. Lawrence in Thanet. This church is on the outskirts of Ramsgate, and near Sir William Garrow's villa by the sea on Pegwell Bay. It is also the church where Sir William Garrow's remains now lie buried. By the time young David William was baptized the Garrows had owned the villa for about twenty years, and it must have served as a family gathering place. Little has been recorded of young David William's life other than that he became a cadet in the Madras Army in 1827, at the time of his father's death. He was in the Madras Army eighteen years until he resigned on 31 March 1845 and died in Madras sometime later.

Arabella (1811?-1868) While records of her birth and early life have not been found, Arabella remained unmarried during the life of Sir William Garrow. She was present at the Priory with three of her four sisters at the death of her mother, as recorded in the census of 6 June 1841. Later, at age 35, she married Waldo Hicks Philips on 5 March 1846 at the parish church of Carisbrooke on the Isle of Wight. The marriage certificate states that Waldo Hicks Philips was a gentleman, and Arabella Garrow was a spinster, and daughter of David William Garrow, D.D. The marriage was performed in the presence of Thomas Philips, a clerical Clerk, and father of Waldo. Also present as a witness was Anna Maria Garrow. Anna Maria was a sister of Arabella. Waldo and Arabella made their home at Hunny Hill, Newport, Isle of Wight, and according to family tradition, a home in London. Their only child, Carolina Georgina, was born on 15 December 1847 at Lopen in Somerset, across the English Channel from the Isle of Wight, and near Toller Fratrum where the parish in which Thomas Philips served was located.

Eight and one half months before the birth of her daughter, Arabella signed a most interesting will. It is apparent that Waldo had become acquainted with the specific terms of the trust set up by Sir William Garrow through which Arabella had access to a considerable sum of interest money. The trust has already been described in detail in the previous chapter. As we have seen, and simply stated, female descendants of Sir William were to receive only the interest on their share of the trust, the money was for their use only and could not be assigned away. Her children, if male, would receive the principal, ending their rights to the trust money. However, if the child were female, then again she would have access to the interest on her share of the money, passing the principal to the next generation. Arabella clearly had access only to interest money. However, it would take a lawyer to unravel the logic of Arabella's will. Simply stated, Waldo wanted the money. Arabella signed a will that restated and inaccurately interpreted the details of Sir William Garrow's trust. Arabella's will, in part, then stated:

> Now I the said Arabella Philips, wife of the said Waldo Hicks Philips, formerly Arabella Garrow, Spinster, one of the daughters of the said David William Garrow, having attained the age of twenty one years pursuant to and by force and virtue and in exercise and execution of the power or authority to me for this purpose given by the said hereinbefore recited Indenture of Settlement and of every other power or authority in anywise enabling me in this behalf Do by this my last Will and Testament in writing executed by me in the presence of and attested by the two credible witnesses whose name are hereunder written as witnesses hereto direct and appoint give devise and bequeath unto the said Waldo Hicks Philips of Lopen aforesaid in the County of Somerset all and every my Original and every additional part share and proportion of and in the said trust monies stock funds and securities and all other the part share and proportion of and in the said trust monies stock funds and securities and the dividends and interest thereof to which I now am or may hereafter become entitled by survivorship, accruorship or otherwise ....[8]

Waldo's plans to capture the money were never accomplished. He apparently died before Arabella. Arabella died at Ramsgate on 30 April 1869 after a long illness. Burial records indicated her age was fifty-eight. Her only daughter, Caroline Georgina, became entitled to her mother's personal estate, "and objects over which she had no disposing power." Caroline had two marriages. In her first she gave birth to two children before her husband died. In her second marriage again she gave birth to two children. The last of these children was Edith Elizabeth. It was the stories told by Edith Elizabeth Hacker Snead to her grandson, Richard Braby, that created the interest for this study. (Note: Waldo Hicks Philips gave his wife Arabella Philips a Bible dated 5 February 1851. This became the family Bible of Caroline Georgina in

---

8. Last Will and Testament of Arabella Philips, signed 9 March 1830. The National Archives, London.

which she recorded her weddings and the births of her four children. It is now held by the author, Richard Braby.)

There is an interesting footnote on Waldo Hicks Philips. Before marrying Arabella, Waldo Hicks Philips had an affair with Harriet Linnington, who gave birth to their daughter, Clara. The records indicate that Waldo was 19 and Harriet was 21. The birth took place at Chale on the Isle of Wight on 21 January 1839. Clara Linnington grew up and married William George Scudamore, a shipwright at Portsmouth. They raised five children, and the youngest was Daisy Bertha Mary Scudamore who was born in 1881. Daisy left home at 18, and found her way to the offices of theatrical agent Sir John Denton. Introducing herself as Daisy Scudamore, Sir John Denton thought she was the youngest daughter of a well known actor Frank Scudamore, and gave her "Scudie's" address at Castelnau Mansions, Barnes. Daisy promptly presented herself as a long lost daughter, apparently unaware of some intrigues that Frank Scudamore had perpetuated. It seems that Frank had originally been known as Frank Davis, but thought that name lacked the appearance of pedigree and changed it to Fortunatus Agustine Davis Scudamore. Scudie maintained Daisy's charade. He flung his arms around her with the words, "if you are not my daughter, I don't know whose daughter you might be."[9]

And so Daisy was introduced to the theatrical scene. Daisy met a successful internationally touring actor, Roy Redgrave, while he appeared at the Grand Theatre in Brighton. They married at Glasgow Registry Office in 1907 while touring in the north. It was not his first or last marriage, but in this marriage with Daisy they had one child, Michael, who would become Sir Michael Redgrave, the actor and father of actors Vanessa, Lynn and Corin Redgrave. However six months after Michael's birth, Roy returned to Australia where he had previously toured and never returned. Back in England the forsaken Daisy changed her name to Margaret and married Captain James Anderson, a wealthy tea planter. Daisy's son Michael started acting, and the rest is well-known theatrical history – the Redgrave acting dynasty was born.

Georgina Laetitia (1812-1888) Little is known about Georgina Laetitia's early life. She was twenty-eight when her grandfather, Sir William Garrow, died. Georgina Laetitia was with three of her sisters at the Priory in Totteridge, Hertfordshire on June 6 during the 1841 census, at the death of her mother and is included in that census report and is recorded as unmarried. When she did marry on 2 January 1858 at the age of about forty-six she married her first cousin Robert Crawford J.P., D.L., of Saint Hill, Sussex, and was his second wife. Robert was the only child of Charles Payne Crawford J.P., M.A., by his wife Arabella, the eldest daughter of Reverend Narcissus Charles Proby. Georgina and Robert apparently lived together for twenty-

---

9. The story of Daisy Scudamore meeting Sir John Denton is found under Margaret Scudamore in Wikipedia.

five years. Their home was 1 Gordon Place, Tavistock Square, in the heart of the Bloomsbury district of London. Robert died in March 1883, and Georgina Laetitia (age seventy-one) moved in with her sister's son, William Carolus Bradstreet at 1 Osborne Road, Windsor. She lived another five years and died on 23 May 1888 at Windsor. Georgina and Robert had no children. In her will, she also discussed at some length the trust of her late grandfather, Sir William Garrow. She attempted to leave the trust income, as it came due, but not by way of anticipation, to her sister Katherine Caroline Bradstreet.

Following the death of her sister, trust funds were to go to her sister's two children, William Carolus Bradstreet and Caroline Anna Bradstreet. The will stipulated that for Caroline Anna there was the now standard condition, the income was "to be for her sole and separate use free from the debts control or engagements of any husband with whom she may intermarry". The will was a convoluted complex of legal statements. However, in a Codicil written shortly after the will, she simplified things. She revoked her current will and left everything to her sister, Katherine Caroline Bradstreet. William Carolus Bradstreet was one of the Executors of the will. The value of her estate was £9175 .. 1s .. 8d, in addition to her interests in the Garrow trust, a considerable sum of money in that day.

Anna Maria (1813-1853) Again, little is known of Anna Maria's life, but she would have been twenty-seven at the death of her grandfather, Sir William Garrow. She was the only sister not present during the census taken at the Priory on 6 June 1841. Living in Canterbury, she was, as previously noted, a witness at the wedding of her sister, Arabella. She died in Canterbury in the parish of St. Mary (Bredin) on 24 August 1853 at the age of forty. Three months before her death (4 June 1853) Anna Maria gave a small Bible to Georgina C. Philips, who was then six and a half years old. The handwritten notes states: "This book was always used by her dear Aunt Annamaria." (This Bible is now held by the author, Richard Braby.) The administration of her estate was granted to Georgina Laetitia Garrow, and the value was set under £3000.

Katherine Caroline (1814-1904) She was born on 8 August 1814 at Sutton and was married at Totteridge, Hertfordshire to the Reverend William Bradstreet, esq. of Oaklands, Hants on 22 March 1838, two years before Sir William Garrow died.

Katherine Caroline's son, William Carolus, was listed with his mother during the census taken at the Priory on 6 June 1841 and was recorded as two years old. It is possible that young William Carolus saw his great grandfather, Sir William Garrow, before he died. Katherine Caroline had a second child, Caroline Anna. Katherine Caroline's husband, William Bradstreet, attended Emmanuel College, Cambridge University, where he earned a Master of Arts degree and then took holy orders and was successively vicar of Nackington, Kent and rector of Theberton, Suffolk. As noted previously, Katherine Caroline received the estate of her sister Georgina Laetitia Crawford, upon her sister's death.

This photograph of the Theberton Rectory, Katherine Caroline's home, has been passed down through the family and is the earliest photograph in the Garrow family story.[10]

The photography of the Theberton Rectory labeled "Theberton Rectory, finished April 1866. For dear A.P." has been passed down through the generations that preceded Edith Elizabeth Hacker Snead. Apparently this was a photograph taken of Katherine Caroline in front of the newly finished rectory. William Bradstreet's business transactions necessary to build this home were recently located by Douglas Monk and show the complicated financial arrangements necessary at that time to organize the wealth necessary for such a project.

The photograph celebrating the completion of the project was sent by Katherine Caroline to her sister, Arabella Philips, at the beginning of Arabella's extended sickness that led to her death three years later. Katherine Caroline finished her days at Caldicot, Windsor, in the home of her son. Her daughter, Caroline Anna Bradstreet, never married but lived for many years in Florence, Italy, dying there in 1938. She was entitled to Garrow Trust money, and may have been the last to enjoy the wealth that he was able to acquire in life, and leave in trust following his death.

10. Photo owned by Richard Braby.

Edward William (1815-1896) He was born on 18 October 1815 and baptized by his father at Monken Hadley on the same day. Ironically the baptism was omitted from the parish register on that date but was rectified many years later by an affidavit by his mother. Edward was twelve when his father died, and twenty-five when his grandfather, Sir William Garrow, died. He was educated at Charterhouse, as was his father, and graduated from Brasenose College, Oxford University with a Bachelor of Arts. (1839) and Master of Arts (1842). He was ordained a deacon in 1839 and priest in 1840. During June 1847 Edward married his cousin, Louisa Harriet Elliot in Northleach, and in 1847 he became the parish clerk, the junior minister, at Abdale, Gloucestershire, a position he held for twenty years. He then served as Rector of Bilsthorpe, Nottinghamshire (1867-1896). The Rev. Edward William Garrow died on 29 March 1896 at the age of eighty, the same number of years lived by his grandfather, Sir William Garrow. He and Louisa Harriet had no children.

George William (1818-1847) George was born on 27 October 1818 and was nine when his father died, twenty-two when his grandfather, Sir William Garrow, died, and twenty-three when his mother died. He was also educated at Charterhouse, and then at Eton. He graduated from Worcester College, Oxford University with a Bachelor of Arts in 1841, and then served as a clergyman at Tamworth, Warwickshire, before becoming a Royal Naval Chaplain. He remained unmarried and died at Port Royal, Jamaica, on 16 October 1847, where there is a monumental inscription to him.

DAUGHTER ELIZA SOPHIA AND FAMILY

Eliza Sophia Garrow (1784-1857) Sir William Garrow's daughter, Eliza Sophia, married Samuel Fothergill Lettsom, a Quaker, and gave birth to five children. Two of her sons died within the first year, and a daughter died in her teens. One of her sons achieved significant success as a diplomat and naturalist. Her husband inherited a substantial business, but became bankrupt and fled to France to avoid his creditors and remained there. Eliza Sophia remained in England to raise her family.

Sir William Garrow's daughter was born on 18 June 1784, and was baptized at St. Andrew's, Holborn, in London on 30 September of the same year and was given the name Eliza Sophia. She grew up in London and Pegwell and on 6 April 1802 when she was nearing her eighteenth birthday she married Samuel Fothergill Lettsom at St. George's Church in Bloomsbury. Samuel Fothergill Lettsom was the second son of the prominent Quaker physician, Dr. John Coakley Lettsom.

Eliza's father-in-law, Dr. John Coakley Lettsom, had a large medical practice, and was a writer and biographer of the famous Quaker physician and botanist John Fothergill. His son was named Fothergill after his father's esteemed friend. The relationship between William Garrow and John Coakley Lettsom remains an interesting sidelight to this family story. In 1805 William Garrow negotiated a libel action against Dr. John Coakley Lettsom that was settled before it went to trial, saving Dr. Lettsom considerable money. It seemed that in some of his writing, Dr. Lettsom had challenged the reputation of a fellow physician. Garrow had considerable experience in these types of cases, and saw that Lettsom had no defence. He guided Dr. Lettsom in printing a retraction that was acceptable to both parties. In another sidelight, Dr. Lettsom founded the Royal Sea Bathing Hospital at Margate. This was not far from Garrow's home on Pegwell Bay. Under Dr. Lettsom's influence, William Garrow became involved in the financing of this operation and directed some fundraising events. In April 1809, William Garrow, no doubt through Dr. Lettsom's influence and their family connection, was named as Vice-President of the Royal Humane Society.

When Eliza Sophia Garrow married Samuel Fothergill Lettsom, it was the second time a Lettsom child married outside the Quaker connection. A Lettsom biographer called attention to this fact to illustrate a not uncommon happening in the first quarter of the nineteenth century, when the Quaker sect began to mix more and more with the outside world, and its distinctive costumes and methods of "theeing" and "thouing" were becoming obsolete.

Samuel Fothergill Lettsom's occupation in life was practically settled when he was a nine year old boy. His uncle willed the family tinplate works in Glamorgan in Wales to him, along with his cousin. The two cousins took over the business in 1799. In 1810 acute differences of policy arose. Fothergill Lettsom was all for pushing out, expanding. His cousin and partner was for conserving, watching, going cautiously. And so they parted, each taking half of the company. Fothergill Lettsom launched out into ambitious schemes, and sought to build up a great industry. He drew his father-in-law, Sir William Garrow, into his schemes. Garrow was a wealthy man, but soon found that his son-in-law's need for money was too great and too persistent even for his purse. Eventually he withdrew his support. Lettsom's ideas apparently were too grandiose for the cautious lawyer blood of his father-in-law. Disaster followed. Fothergill Lettsom failed heavily in 1823, and the tinworks business was taken over by his creditors. To avoid his creditors, Fothergill Lettsom left England and went to Boulogne, France, where he remained for the rest of his life. He died there on 28 October 1844 leaving a large debt for his children to pay.

The genealogist and biographer of the Lettsom family, James Johnston Abraham, who is the main source for this part of the family story, stated:

> Samuel Fothergill Lettsom had his father's weaknesses without his strength. He was a man of grandiose but impractical ideas, and was constitutionally incapable of appreciating the value of money.[11]

---

11. James Johnston Abraham (1933). *Lettsom, His Life, Times, Friends and Descendants.* London, William

Eliza Sophia and Samual Fothergill Lettsom's three children that survived childhood are listed below. A brief description of each child will be presented at this point, with a more detailed story to follow. The Lettsom children were:

William Garrow (1805-1887) He entered the diplomatic service, and served with distinction ending his career as the Consul-General and Charge d'Affaires to Uruguay. As a scientist and author he was interested in any subject associated with Natural History. He is best known as part author of a Manual of Mineralogy. He never married.

Samuel (1807-1851) He became a soldier and rose to the rank of Major in the 80th Regiment. Samuel married but there were no children.

Eliza Garrow (1813-1830) She was the only daughter and died at the age of sixteen without marrying or having children.

When Samuel Fothergill Lettsom fled to Boulogne, he left Eliza (thirty-nine) with the three children, the boys were eighteen and sixteen and the little girl was ten years old.

Fothergill Lettsom's business failure had considerable impact on Sir William Garrow's life. First, Garrow may have had a hand in forcing bankruptcy on his son-in-law. We can assume that Garrow lost a lot of money. He also acquired title to some of the assets, which would make up a portion of the trust he would establish just before he retired.

Garrow's problems with his son-in-law may have influenced the way he drew up the terms of his trust. In addition, Eliza Sophia apparently moved into his home on Great George Street to raise her family there. This idea is supported by the note in the diary of John Asplin, a Doctor at Prittlewell, Essex, who had been doctor to the British residents in Paris. We read: "Dec. 6th 1826 - Took a coach to Great George Street and saw Mrs. Lettsom at Sir William Garrow's." Eventually Eliza retired to Folkestone on the coast south of the white cliffs of Dover and not too far from the site of Garrow's marine villa near Ramsgate. The 1851 Census in Folkestone lists E. S. Lettsom, widow, aged sixty-two, annuitant born in Bloomsbury. (Living with her was C. (?) Lettsom, widow aged twenty-six, daughter-in-law, born in Islington.) This would have been Eliza Hook, who had married the now deceased Samuel Lettsom. Eliza Sophia Garrow Lettsom eventually died on 21 August 1857 while living at Folkestone. She was seventy-three.

A more in-depth look at the lives of some of the Lettsom children is possible.

Heinemann Medical Books Ltd. p. 451.

William Garrow Lettsom (1805-1887) This Lettsom, obviously named after his grandfather, was born on 24 March 1805 in Fulham in the heart of London and was educated at Westminster. It is thought that when he was eighteen he moved into the home of his grandfather, Sir William Garrow ,who had entered Parliament and was the prosecutor on treason trials for the Crown. It was intended that young William Garrow Lettsom would follow his grandfather's footsteps and enter the legal profession. But his tastes were otherwise. James Johnston Abraham, in his study of the Lettsom family states:

> . . . he entered the diplomatic service in 1831. He appears to have been a man of great personal charm, and considerable literary and artistic ability. He was a friend of Thackeray and Cruikshank, and contributed to the Omnibus under the signature of Dr. Bulgardo.
>
> His first appointment in the diplomatic service was attaché at Berlin. This was followed by periods of service in Munich, Washington, Turin and Madrid. He was next appointed Secretary to the Legation in Mexico, and shortly afterwards became Charge d'Affaires. Whilst in Mexico, the British Government suspended diplomatic relations with that country, owing to representations from Lettsom of grievances which were not redressed. This made him exceedingly unpopular, and his life was attempted unsuccessfully. On a satisfactory termination of the dispute, he was presented with a testimonial by the British residents whose liberties he had defended so courageously. In 1859 he was appointed Consul-General and Charge d'Affaires to Uruguay. He remained at Montevideo until 1869, in which year he retired from the service.[12]

All his life he appeared to have been keen on any subject associated with Natural History. He is best known, however, as part author of a *Manual of Mineralogy* which was the most complete and accurate work that had appeared relating especially to the mineralogy of the British isles. He wrote also on spectroscopic subjects, and on geology. He died of acute bronchitis on 14 December 1887, at 142 Norwood Road, Lower Norwood, and was buried in Norwood Cemetery (south of Brixton in the London). He was a Fellow of the Royal Astronomical Society, to which he was elected on 13 April 1849. The mineral "Lettsomite," a hydrous sulphate, is called after him. He was the last of the Lettsom's descendants in the male line. With him the name Lettsom became extinct in 1887.

Samuel Lettsom (1807-1851) The second surviving son of Eliza Sophia and Samuel Fothergill Lettsom was born on 17 May 1807. He was thirty-three when his grandfather, Sir William Garrow, died. Samuel became a soldier and would have been in the army during the last years of Garrow's life. Samuel rose to the rank of Major in the 80th Regiment. He married Eliza Hook, a daughter of James Hook, but had no children by her. Samuel Lettsom's death occurred on 16 January 1851 and he is buried in the Brompton Cemetery. Eliza survived his death and married again.

---

12. *Ibid.* pp. 452-3.

Elizabeth Garrow Lettsom (1813-1830) This Lettsom was the only daughter of Eliza Sophia and Samuel Fothergill Lettsom, and she was ten years old when it is thought she moved into the Sir William Garrow home with her mother and brothers. It is assumed that when she died unmarried on 28 March 1830 at sixteen years of age, she was still living in William Garrow's home on Great George Street. She was buried with her Garrow relatives in the churchyard at Monken Hadley, Hertfordshire, north of London.

The other Lettsom who played an important role in Sir William Garrow's life was **William Nanson Lettsom** (1796-1865). He was the son of Samuel Fothergill Lettsom's brother John Miers Lettsom. Sir William Garrow must have had great confidence in this person because when he set up his trust in 1830 he made William Nanson Lettsom one of the trustees to oversee the management and eventual distribution of his wealth. It is interesting to consider how a Shakespearean scholar became qualified to make decisions on who gets the money. But that was the case. Thus he is important in this story. William Nanson Lettsom was wealthy in his own right. He had inherited a huge fortune left to him by an uncle. His grandfather John Coakley Lettsom had great faith in him also. He is reported by Abraham to have spoken of his grandson with these words: "My grandson, Wm. Nanson Lettsom has just entered at Trinity College, Cambridge. He is a youth of great promise, and of a character unblemished; no way presuming on the prospect of the vast fortune that awaits him."[13]

Abraham also noted that William Nanson Lettsom was educated at Eton and Trinity College, Cambridge. B.A. 1818, M.A. 1822 and that he spent his life in the study of literature. He became a distinguished critical writer and edited W.S. Walker's *Shakespeare's Versification,* 1854, and his *Critical Examination of the Text of Shakespeare,* 1860. He also assisted Alexander Dyce in his edition of Shakespeare. He died unmarried, after a long leisurely life devoted to literature, on 3 September 1865 at Westbourne Park, aged sixty-nine, and was buried in Paddington Cemetery.

WILLIAM ARTHUR DOREHILL AND FAMILY[14]

William Arthur Dorehill (1779-1849/50) He was born in 1779, and was the only child of Sarah Dore and Arthur Hill who, after his liaison with Sarah, became the 2nd Marquis of Downshire. William Arthur Dore Hill was an active part of the immediate and extended family of Sir William Garrow. Young William Arthur was raised in the Garrow household. This is made clear in Arthur Hill's will, written

13. *Ibid.* p. 449.
14. All information, unless otherwise noted, on the Dorehill families comes from family records held by a descendent, Jan Dalton.

when he became the 2nd Marquis of Downshire and provided financial support for young William Arthur's education and other needs. Young William Arthur changed his sir name from Dore Hill to Dorehill upon his marriage. Through the Hill parentage, William Arthur Dorehill's linage is traced back to royalty, through Michael Hill (1672-1699) and Ann Trevor (1669-1747) to a connection with the late Queen Mother, Elizabeth Bowes-Lyon, mother of Queen Elizabeth II, and a lineage traced back three ways to King Edward I.

Through stories passed down in the Dorehill family it appears that William Arthur Dore Hill spent much of his time between the homes of Sir William Garrow and Downshire House, Belgrave Square in London. When a boy he lived sometimes with the Downshires and sometimes with the Garrows and was on most friendly terms with both families. He was very well off, kept very fashionable society and was most extravagant, but had no occupation. To use the phrase of his daughter-in-law Margaret Dorehill (nee Mitchell) "He never did a stroke of work in his life."

In the year 1800 on 3 July William Arthur Dore Hill married Mary Mair, (1780-1866). She was the daughter of Philip Mair of Thong, near Rochester, Kent. Two of the witnesses were William Dore Jnr. and David W. Garrow. After his marriage, he took up his abode in Bath. While he lived the life of a gentleman, obtaining an income to sustain this lifestyle without personal wealth was a struggle. He was totally dependent upon the Marquis of Downshire for his support, and this required the art of routinely requesting this support from the Downshire estate, an art form he perfected.

A series of letters exchanged between William Arthur Dorehill and Lord Downshire have been preserved in the Public Record Office of Northern Ireland in Belfast. These letters help us understand the relationship between William Arthur and the Downshire family. The letters generally concern money, requesting funds not only for his routine support but also to meet specific emergencies and to buy an army commission for his son. They also give a first hand account over the years of their relationship. In one instance they describe the Marquis' and Dorehill's reaction to Dorehill's administrative appointment to Tortola in the West Indies, and Dorehill's decision to decline the appointment. His reasons for not carrying out the appointment were inadequate income, his family's declining health, and the local weather in the West Indies. It would have resulted in a radical change in his comfortable lifestyle. Lord Downshire's response to William Arthur on his decision to not carry out his appointment is most revealing of the relationship between William Arthur and the Downshires. Lord Downshire writes:

Easthampstead Park

9th Feby 1822

My dear Mr Dorehill

I have received both your Letters this day and derive very great satisfaction in finding from their contents, also from Mr. Handley's previous Communications after having seen Miss Dorehill (Sarah Ann) herself, that what I have proposed to do after having consulted with my Mother Lady Downshire has so much relieved your mind and that of Miss Dorehill from the anxiety and distress which would have arised from your undertaking the distant voyage to the West Indies. Your warm and kind feelings of acknowledgement are most gratifying to me, but I request that you will not attribute more to what I have been desirous of doing, that it ... for neither my Mother Lady Downshire or myself could feel happy in agreeing to your voyage, after the account Mr. Handley had given of the Climate of Tortola, and I am glad to hear that you have decided to surrender the appointment. With respect to the mode of doing so I recommend you to see Mr Handley and to be guided by his good advice. As my mother obtained it for you and as I have learnt this day by a letter from Paris that it is her intention to return to England immediately, it may perhaps by more agreeable to her that you should postpone the relinquishment of the office until her arrival and the delay cannot be of any consequence.

Your mind being now relieved from the distress which a separation from your Family and the delicate state of your health must have occasioned to you and to Miss Dorehill, I hope you will hereafter be enabled to be more comfortable, and I shall always be happy to contribute my assistance as well as my best wishes as much as lays in my power. I believe Mr. Handley has not settled finally with you the amount of the increase of the annuity from me to you, but I am ready to do so whenever it is found necessary.

Believe me, very sincerely yours,

Downshire.

These letters provide evidence of a statement passed down through the generations concerning William Arthur Dorehill's reaction to being left out of Sir William Garrow's will. In his letter to the Marquis of Downshire he writes:

9. Edward Street, Bath

29th Dec. 1840

My Dear Lord

Your princely generosity in releasing me from the heavy Debt, which I most unavoidably contracted with your Lordship has made an indelible impression of profound gratitude upon my heart, and I cherish it with greater feeling when I contrast your noble conduct with the cruelty of my Stepfather, the late Right Honourable Sir William Garrow, who died about 4 months since, and never left me a single shilling or mere mention of my name in his Will, and did not even secure to me the enjoyment of a small Annuity of £60 per Annum, which now consequently ceases; I feel the unkindness the more, as he thought of others, who had not the lightest claim, upon his testamentary consideration, and I well remember the time, when in early life, he was for many years under the greatest pecuniary obligation to your Lordship's much lamented, and revered good father, my generous Benefactor, and kind patron; I am therefore quite at a loss to account for his having so entirely overlooked me - at first I was sensibly affected, but I now console myself with the pleasing reflection that I possess at least a warm friend in your Lordship who will never forsake me or mine.

Apparently, Sir William Garrow decided to leave the support of William Arthur Dorehill to the deep pockets of the Downshires. It is also apparent that the Downshire family, over two generations, accepted responsibility for the care of William Arthur and his family.

Another letter indicates the level of family financial support William Arthur received from the Downshire estate as an adult. After responding to information on the health of William Arthur's family, it continues:

The statement, which you have given me of your income and the increased expenses to which you have been subjected from your family growing up, are powerful reasons in favor of my complying with your request "that I should add to the sum of (four ?) hundred ninety pounds which has been hitherto paid to you." I have therefore determined to set apart for your acceptance two hundred guineas a year which will bring the whole amount to six hundred pounds to commence from the last half year Day. And I shall be happy if this arrangement meets your expectations - that it may contribute to make Mrs Dorehill and yourself more comfortable.

There are other indications of the relationship of William Arthur Dorehill and the Downshire family. When William Arthur's daughter, Sarah Ann, was married, Lady Downshire presented her with a trousseau, and also gave her a necklace, a keepsake still held in the family.

William Arthur Dorehill was described by his granddaughter as, "a dapper little man, dressed in the height of fashion. He used to frequently go down to Iron Acton in Gloucestershire, to visit with his father-in-laws brother John Mair where they used to read the "Riot Act" to each other, and granddaughter Julia, then a little girl used to creep under the table to hide during the reading of the "Act". What it was all about I have not the faintest idea, so one has to guess all sorts of funny things."[15]

After William Arthur's family grew up and relocated, he lived sometimes on the continent in Holland. Towards the end of his life he took a house in Dover, and on a visit to his daughter, Eliza Leroux, in Calais, France, he died suddenly of Gout in the stomach, in his 70th year, 1849/50, and is buried at Calais, France.

A brief description of the lives lived by each of the children of William Arthur Dorehill who lived to adulthood is presented next, followed by a more in depth discussion of the three male descendents for which more information is available.

Eliza Sophia (1802-1888) It was Eliza Sophia who expressed concern to the Marquis of Downshire that her father's assignment to Tortola was inappropriate. She married a wealthy French Surgeon, Dr. Midford George Leroux on at Chalk, Kent, and lived sometimes in England and sometimes in Calais, France. Eliza died on 6 September 1888 and is buried at Kensal Green Cemetery, London.

Charlotte Emma (baptized 2 June 1814) She had two marriages. She married Henry Charles Fraser (a Scotsman) on 21 April 1829 at Chalk, Kent. In the army, he was accidentally killed 'pig sticking' in India. Her second marriage was with Dr. John Drummond, another Scotsman who was on Lord Aukland's staff in India.

Sarah Ann (baptized 2 June 1814) She is the person who as a little girl was riding in a coach from Ramsgate to London with her grandmother, Sarah Garrow, when they were attached by highwaymen and robbed. Minutes later the highwaymen again stopped the coach and returned what they had taken. The full story is presented in the chapter on Sarah Dore. Sarah Ann married H. A. Dalton of Broadpark, Ilfracombe, Deven. For her wedding Lady Downshire presented Sarah Ann with a trousseau and a necklace.

Arthur Lettsom (1813-1899) He was the eldest son of William Arthur. He served seven years in the Navy and then went to the Continent to study. After a short time

---

15. In a family story now held by Jan Dalton.

he returned to England where he married and lived in Bath. The family recollection is that Arthur Lettsom Dorehill and William Garrow were great friends.

William John (1815-1885) He entered the Army in 1835 as an ensign and after a distinguished career in Australia, India and Ireland, as well as in England, and retired with the rank of Major General. He married Margaret Mitchell on 9 December 1848 and had six sons, One of these sons, Lewis Henry Dorehill, became the grandfather of Jan Dalton who has provided the Dorehill family records for this book.

George (1819-1894) His career was in the army, where he served in India and Aden. Owing to ill health he retired early after obtaining the rank of Major. He married Agnes King on 29 April 1857 and raised a son and daughter.

A more detailed account of the male children of William Arthur Dorehill can be presented to expand the family story of this interesting group of members of Sir William Garrow's extended family.

Arthur Lettsom Dorehill (1813-1899) Baptized on 2 June 1814 at St Mary Lamberth, London, he was appointed a Midshipman in 1826, and was present at the battle of Navarino on board the flag ship "Asia", a metal ship, and was about six hours on the quarter deck under fire. Arthur's report of the battle as recalled by his nephew, Lewis Dorehill, is interesting. Asked why the Asia was more injured than the other ships which took part in the engagement, he told Lewis that the Asia took up her position opposite a fort and received its fire as well as from the enemy ships. He also told him that owing to the absence of wind, the smoke hung so that it was difficult to see the ships except the tops of their masts. He also served in the North Sea and in the West Indies. After seven years service, he left the Navy and went to the Continent to study and lived there for two or three years. On his return to England he was given a Civil Service position in Somerset House, but only held the position a short time. He married his first cousin Eliza Baker and settled in Bath's 9 Somerset Place, and lived there for about fifty years. He died 12 April, 1899, aged 86 years, and is buried in the Bath Cemetery. Eliza died 7 November 1902 aged 86 years and is buried in the same cemetery.

The Dorehill family record indicates that Arthur Lettsom Dorehill was a strong, vigorous man and used frequently to walk from his house to the Bath Club, and had it not been for a fall whereby he fractured his collarbone he might have attained a greater age than 86 years. He was great friends with Baron Sir William Garrow. There were few men more respected at that time than Arthur Lettsom. Arthur and Eliza had no children.

William John Dorehill (1815-1885) Remembered as Major General Dorehill, he was born 14 August 1815, and entered the Army in 1835 as an ensign of the Buffs (3rd East Kent Regiment). His commission was signed by William IV. Twice he went to India, - two spells of seven years-, fourteen years altogether. The rest of his Military career was chiefly in Ireland. When he went to India the second time he was accompanied by his wife Margaret and two children, George and baby Philip. They were twenty-one weeks at sea, and it was during this time that baby Philip was accidentally killed on board the ship. They were in India when the "Mutiny" broke out, and as William Dorehill had been appointed "Brigade Major" to the Sauger Field Division, he sent his wife, and child George, and a new baby, Robert, back to England by the Overland Route, viz. by steamer to Egypt and as there was no Suez Canal in those days, they crossed the desert on a camel via Cairo, and then on to Alexandra and from there they took the P&O Steamer home. Stories told of his military adventures include the following.

Shortly after joining he took a half company of the Buffs to Australia as guard over a batch of convicts. On his return to England he went to India with his regiment and saw service in the "Gwalior Campaign", and commanded the "Light Company of the Buffs at the battle of Punniar" on 29 December 1843 for which he received the Bronze Star and was severely wounded. A spent grape-shot from one of the guns they took hit him in the chest just below the throat. On the return of the "Buffs" to England, the regiment marched through the City of London with fixed bayonets and colours flying. They were charged by a herd of bullocks which were being driven to Southfield Market and a boy was killed close to him, and several people were injured.

The Duke of Wellington recommended Lieutenant William John Dorehill for promotion, and he then he received his Company. He then went to India for a second time, where he took part in various actions from 24 December 1857 to 19 July 1859, including quelling a mutiny.

On his return to England he was appointed Staff Officer of Pensioners at Clonmel, County Tipperary, and part of the counties of Waterford and Cork, Ireland. He had command of what in those days were the reserve forces. He took part in the suppression of the "Fenian Rising" of 1868. Of the many hundred men he had under him in the Service of Pensioners, only one man joined in the uprising. His men were all Irishmen living in their native land, among their civilian friends and relations, Catholic in religion, whose sympathies, rightly or wrongly, were with those who were opposing British rule and were with those conspiring to overthrow the Union. However, they remained loyal to their oath, and except for one man, did not join in the revolt. This was thought to be a high tribute to William John Dorehill's influence.

He retired in 1876 with the rank of Major General. On his retirement he took up his abode in Dover, where he died on 3 April 1885 and is buried in Copps Hill Cemetery, Dover near the grave of his mother.

George Dorehill (baptized 1819-1894) The last of the three sons of William Arthur and Mary Dorehill, George married Agnes King, the daughter of Charles King, Esquire, on April 29, 1857 at the Catholic Church, Chelmsforrd, by her brother, the Rev. C.R. King. As a Major, he served with the 97th Regiment and the 94th Regiment and was in India, but saw no active service and was for sometime quartered in Aden. Owing to ill health he retired on half pay, and lived in Dover. He was considered to be a tall handsome man, and a very devout. He became a Roman Catholic about the time of his marriage. He was remembered as good-natured and amiable with a vein of humour, and a staunch conservative. They had a son and daughter. He died on 20 September 1894 and is buried at Haywards Heath, Sussex.

SIR WILLIAM GARROW'S BROTHERS AND SISTERS

William Garrow had two brothers and two sisters who survived to adulthood. He was the youngest to survive to adulthood in this family. While William Garrow was struggling to learn his craft in the Old Bailey, his two brothers were making fortunes in India, and one of his sisters was making a good marriage and starting a large family. His eldest sister devoted her life to giving loving care to their parents. A brief description of the lives of these brothers and sisters is presented next, followed by a more detailed description.

Edward (1751-1820) He was the oldest child and was born nine years before William. Having made a fortune in India with the East India Company, and having served as Mayor of Madras, he returned to England to play an important role in his community. His story illustrates and emphasizes how the extended Garrow family was deeply involved in the affairs of India.

Eleanora (1752-1805) She remained a spinster and resided at home at the Priory where she took care of her parents. She continued to live at the Priory until her death (aged fifty-one), at which time William Garrow was just entering the national political picture.

Jane (1754-1841) Six years older than William, she lived eighty-seven years and outlived him. Married to William Monk, a gentleman farmer, she raised a large family and played a prominent role in the extended family of William Garrow.

Joseph (1757-1792) As an employee of the East India Company, he became a person of considerable means. After his death in India in 1792, his son, Joseph, by Sultan, perhaps a high caste Brahmin, would come to live in William Garrow's home in London.

A more detailed account of these brothers and sisters of William Garrow is presented.

Edward Garrow (1751-1820). He was educated in his father's school and petitioned to join the East India Company in 1768 where he was appointed a Writer in 1769 (age eighteen). He advanced to Junior Merchant in 1778, to Senior Merchant in 1780, and then paymaster, and Storekeeper at Trinchinoply, making his fortune with the East India Company. He lived in India until 1795 (twenty-six years).

While in India he married Sophia Dawson from England on 22 March 1773. The wedding took place at Fort St George, Madras, India. However, during May of the same year his first child, George Garrow, was born, but to an unnamed presumably native woman. In subsequent years two more children were born to unknown presumably native women. They were Myra and William Garrow. His Indian family was well established in India. Sons George and William remained in India and served with distinction in the East India Company spending much or all of their lives in India. They married there and were very productive in a family sense, generating many generations of Garrows in India. Myra, as well as English born David married and had families and spent most of their lives in England.

Edward was an enlightened and capable administrator. While he was Mayor of Madras in 1782 there was a project within the East India Company to extend the Port of Madras. A Hindu temple was in the way. Edward was not prepared just to remove the temple to make way for the port without giving the people another temple. The temple was removed and, in part, rebuilt. Edward was in the forefront in raising funds for the project and he contributed to it.

Leaving the East India Company in 1795, Edward returned to England. There Sophia gave him his English born son, David, on 26 March 1796. Edward and Sophia first resided at 'The Mount", a large 18th Century house on Hadley Common, later, and for the rest of his life, Edward lived at Totteridge, Hertfordshire. From the will of his uncle, Dr. William Garrow, he received various parcels of land including some in Hadley. Edward was made High Sheriff of Hertfordshire in 1804, and served as Governor of Barnet Grammar School and Justice of the Peace.

Edward died in 1820 in Totteridge and left a most interesting will dated 6 March 1819. This will suggests something of his lifestyle and leaves some intriguing questions unanswered. He left the bulk of his estate to be divided equally between his son George and his daughter, Myra, the wife of George Taylor, who was one of the

Executors. He gave his son, David, £110 at his death and then £105 a year during David's life, a small amount compared with the wealth he shared with others.

According to Edward's will, Mrs. Jane Monk, his sister, was to receive £350. His third son, William, served with distinction in India, raised seven children, and died there before his father's death, and was not mentioned in his will.

Mentioned prominently in the will were a series of women and their children. The sum of £2,660.13.4d was given to a Mrs. Sophia Warren, and £1,333.6.8d to her eldest son (Edward Smith) and £2000 to her older daughter (Sophia Smith). Sophia's four youngest children, when they reached twenty-one, were each to received £1,333.6.8d. Until that time they were to receive the interest on these investments to pay for their maintenance and education. (By a Codicil executed one week after the will, the six Smith children of Mrs. Sophia Warren were to be paid £50 a year for six years - from the Totteridge property sale proceeds. He also remembered his housemaid, housekeeper and footman with a payment to cover "proper mourning" to the value of £25 plus one year's wages.) Also the interest on £2000 was left to the two children of Ann Jordan for their education and maintenance. And to Ann Jordan was left £30 yearly for five years to be paid in increments every six months. Then he gave to Mary Warr, an apprentice, £200 to be invested by his executors until she reached the age of twenty-one, at which time she was to get the invested sum. In addition Mary Warr was to receive £15 a year for her maintenance until she became twenty-one.

It appears that Edward Garrow had an ongoing interest in a number of women, and their children, and a personal sense of responsibility for their care.

A brief description of the lives lived by each of the children of Edward Garrow is presented next, followed by a more in depth discussion where more information is available.

George (1773-1838) Born to a native woman, he lived in India and worked in various positions in the East India Company, and assumed substantial responsibilities within the company. He married Eliza Jane Baker and had two children. He died and was buried in India. His children returned to England, married and produced large families, and perpetuated the name Garrow, in both England and India. With his sister, Myra, he inherited the bulk of his father's fortune.

Myra (1774-about 1846) Also born to a native woman, she married George Taylor and lived much of her life in England where she raised a large family and inherited substantial wealth from her father.

William (1776-1815) Also born of a native woman, he was successful in obtaining an appointment with the East India Company, and rose to carry substantial responsibility. His life was in India, where he married Mary Inch and raised seven children. He is remembered today in Coimbatore where it is claimed he worshiped a Hindu goddess. The following information is being displayed to attract tourists to that area.

> The Sangameshwarar temple at Bhavani is situated at the confluence of the rivers Bhavani and the Cauvery. This place is called as "Tiruveni of South India". It is an important pilgrim center. Lord Sangameshwarer with His consort Vedanayaki is the presiding deity. It is said that during the East India Company regime the then Collector of Coimbatore and Salem Districts, William Garrow, who had his headquarters at Bhavani, worshipped the Goddess Vedanayaki. One night the Goddess directed him in his dream to vacate his bungalow immediately. The moment he vacated, the entire bungalow collapsed. In reverence of this miracle, he presented to the temple an ivory cradle which is still in the temple with his signature.[16]

He died almost five years before his father and was not mentioned in his will, but perpetuated the name of Garrow through many generations.

David (1796-1866) Born in England to Edward and Sophia Garrow, he apparently was in disfavour with his father, who gave him a small inheritance. However, following his father's death, David completed his studies at St. Johns College, Cambridge, and was ordained a deacon. David published a book, The History of Lymington, and its Immediate Vicinity, in the County of Southampton: Containing a Brief Account of its Animal, Vegetable, & Mineral Productions. For a while he served as a Chaplain in the Bengal Establishment, but did not remain active in the ministry. He returned to London where he worked at the Board of Trade. He married twice and had three children by the first marriage and one by the second. He died in London and on his death certificate he was described as a "clergyman having no cure of souls".

Eleanora Garrow (1752-1805). William Garrow's oldest sister remained unmarried and lived in the "Priory" all her life. She took care of her father as he became aged, and died three months after her father's death.

Her will, which she wrote herself, is described here in more detail here than similar documents on other members of the family. To a genealogist it is a most interesting document, and should be inspected for details. To the person interested in the family life of William Garrow in order to better understand his professional accomplishments, this document can be used as a time capsule to glimpse what was valued within the family, and of their affluence. Its more significant contents are described below.

First she attempted to meet her obligations to young Joseph Garrow, her brother's son by the Indian lady. She did this is a variety of ways. As will be noted, Joseph

---

16. In a family story now held by Jan Dalton.

Garrow, the father, in his deathbed will in India had given Eleanora £1000 to take care of young Joseph's education once he reached the age of sixteen. At the time of Eleanora's death, young Joseph was four months short of being sixteen.

It appears that she hoped her friend John Wright would help her keep this commitment. Perhaps with this thought in mind she included the following gifts and instructions in her will. She gave £1000 to "her dear friend" Mr. John Wright, her father's nephew of Caius College, Cambridge. In addition she also gave him a large silver salver (a tray on which letters, visiting cards and refreshments are presented) that had belonged to her uncle, Dr. William Garrow of Barnet, and a silver coffee pot and a large ladle. Also she gave him twenty Guineas "for a ring as a mark of my esteem" and "in expectation that he would continue as far as lies in his power to be a kind friend to the dear son of my late worthy brother Joseph". In a codicil written two weeks after her father's death she wrote: "The money my dear Father has bequeathed to me by his will I leave in manner following in addition to what I may have left in my will to my cousin John Wright A.B. of Caius College, Cambridge, it is my wish that the sum of one thousand pounds three per cents may be made over to him." Earlier in the will she stated she wished "that he be one of those who attend as a mourner at my funeral." Concerning her direct support of young Joseph Garrow, she also left £1000 to him to be paid to him when he reached the age of twenty-one years. He also received a miniature picture of his father and a "Flat" silver candle-stick. It should be noted that young Joseph attended St. John's Cambridge starting in 1808. This was approximately three years after Eleanora's death.

Second, she gave £2000 to her sister, Mrs. Monk. The money was in an investment at four per cent interest and the dividends from it were "for her own sole and separate use without the control of her husband and at her death to be equally divided among her children." She also left her sister five shares in the London Bridge Water Works "for her life which at her demise are to go to the eldest surviving daughter and so on ever to remain in the female branch of our family." It appears that Eleanora had strong feminist views long before such views became fashionable.

She left "merely" ten guineas for a ring to each of her brothers, Mrs. William Garrow and her son David Garrow - a small gift was appropriate because of their affluence. She left this same ten guineas gift to a number of others, including Mr. Lettsom and Mrs. Lettsom, as well as her three nephews George, William and David Garrow, and to the sons of her brother Edward. It appears that she also left money for a ring to Mrs. Taylor (her niece), and Edward Taylor (her godson), Mr. Monk and his eldest son William. This William was also to receive the mourning ring Eleanora had inherited from her uncle with his initials W. G. She also left a silver teapot and stand, a small waiter and fish trowel to Mrs. Lettsom, daughter of Sir. William Garrow.

To her brother Edward she gave a miniature picture of his son George and daughter Myra set round with pearl. To Eliza Eleonora Monk she left her gold watch and chain, seal, and enamelled case, one dozen dessert spoons, a silver soup ladle, sugar dish and cream jug, and her best suit of lace, her damask table linen, chintz furniture described as "bed and down bed, and all thereunto belonging complete" and one shawl.

To Myra Monk, her niece, she left her "white dimity bed with furniture and bedding all complete and shawl and such muslin or apparel as have not been made up, also two pair of silver candlesticks and snuffer, dish and silver frame for tricots."

To her "much respected cousin, Jane Alloway" she bequeathed £1000 "in the four per cent to be for her own sole and separate use without control of any husband she may ever have" and leaving her free to make her own choice of trustees. Also she was to receive Eleonora's wearing apparel and household furniture which was not specified elsewhere, and ten guineas and a small amethyst ring set around with yellow stones. In addition she requested that Jane Alloway serve as executrix to the will with Mrs. Monk, her sister. Jane also was to receive the remainder of the equity that Eleonora was to receive from her father's will.

Finally Eleonora did not forget the clergyman who was to bury her. He was to get five guineas, and her friend Mr. Quilter was to receive ten guineas for a ring.

The two documents (Will dated 11 January 1804 and Codicil dated 3 April 1805) which had not had the signatures duly witnessed were found "in a drawer of a cabinet" among her papers of "Moment and Concern" by her brother Edward who observed "that a piece of the paper … had been cut off from the end." On 19 July 1805 at the Court, Edward, with two of Eleanora's close acquaintances, verified the handwriting and "were duly sworn it the truth of the afore going affidavit."

Jane Garrow (1754-1841). William Garrow's younger sister travelled to India presumably to visit one or both of her elder brothers during their service with the East India Company. Upon her return she married William Monk by Licence on 15 April 1785, a gentleman farmer of Bury Green, Cheshunt, Hertfordshire, and raised a large family. Apparently William Monk was an accomplished sportsman since Dr. William Garrow in his will wrote, "I give my long Spanish Gun and my Horsewhips to William Monk Esquire as I think he is the best sportsman in the family." William and Jane Monk made their home at Bury Green in Cheshunt located adjacent to Enfield, north of London.

There were eight Monk children born to this marriage. Six lived to adulthood and led lives of note. These Monks were: William Garrow, Elizabeth Eleanora, Maria (Myra) Charlotte, George Mitford, Charles Edward and Selina Augusta. A brief description of the children of Sir William Garrow's sister, Jane Monk are presented here.

William Garrow (1785-1859) He became a civil servant with the East India Company rising from Writer to Judge, fathering three children in India (mother unknown), marrying Eliza Anne Archer in London and fathering six more children.

Elizabeth Eleanora (1788-1836) She married Rev. Thomas Henry Elwin and created a family of five sons and five daughters. She received £200 in Sir William Garrow's will. The history of this family has been carefully recorded by Elwin Craig Pilkington (now deceased - he died 4 June 1998) and his work is an important source of information on the extended Garrow line.

George Mitford (1790-1858) As a member of the Royal Navy, he became the Lieutenant Superintendent of Royal Hospital Schools. His marriage with Mary Phillips resulted in four children, the eldest George Garrow Monk carried on the name of Garrow. He was the great grandfather of Douglas Monk who is helping to record this family story.

Maria (Myra) Charlotte (1791-1849) She married Thomas Archer and died at fifty-eight after a protracted and painful illness. According to Sir William Garrow's will, following her mother's death, Myra was to receive the £2000 given by Sir William to her mother, her mother having received only the interest on the money. If all went as specified, Myra received the money at about age fifty.

Charles Edward (1795-1832) He became deputy Assistant Commissary in Dominica and died there. He was to receive £200 from Sir William Garrow's will.

Selina Augusta (1796-1839) She married William Francis Balthazar Blanc who was admitted to the Middle Temple where he was called to the bar and later became Attorney-General and President of the Council Dominica in the West Indies. Selina was to receive £200 from Sir William Garrow's will.

Joseph Garrow (1757-1792). Sir William Garrow's brother, Joseph followed the footsteps of his elder brother, Edward, and served with the East India Company, and made his fortune there. He joined the Company as a Writer in 1779 at age twenty-two and became a Senior Merchant in the Company in 1790. He served as Secretary to the Commander-in-Chief, Madras, and acquired considerable means.

On 29 October 1789 his natural son Joseph was born to Sultan. Most sources state that Sultan was a high caste Brahmin, however one writer notes it was impossible for a Brahmin woman to be given the name "Sultan." With this name she was a Moslem. On 10 May 1791 Joseph wrote his remarkable Will in his own hand and in his own words at Fort Saint George in the East Indies, in which he took great care to arrange for the education of his son then aged only eighteen months. He asked his executors to invest £5000, the interest to pay for the expense of his education, "which I desire may be as good as he is capable of receiving in Europe." The surplus interest, after paying the charges of his education, and such allowances judged proper, were to be invested along with the initial investment and this fund to be his when he became twenty-one, "and not before." In addition to a personal legacy of £2000, the father set aside £1000 pounds to be invested and to be available to Eleanora, Joseph's sister, under the conditions that when young Joseph reached the age of sixteen she would take care and attend to his education. In an appended memorandum dated 16 August 1792, one month before his death (age thirty-six), Joseph Garrow took significant additional steps to care for his son. He asked a friend, John Mitford, to send his son in a proper manner by the first good opportunity to England if arrangements for his care in India did not work out.

In his will Joseph spoke to the perpetual care of his child's mother, including provisions for her to receive a monthly allowance for the rest of her natural life. In the deathbed amendment to his will, Joseph took additional steps to care for Sultan. The house he recently purchased in Black Town was given to Sultan during her lifetime in addition to the allowance previously made for her care.

Joseph left substantial money to a variety of other people, members of his family in India and England, co-workers and servants. It is interesting to note that he left to his Moonshey (a Mohammedan professor; a teacher of languages; a secretary or interpreter) a gift of money and "to have the choice of what horses I may leave behind me." He also stated: "I request my Hon Father the Reverend David Garrow of Hadley Middlesex to accept of the Sum of £2000 Sterling to enable him more fully to follow the dictates of his benevolent heart in relieving the wants of the poor and needy, this sum to be paid as soon as possible."

He established two executors to carry out his Will in India, including his older brother Edward. He also named two executors in England, his younger brother William, and his sister's husband, William Monk. After all his debts and legacies were paid, the residue of his estate was to go to his brother, William Garrow.

Joseph died on 19 September 1792 at Fort St. George, Madras, and was buried at St. Mary's Cemetery, Madras, where there was a monument erected to his memory.[17]

As observed previously, when Joseph Garrow died, young Joseph was sent immediately to England, and it appears that he lived in the William Garrow home. As noted, Eleanora died four months before young Joseph reached sixteen. However, she arranged for John Wright, her cousin at Cambridge, to assume her responsibility.

The story of the life of Joseph Garrow's family in Florence, their role in the artistic expression of that community, and how the daughter became a national hero

---

17. Tamil Nadu Tourism Development website for Bhavani, India.

of the Italian revolution, are the subjects of the next chapter.

CHAPTER 15

Joseph Garrow's Literary Legacy

Evidently William and Sarah Garrow had substantial responsibility in raising Joseph Garrow, the son of William's brother Joseph. The literary experiences of young Joseph Garrow and his family is an interesting story.

In telling this story, the present chapter contains episodes from the life of Joseph Garrow, the son of Joseph, the English merchant of the East India Company, and Sultan, a native woman of India. Also presented here is a glimpse into the life of Theodosia, the Jewish woman who became young Joseph Garrow's wife. Then presented are stories about their daughter, young Theodosia, who became a hero of the Italian Revolution, and her husband, Thomas Trollope, who became a recognized author. And there are descriptions of Frances Trollope, young Theodosia's mother-in-law, who lived with them and was recognized as one of the most important novelists of her day.

Pastel by Russell (1792) of William Garrow, his daughter Eliza Sophia, and young Joseph Garrow, his brother's child, shortly after arriving from India.[1]

---

1. *Watercolours and Portrait Miniatures*, to be sold by auction Tuesday 7 November 1995 at 11 am, London Phillips, Son & Neale p. 7. This is an auction catalogue. (Information in the catalogue is not correct concerning the two children.)

Most of these observations are about this extended family when they were living in Florence, Italy. While in Florence they became a part of a special literary community of English expatriates that flourished there.

To understand the story of young Joseph Garrow, one must go back to Fort St. George, India, and to his father's deathbed will, including the memorandum to that will signed 16 August 1792, three days before his death. As previously mentioned, William Garrow and William Monk were named executors of this will in England, and William Garrow was to receive "the residue of my Fortune." In the Memorandum to the will, Joseph Garrow directed that if arrangements for taking care of his son in India did not work out, his son was to be sent in a proper manner by the first good opportunity to England. We know that Joseph was soon sent back to England and appears in a family picture with William Garrow and his daughter Eliza Sophia. It is believed that Joseph was raised in the William Garrow household. Indeed, in William Garrow's will, it is Joseph Garrow who is mentioned first. He was to receive £1000, and if young Joseph Garrow was deceased at the time of William Garrow's death, then the sum was to be given to Theodosia, his daughter. Further, he was living in William Garrow's home at the time of his wedding. It should be apparent that some notice of Joseph and Theodosia should be a part of the William Garrow story.

MARRIAGE

As young Joseph Garrow grew to adulthood, he attended St. John's, Cambridge where he matriculated in 1808, received a Bachelor of Arts degree in 1812 and a Master of Arts in 1818. He was admitted by Lincoln's Inn on 26 November 1810. Some sixteen months later, The *Gentleman's Magazine* included the simple note that on 17 March 1812, Joseph Garrow of Great George Street married Mrs. Fisher, of Torquay, Devon. A Marriage Settlement was executed and dated 14 March 1812, three days before the wedding ceremony. Mrs. Theodosia Fisher was the widow of a naval officer, a mother with two children, and was thought to be twice the age of her new husband. It was a strange arrangement.

Theodosia's maiden name was Abrams. She was from a Jewish heritage, and was a musician and one part of a popular Abrams Sisters Trio. Her two brothers were accomplished musicians also. They composed and published music, and presented concerts in London and were very much a part of the musical scene in London where they made a comfortable living with their musical careers. With her sisters, Harriet and Eliza, she sang Scottish airs among other types of music, and published a collection of Scottish airs arranged for three voices. One music critic, called attention to Theodosia. He wrote: "… Miss Theodosa, now Mrs Garrow, whose voice was the most beautiful contralto I ever heard."[2]

Joseph Garrow's financial situation was enhanced by his marriage. Theodosia was a well-to-do widow. However, shortly after Theodosia married Joseph Garrow, she and her sister Harriet petitioned the King to give Joseph a job in the government because his fortune was too small for them to live comfortably. Joseph Garrow became a magistrate in Torquay and along with his wife and her sisters, became active in the musical life of Devon. Joseph was viewed as an accomplished violinist. Theodosia's sisters, Harriet and Eliza, lived with the Garrows, when not in London, for the rest of their lives. For twenty-three years the Joseph Garrows lived in Torquay. They lived in an estate called The Braddons in middle-class comfort. [3]

During this period, in 1824, their daughter Theodosia was born. The rumours surrounding this birth have given voice to speculation concerning the real mother. The stories that have circulated about this birth are presented here, only because they have been a colourful part of Joseph Garrow's story, and with the hope of shedding some light on innuendos that have passed as history. Theodosia, Joseph Garrow's wife, would have been in her 50s, some say 59 years old, at the time of the birth of daughter Theodosia according to Pamela Neville-Sington, in her book *Fanny Trollope, The Life and Adventures of a Clever Woman*. She states:

> Theodosia was extremely fond of her half-sister, Harriet (her mother's daughter by a first marriage to naval officer Fisher), "neither specially clever nor specially pretty, but," as Tom (Thomas Trollope) recalled, "the most absolutely unselfish human being I ever knew, and one of the most loving hearts." However, as Tom put it, Mrs Garrow "was not, I think, an amiable woman," nor very bright. She was, moreover, jealous of Theodosia's close relationship with her father - so much so that, Tom states, "I am afraid that Mrs Garrow did not love her second daughter at all."[4]

On this issue Pamela Neville-Sington adds the speculation of two observers, L. P. and R P. Stebbins, in their book, *The Trollopes: The Chronicle of a Writing Family*, where they conjectured that little Theodosia was in fact the daughter of Harriet, not Theodosia.[5] The intrigue remains.

FLORENCE

While living in Torquay, young Theodosia struck up a friendship with the future Elizabeth Barrett Browning, and also the great poet, Walter Savage Landor, friend-

---

2. O. Baldwin & T.Wilson. (2004) "Tom Trollope's Mother-in-Law," *Trollopiana*. No. 67 of November 2004, the Journal of the Trollope Society.
3. *Ibid.*
4. P. Neville-Sington. (1997) *Fanny Trollope, The Life and Adventures of a Clever Woman*. New York, Viking, p. 325.
5. *Ibid.*

ships renewed later in Florence. Drawn by a variety of reasons, including a need to find a more healthful climate for the delicate young Theodosia, the Garrows moved to Florence, Italy, during 1844. At this time Joseph was fifty-five, his wife Theodosia was reported to be about seventy-four and their daughter Theodosia was twenty.

The Garrows were to become a vital part of the English colony in this historic city. The community was one in which literary giants of the day, Milton, Elizabeth Barrett Browning, Dickens, Landor, and many others created an expatriate way of life that stimulated their artistic work, a lifestyle that carried on the tradition of Florence as the centre for artistic expression. In doing so they also created a piece of England away from the homeland. Note, incidentally, that this good life in Florence cost a fraction of what it would have cost in England, a major factor in the choice of many of these artists to live in Florence.

In Florence, Theodosia Garrow would come into contact with the Trollopes. Frances Trollope (Fanny) was one of the most successful novelists in England at this time. Fanny and her daughter, Cecilia, and her son, Thomas, came to Rome during the winter of 1847-1848 in an attempt to help Cecilia regain her health. Fanny's guest for the season was Theodosia Garrow, described as a petite and delicate young lady with masses of dark hair, gray eyes and an olive complexion thought to be a gift from her grandmother who was an native of India.

The Trollopes

Young Theodosia was drawn to Fanny to find the motherly love that she could not find at home from her now elderly mother. She also found love from another source. By the end of December 1847, Theodosia and Thomas were engaged, to the delight of everyone in the Trollope household. This delight was not shared in the Garrow household. Pamela Neville-Sington records the drama by quoting the words Thomas Trollope wrote in his diary at the time:

> We wrote to Garrow. Much opposition, and very harsh letters in reply. Days of distress and anxiety. Garrow fixed to come here (to Rome) on Thursday. Our anxiety at agony point. He came, awfully savage, terrible scenes!" Eventually, owing partly to Fanny's "tact" and "good sense" and partly to Mrs Garrow's "desire to get Theo out of the house," the engagement was back on.[6]

From her father, young Theodosia inherited aptitudes as a linguist and she was known as a talented writer with a wonderful mastery of Italian. Her father translated Dante's *Vita Nuova*, and he was also known as an able violinist. *The Times Literary Supplement* of 27 May 1920 stated: "it is a curious footnote to the literary annals of Anglo-India which proves that the son of an Indian mother lived to translate Dante and to move in a circle where the Brownings and Landor were the greater lights."

---

6. P. Neville-Sington. *Fanny Trollope, The Life and Adventures of a Clever Woman. Op. cit.* p. 326.

Young Theodosia's romance with Thomas Adolphus Trollope brought on a major change in both the Trollope and Garrow households. By 1850 Joseph Garrow was a widower, and very much wanted to be near his daughter. Fanny Trollope continued to need her son, Thomas, to assist her in her affairs - an arrangement she had depended on much of her adult life. Young Theodosia had a great respect for Fanny, and enjoyed her company.

In 1850, Joseph Garrow, Fanny Trollope, and the recently married couple, Theodosia and Thomas Trollope, entered into a strange arrangement that proved to be most successful. They pooled their resources and purchased a villa in Florence, a three storey home at the north-west corner of the Piazza Maria Antonia (now the Piazza del'Indipendenza). Pamela Neville-Sington notes that "Fanny, Mr. Garrow and the young couple were to inhabit separate floors, each one 'as large as a house in England,' according to Elizabeth Barrett Browning." They called the place Villino Trollope, and it quickly became a fixture in the social life of the expatriate English colony in Florence.

The Villino Trollope, Piazza dell'Indipendenza, Florence, as it appears today.
Reproduced by kind permission of Pamela Neville-Sington

In Villino Trollope, Theodosia and Thomas Trollope created one of the best known literary salons in Italy. The Brownings, the Dickens and many other literary figures were warm friends.

In the *Atlantic Monthly* of December 1864 there is a description of what it was like to visit Villino Trollope:

....Justice prompts to say that no other foreigner of the present day has done so much as Mr. Trollope to familiarize the Anglo-Saxon mind with the genius and aspirations of Italy ...

... Mrs. Trollope, (Theodosia), who from her polyglot accomplishments may be called a many-sided woman, has been, both by Nature and education, most liberally endowed with intellectual gifts. The depressing influence of continual invalidism alone prevents her from taking that literary position which good health and application would soon secure for her.

Nevertheless, Mrs Trollope has for several years been a constant correspondent of the London "Athenaeum," and in all seasons Young Italy has found an enthusiastic friend in her.

... As a translator, Mrs. Trollope possesses very rare ability. Her natural aptitude for language is great. A resident in Italy of seventeen years has made her almost as familiar with the mother-tongue of Dante as with that of Shakespeare....

.....Ah, this Villino Trollope is quaintly fascinating, with its marble pillars, its grim men in armor, staring like sentinels from the walls, and its curiosities greeting you at every step. The antiquary revels in its *majolica,* its old Florentine bridal chests and carved furniture, its beautiful terra-cotta of the Virgin and Child ... The bibliopole grows silently ecstatic, as he sinks quietly into a mediaeval chair and feasts his eyes on a model library, bubbling over with five thousand rare books.... To those who prefer (and who does not?) an earnest talk with the host and hostess on politics, art, religion, or the latest new book, there is the cozy *laisser-faire* study where Miss Puss and Bran, the honest dog, lie side by side on Christian terms, and where the sunbeam (daughter) Beatrice ... will sing to you ... like a nightingale in voice, though with more than youthful expression. Here Anthony Trollope is to be found, when he visits Florence; and it is no ordinary pleasure to enjoy simultaneously the philosophic reasoning of Thomas Trollope ....and the almost boyish enthusiasm and impulsive argumentation of Anthony Trollope, who is a noble specimen of a thoroughly frank and loyal Englishman. The unity of affection existing between these brothers is as charming as it is rare.

Then in spring, when the soft winds kiss the budding foliage and warm it into bloom, the beautiful terrace of Villino Trollope is transformed into a reception-room. Opening upon a garden, with its lofty pillars, its tessellated marble floor, its walls inlaid with terra-cotta, bas-reliefs, inscriptions, and coats-of-arms, with here and there a niche devoted to some antique Madonna, the terrace has the charm of a *campo santo* without the chill of the grave upon it; or were a few cowled monks to walk with folded arms along it space, one might fancy it the cloister of a monastery. And here of a summer's night, burning no other lights than the stars, and sipping iced lemonade, one of the specialties of the place, the intimates of Villo Trollope sit and talk of Italy's future, the last *mot* from Paris, and the last allocution at Rome.

Many charming persons have we met at the Villino, the recollection of whom is as bright and sunny to us as a June day - persons whose lives and motive-power have fully convinced us that the world is not quite as hollow as it is represented, and that all is not vanity of vanities....

It was at Villino Trollope that we first saw the wonderfully clever author, George Eliot. She is a woman of forty, perhaps, of large frame and fair Saxon coloring ... The expression of her face is gentle and amiable, while her manner is particularly timid and retiring. In conversation Mrs. Lewes is most entertaining, and her interest in young writers is a trait which immediately takes captive all persons of this class. We shall never forget with what kindness and earnestness she addressed a young girl who had just begun to handle a pen, how frankly she related her own literary experience, and how gently she suggested advice ... long did English readers rack their brains to discover the sex of George Eliot.

A centrepiece of the Villino Trollope was Young Theodosia. She is remembered as a participant in the Italian Revolution of 1859 during the establishment of the Republic. It was during this revolution that the many independent states of Italy became integrated into Italy as we know it today. Also, the Papal state lost much of its land at this time. Theodosia wrote letters during the revolution to the English publication *Athenaeum* describing how the people of Florence were experiencing the revolution, their enthusiasm for the cause and their emotional moment-by-moment response to the unfolding events. Her eyewitness reports generated important support for the cause in England. These letters were republished in a book: *Social Aspects of the Italian Revolution, in a series of letters from Florence.* Excerpts from *Chapter 1* are presented here.

Florence, April 27, 1859.

We have made at Florence a revolution with rose-water. Since yesterday evening a dynasty has been, not overturned, but calmly put aside; an entire change of national policy effected; a provisional government appointed, and we appear no doubt at this moment to English eyes to be boiling and bubbling, poor souls! in the fiery cauldron of revolution. But truly, considering all these things, the real state of our surroundings on this beautiful starlight night of the 27th of April, when, for the first time, we shall lie down under the shadow of the silver Cross of Savoy, together with the manner in which the citizens of Florence have borne and bear themselves on this occasion, merit a word of notice even in the proud centres of civilization, inasmuch as these social phenomena have deeper meanings in them and point to more enduring and world-wide conclusions than even the political earthquake tremblings which are beginning to shake the Peninsula from Monte Viso to Vesuvius.

... I think ... [that reporters] ... would perforce have confessed, had they lived through this day in Florence, that the last ten years of suffering and humiliation have strangely matured and tempered the fitful impulses and aspirations of the then half-asleep, half-childish, wholly misruled population of Tuscany. A people so conditioned as this, is too often considered by those happily born and bred under more wholesome political influences, to be a totally worn-out, effete, degraded race, fit only for the fate of the savourless salt of the Scripture denunciation. But such a race could not have carried itself as the Florentine people did today - such a race would not, with the army to back it up, and the city absolutely at its mercy, with plenty of excuses for excess, and valid reasons more than enough for bitter retaliation on its rulers, have abstained from every lightest shadow of riot or disorder, nay, of insult to even the most unpopular among them, and effected its will with a dignified enthusiasm and a singleness of purpose as far removed from theatrical bravado as from wavering timidity.

I will venture to say, at the risk of seeming to exaggerate the merits of our bloodless revolutionaries and the admirable guidance of the leaders of the movement, that neither London nor Paris, high places of civilization though they be, would, under similar circumstances, have presented a like aspect.[7]

Be it remembered that the story (I am about to tell) is no mere flying rumour hatched in the heat of revolutionary ferment, but the unvarnished tale of an eye-and-ear-witness of the circumstances . . . It appears that certain papers containing sealed orders had been deposited as much as two years back . . . at our two fortresses . . . as well as at every other *corps de garde* in the city.[8]

She described how at the start of the uprising the sealed orders were not opened and carried out and instead there was a fraternization of the troops with the people. The guns kept a discreet silence.

The Grand-Duke was at that moment at the Council, doggedly refusing every concession to the entreaties of his people. Arrived at the fortress, their Royal Highnesses summoned the whole of the officers to their presence, and caused the Commandant to open and read aloud the sealed orders. The reading lasted some twenty minutes, and at its close the whole audience, with the exception of the Royal visitors, stood breathless with wonder and indignation - as well they might. The sealed orders prepared so long before contained a minutely-particular-ized plan for the repression of any popular movement by the following infallible means. While both the fortresses were to fire down upon the defenceless city, the troops were directed to advance through all the great throughfares in triple file, that in the center with fixed bayonets, and those on the right and left trottoirs firing in each at the windows of the houses on the opposite side of the street!

Truly, a more atrocious project for trampling out in blood the aspirations of a people, at least in modern time . . . was never laid as a damning sin at the door of any ruler. A dead silence followed the reading of this precious document. The officers stood with heads bowed down, and did not venture to look each other in the face. At last, the Archduke said, "Gentlemen! You have heard your orders. I think no comment is needed. It is for you now to do your duty." And with that he would have dismissed them forthwith. But one of the young officers present respectfully but firmly answered him, "I think your Highness cannot be aware of the state of the city, nor of the disposition of the troops, or you would not require of us the pursuance of such a line of conduct. The movement is a national one, and expresses our desire as well as those of the people." "Be silent!" broke in the Archduke, "what right have you to speak?" but the stouthearted officer did speak, nothing daunted, while he owned that the so doing was in fact an act of insubordination; and so much to the purpose did he speak that the Archduke could no longer doubt that no co-operation was to be expected from the military in opposition to the popular movement

. . . (The Grand-Duchess harangued) the assembled officers with most eloquent invectives, and crying, 'So you are all of you traitors to us, are you? Not even our persons are safe now

7. T. Trollope. (1861) *Social Aspects of the Italian Revolution, in a series of Letters from Florence.* London. Chapman and Hall. pp. 1-3.
8. *Ibid.* p. 6.

in your hands.' 'Nay,' replied one of the officers, 'we are ready to defend your Highness and your family with our lives if need be, as is our duty; but that which your Highness demands of us lies beyond our duty, and therefore we cannot do it.' So after a stormy discussion, in high and impotent wrath the royal personages broke up the conference, and the result is already a matter of notoriety. And thus was accomplished a revolution not only unmarked by any act of violence, but unaccompanied ever by the interruption of the ordinary avocations of the citizens, or so much as a harsh word except those of the royal personages above recorded.[9]

Theodosia wrote twenty-seven letters to the *Athenaeum* on the revolution as she witnessed it from her vantage point in Florence. For this vivid and very personal unfolding account of the Revolution she is honoured with a plaque on the house where she lived in Florence, the site of the Villino Trollope.

Before leaving this Joseph Garrow story it is important to more fully introduce readers to Frances Trollope and to the literary career of her two sons, Thomas and Anthony. Her connection with America will be of special interest.

James C. Simmons, in his book *Star-Spangled Eden* published in 2000, describes Frances Trollope, and depicts mainly in her own words her twenty-five month stay in Cincinnati - from February 1828 to March 1830. Her husband's financial troubles had brought on a change from a comfortable lifestyle, to one of marginal existence and struggle.

To change her circumstances, Frances came to America with three of her young children, and eventually selected Cincinnati where she would attempt to use her charm, her wit, and her never-ending resource of ideas, to achieve her material comfort and financial security. Cincinnati, although recently an area of wilderness, was now becoming a centre for western migration, and was growing at a remarkable rate, with new factories, newspapers, schools, and a theatre that was reputed to be the finest in America, after New York's and Philadelphia's. It was here that Frances tried a series of business adventures. After initial success each in turn failed.

Frances hated Cincinnati. She found the people ill-mannered and uncouth. She confessed, "I do not like their principles. I do not like their manners. I do not like their opinions." She grew to believe that the American experiment was a giant step back toward barbarism, an unruly triumph of the mob. However she was a shrewd, if prejudiced, observer of the American frontier.

9. *Ibid.* p. 10.

The plaque in Italian, when translated into English states:

On 13 April 1865
there died in this house
Theodosia Garrow Trollope
who wrote in English with an Italian soul
about the struggles and triumph of liberty.

She returned to England, now aged fifty-three, and wrote a book of her experience in America. It was her first book, and she called it *Domestic Manners of the Americans*.[10] She described Cincinnati as she had experienced it, with an acid wit in the telling. Her book quickly became a best seller in both England and America. In America an outraged citizenry bought up copies as fast as publishers could print them. As James Simmons describes her, "No English citizen since King George III enjoyed such notoriety in America as did Mrs. Trollope. She was lampooned, parodied, travestied, and caricatured everywhere, until she became a folk character. ...... And *trollop* in America became a universal slang term of reproval to be hurled at ill-mannered and uncouth brethren. In England many people were still hostile [to] the United States over the War of 1812 and were ready to find her tart, critical tone amusing. Conservative politicians were struggling against bills in Parliament that would give voting rights to many unfranchised people, and used *Domestic Manners* to make the point that giving voting rights to the common man would be a disaster."

10. Frances Milton Trollope. (1832) *Domestic Manners of the Americans*. New York, Whittaker, Treacher & Co.

Space is available for one illustration of an aspect of life in Cincinniti that Frances found extremely challenging and disruptive of her comfort. Simmons tells Mrs. Trollope's story in these words.

> Finally, Mrs. Trollope and her group were settled into a house that was both neat and comfortable. But life in Cincinnati lacked many of the amenities she had taken for granted in London. Her house had no pump, cistern, or drain. And no dustman's cart stopped regularly to collect the garbage. "What," she demanded of her landlord, "are we to do with our refuse?" "Your help will have to fix them all into the middle of the street, but you must mind, old woman, that it is the middle ... I expect you don't know as we have got a law that forbids throwing such things at the sides of the streets. They must all be cast right into the middle, and the pigs soon take them off.[11]

The author of that work also noted that Cincinnati was at the time "one giant pigsty" with the animals roaming the streets and rooting about.

Domestic Manners established Frances Trollope as a successful author, and with it she commenced a long and celebrated career in writing travel books and novels. She became one of the most commercially successful authors of her day.

A more reasoned American view of Fanny Trollope appeared in the *Atlantic Monthly* (December 1864) article on English authors in Florence:

> But ere turning away, we pause before one face, now no longer of the living, that of Mrs. Frances Trollope. Knowing how thoroughly erroneous an estimate has been put upon Mrs. Trollope's character in this country, we desire to give a glimpse of the real woman, now that her death has removed the seal of silence ...
>
> Mrs. Trollope's works, beginning with the *Domestic Manners of the Americans*, published in 1832, and ending with *Paris and London*, which appeared in 1856, amount to one hundred and fourteen volumes, all, be it remembered, written after her fiftieth year. Of her novels perhaps the most successful and widely known...(was) the *Vicar of Wrexhill*, a violent satire on the Evangelical religionists, published in 1837 ....
>
> ... In Florence she gathered around her persons of eminence, both foreign and native, and her interest in men and things remained undiminished until within a very few years of her death. Even at an advanced age her mind was ready to receive new ideas, and to deal with them candidly.[12]

Thomas Trollope was also an acclaimed author in his day. Most of his works were written in Florence or after that period of his life, and concerned Italian history, or fiction in an Italian setting. The *Dictionary of National Biography* states that between 1840 and 1890 he wrote some 60 volumes. It observed that this was "trifling" beside the records achieved by his brother Anthony and his mother Frances. It also noted that when you add his contributions to periodicals and other journalistic work, that

---

11. J.C. Simmons. (2000) *Star-Spangled Eden*. New York, James C. Simmons. pp. 29-30.
12. "English Authors in Florence". (1864) *Atlantic Monthly*. vol. xiv. pp. 660-671.

he probably published more than any of his family

Anthony Trollope, while just beginning to find success in his writing at the time of the Villino Trollope, became the most famous author of the four Trollopes and is considered one of the great English novelists. Besides his novels he wrote travel books, biographies, and an autobiography. He worked a regular and rigorous schedule, rising at 5:30 a.m., standing at a high desk, he would write until 11:00 a.m. His work presents a microcosm of Victorian society.

Sir William Garrow, by dying in 1840, left the scene eight years before the Trollopes became a part of his extended family by the marriage of young Theodosia to Thomas Adolphus Trollope. However, Joseph Garrow lived nine years after his daughter's marriage and would have been in the middle of this whirl of the social and literary life of eminent creators of the literature of the day as they met together in the Villino Trollope.

Joseph Garrow and his daughter, Theodosia Garrow Trollope, along with Frances Trollope, lie buried in the English Cemetery in Florence, within a few feet from the grave of their friend Elizabeth Barrett Browning. Theodosia's daughter Bice (Beatrice) married Charles Stuart-Wortley on August 16, 1880, and they had a child, Beatrice Susan Theodosia Stuart-Wortley on July 15, 1881, who married Arthur William James Cecil (a Captain in the Grenadier Guards) during 1906.

The graves of Joseph Garrow, Theodosia Garrow Trollope and Fanny Trollope in the vicinity of Elizabeth Barrett Browning's (foreground), English Cemetery in Florence.

CHAPTER 16

Published Stories

Stories about Garrow appeared in the newspapers, professional journals and in popular books published from time to time throughout his professional career, after his retirement and even immediately after his death. He was considered good copy in the London press for over sixty years. Four biographical sketches on Garrow were published during this time period. All four have frequently been quoted in this current work. Some additional mention of these sources will be made here.

PUBLIC CHARACTERS

The first was "Mr. Garrow" in *Public Characters* published in a volume around 1809 but clearly written and published individually at an earlier stage in his career. It describes his private practice in the Old Bailey on the Assize circuits, and Westminster Hall, before he started his work as a public prosecutor. Garrow's newly established style and notoriety for examining and cross-examining witnesses is carefully noted, and it was observed that trials in which Garrow was brought in to examine witnesses became a form of public entertainment. The author then gives his thoughts on how Garrow's career will unfold, or in this case, not unfold.

> Mr. Garrow is likely to remain stationary; he never appears solicitous for a higher station than that which he at present fills; he certainly does not look to the bench, and makes no pretensions to the great law offices of state. Mr. Garrow probably is content with the honours of Westminster-hall; he has never, we believe, had any ambition to possess a seat in parliament; indeed, he well knows that such a seat would be but a losing bargain, as it would deprive him of some very lucrative practice before election committees.[1]

Each of these predictions proved to be wrong, but the qualities which were depicted in this early biographical profile, his special skills in examining witnesses, are what is remembered most clearly today. The author closes his biographical sketch with a note to students studying law. He states:

> He will learn in the life of Mr. Garrow, the great importance of cultivating a general and extensive acquaintance with the world, and pursuing life through all its varieties and circumstances, which has chiefly, if not singly, advanced the subject of this memoir to his present eminence; he will, moreover, learn the necessity of cultivating the art of public speaking, and the talent of cross-examination . . .[2]

---

1. "Mr. Garrow". *Public Characters*. (1799-1809) 4th edition. vol. x. London.
2. *Ibid.*

Public Characters is a difficult document to find in any but the most comprehensive of public archives, and therefore is reproduced here in Appendix 3 for students of Garrow's life and career.

THE LEGAL OBSERVER

The second biographical sketch, *Judicial Characters, No. V. Sir William Garrow* was published at the time of his retirement in *The Legal Observer,* on 18 February 1832.[3] This was just after his plans to retire were announced and before his last day in office of 22 February. It describes, in a straightforward manner, the career of this public figure who had for almost 50 years been a prominent part of the legal scene. Even Brougham, who later would write his own colourful memoir of Garrow, stated that he considered it to be a well-written and authentic memoir.[4] Information in this piece not found in other sources includes a list of memorable speeches delivered by Garrow. In part it states:

> Of the style and force of his eloquence there remain records in the State Trials, and in other publications of legal proceedings of interest, in which he was engaged. It would be difficult perhaps on a deliberate exercise of the judgment, to direct attention to the recorded speeches most worthy of notice; but we may merely, from memory, as affording specimens of varied and superior abilities, advert to the defence of Dr. Symonds, the prosecutions against Picton, against Bligh, against Codling, Reid and others; the case of Doherty v. Wyatt; and to a very short, but powerful and conclusive address to the jury, for the defendant, in the King v. Faulder.[5]

Of this list we have presented in *Chapter 7* Garrow's prosecution of Picton, leaving the other exemplary cases for others to discover in the legal archives. However, the entire *Legal Observer* memoir of Garrow is also available in *Appendix 3.*

MONTHLY MAGAZINE

The third biographical sketch of Garrow was published in *The Times* on 7 November 1840, less than two months after Garrow died on 14 September 1840.[6] It was reprinted from the *Monthly Magazine.* This article was prominently displayed on the first page of news in *The Times,* in two complete columns. It could not have been more prominently displayed. We, as well as others who have written about William Garrow, frequently refer to this biographical source. Indeed, quotable statements are found throughout the piece. Two are noted here. The first concerns the special skills

3. "Sir William Garrow", *The Legal Observer.* (18 February 1832) .vol. iii. pp. 253-6.
4. Lord Brougham, "Memoir of Mr. Baron Garrow". (1844-5) 1 *Law Review.* p. 318.
5. "Sir William Garrow", *The Legal Observer. Op. cit.* p. 255.
6. *The Times.* (7 November 1840)

for which he was remembered then and now.

> But the faculty for which, above all others, Mr. Garrow was celebrated and admired, was the examination of witnesses. In that he had neither model, rival, nor successor. To the casual or superficial observer, cross-examination presents the greatest and most frequent topics of admiration; but they who understand the arcane of the profession know that examinations in chief requires much greater skill, ability, and circumspection . . . With consummate ability and address, Garrow could simplify an entangled or difficult statement into a series of direct, intelligible, apt, and perspicuous questions; and without trespassing on forbidden ground, by leading his witness, would extract the facts he wanted to prove by indicating them in a manner afforded to his opponents no ground of objection. His re-examination never failed to strip from the evidence all the collateral circumstances which might tend to perplex and mislead the jury, leaving most prominently before them the true and real points, and nothing else. In cross-examination severity and sternness were sometimes necessary, and in them he was not deficient; but his greatest was shown in suggesting facts, in a manner which would entangle a dishonest witness, or put one whose conscience was a little more tender in such good humour with himself, that he let escape the truth he had been desirous to conceal.[7]

The second quote from this memoir concerns his view of slavery, and is related to his claim to have prosecuted the first case in violation of a new anti-slavery law in England. In *The Times* article, however, his feeling about the practice is clearly expressed.

> With all the zeal which he was ever ready to display in causes confided to him, with all the desire of wealth and honour which could inflame a youthful mind, Garrow was never ready to undertake a case which would oblige him to profess, in a public manner, opinions which were repugnant to his principles. Thus, at an early period of his life, when the question concerning the manner in which Negroes were obtained, and conveyed from Africa to the West Indies, was in agitation, he had formed a most decided judgment on the facts and on the traffic. One day Mr. Fuller (Jack Fuller, of Rose-Hill, as he called himself), a great West India proprietor, meeting him in the street, said, "Well, Mr. Garrow, here is plenty of business, and plenty of money for you; the committee have determined to retain you, and give you the management of all their business in Parliament and elsewhere." He answered, "Sir, if your committee would give me their whole incomes, and all their estates, I would not be seen as the advocate of practices which I abhor, and a system which I detest.[8]

The entire memoir is also presented in *Appendix 3*.

THE LAW REVIEW

The fourth biographical sketch was 'Mr. Baron Garrow' and was published in the *Law Review* in vol. i. November1844-February 1845, four years following Garrow's

---

7. *Ibid.*
8. *Ibid.*

death.[9] Although the article is unsigned, the publication was edited by Henry Brougham, and there is general agreement that Brougham wrote the article. It has all the qualities of a Brougham piece of work. As previously noted in *Chapter 9, Garrow vs. Brougham*, Henry Brougham had a way of writing quotable text, and in the course of history, certain of his quotable statements have found their way into the work of many who have followed him in discussing Garrow's merits and shortcomings. It is an example of the generally accepted proverb that how one is remembered in history is determined by the work of a good biographer. For Garrow, and until recently, Henry Brougham was that biographer. His lead sentence in his "Mr. Baron Garrow" was:

> Mr. Garrow was, in a certain line of the legal profession, without an equal, certainly - in a portion of that line, without a rival.[10]

Two paragraphs later he continues:

> There have probably been few more ignorant men in the profession than this celebrated leader. To law, or anything like law, he made no pretence . . . Then with so slender a provision of law, his ignorance of all beside, of all that constitutes science, or learning, or indeed general information, was perfect; and yet one important branch of knowledge had become familiar to him – his intercourse with prisoners, with juries, above all with witnesses, had given him extensive knowledge of human nature – though not certainly in its higher, more refined, or even more respectable forms.[11]

In reading Brougham on William Garrow, it is important to keep in mind the dynamics of the relationship of these two men. Brougham's father was a squire with an estate in Westmorland the centre of which was Brougham Hall. He was educated at Edinburgh University, joined Lincoln's Inn on 14 November 1803 and was called to the Engish Bar on 22 November 1808. He was perhaps the most influential law reformer of the nineteenth century but in his personal relations was intolerant and showed a serious lack of balance. He very nearly became prime minister of England but, because of his unreliability, was diverted to the Woolsack where, as Lord Chancellor, he secured serious reform of the Court of Chancery. He was a fop and man-about-town. Although a brilliant lawyer, his contempt for 'lesser mortals' extended to jurors with whom, unlike Garrow, he was thus less than successful.

It seems likely that he was also contemptuous of Garrow as having come from a relatively poor background and failing to secure a university education. This comes across in his assessment of Garrow but such was Garrow's success and achievement that Brougham could not fail to acknowledge it. In consequence his biography of

Garrow is a curious mixture of disdain and praise and the criticisms reveal more about Brougham than Garrow and should be taken with a large pinch of salt.

With this background, Brougham's entire biographical sketch of Garrow can be read, and put in a meaningful perspective, appropriate for the way Garrow is being remembered today. It also is presented in full in *Appendix 3.*

As a colourful character in the London scene, Garrow was often mentioned in the newspapers and other magazines. A small collection of these human interest stories is presented here to illustrate how the press treated him. Also, they are remarkably good story material.

MUSICAL MEMOIRS

There is a quote that refers to Garrow's villa on Pegwell Bay which gives a glimpse of the humour of Garrow. It is an observation by W. T. Parkes in his *Musical Memories - An Account of the General State of Music in England 1784 - 1830.* It also illustrates how people enjoyed telling stories about Garrow.

> When the music meeting at Canterbury was ended, I proceeded from the city to pass a fortnight at Ramsgate, about 17 miles distant. On leaving that fashionable watering place in a diligence [a carriage then in general use for travelling] in company with a lady, we stopped at a house in the suburbs of the town near Pegwell Bay to take up the third passenger. It not being quite daylight when we arrived there, I was ignorant of the name and rank of our new associate, but I shortly ascertained that he was the distinguished barrister Mr. G . . . That gentleman's conversation was animated and polite: but I thought that in one instance he went a little too far, by subsequently saying to a strange lady who, as well as himself, had for a few minutes slumbered, 'Now madam, I can say that I have had the pleasure of sleeping with you.' It ought however to be observed that Mr. G. was at that time a young man, and consequently not a judge. That gentleman's practice was chiefly at the Old Bailey, whither he was proceeding to attend the September sessions.[12]

THE TIMES

In 1840 *The Times* described Garrow's insights into Erskine's style in preparing for a trial, and shows intimate knowledge into his friend's character. Shortly after Garrow's death, a correspondent to *The Times* wrote the following account.

> I dined with Garrow upon one occasion when he was residing in Great George Street, Westminster. He was at the time a Baron in the Court of Exchequer. After dinner, the conversation turned upon the late Lord Erskine, Mingay, and other eminent counselors of their day. Garrow observed in his pleasant manner of communication, that very few persons were aware of Erskine's tact when he was desirous of "firing off a speech," using his own words. "He

---

12. W.T. Parkes. *Musical Memories – An Account of the General State of Music in England 1784-1830.*

would . . . so ingeniously and so happily blend imagery with argument, that when you heard him deliver himself upon one of those occasions you would have been led to fancy that he was largely inspired, and yet to my knowledge," added Sir William, "Erskine was in the frequent habit of concocting some favorite tropes and figures, which he would commit to paper, and be thus prepared to adorn his harangues with so much aptitude of expression, and light up his speeches with such brilliant outbursts of eloquence, that no person unacquainted with Erskine's *art rhetorica* and heard him speak would have suspected that he availed himself of such advantages."[13]

Three stories that appeared in *The Times* further illustrate this point of Garrow being good story material in his day. The first concerns obscure penmanship, a topic that would touch the lives of many readers.

> Unintelligible Writing. In a case tried at Monmouth, before Mr. Baron Garrow, that learned Judge took occasion to remark upon the obscurity of the hand writing of the Mayor of Bristol, who, he said, had signed his name in a very fine and clerk-like hand, and with a great number of flourishes, but in a way that was quite unintelligible to those who did not previously know what his name was. This, the learned Judge observed, was by no means a singular instance, for a respected friend of his, in the city of London, would sign his name on the outside of letters, in such a way as to defy the skill of every man in the court, even if assisted by the other sex, in finding out what his signature could possibly be meant for. The Post-Office indeed, knew that a certain number of straight strokes up and down meant W. Curtis, but probably that was not because they could read the signature, but because nothing else at all like it ever came there.[14]

Not all articles about Garrow were flattering. Indeed, the press in England, even *The Times* could fling a barb at the "distinguished gentleman."

> A Judge - asked a brother Judge after dinner, what he thought of Mr. Garrow's speech - think, says the other - 'I think it is like a race horse, it runs fast because it carries a feather.'[15]

Today, as the internet makes readily available bits and pieces of history, short stories often embedded in longer pieces of rarely read documents in archives around the world, new Garrow stories – new to this age – seem to jump onto the computer screen. Included are lawyer jokes such as this one on a page styled "English Verbal Distinctions" amongst the entries there are as follows:

> Maid a virgin
> Made preterite of make

> 'Counsellor Garrow, during his cross-examination of a prevaricating old female witness, by which it was essential to prove that a tender of money had been made, had a scrap of paper thrown to him by a counsel on the other side, and on it was written,' - 'Garrow submit - that

---

13. *Ibid* (11 November 1840) "The Late Sir William Garrow".
14. *The Times.* (23 October 1827)
15. *Ibid.* 5 August 1790.

tough old jade can never prove - a tender maid!'[16]

Stories of incidents with royalty sometimes emerge. In a series entitled, *The Education of a Royal Princess*, there is information taken from a small volume called *Victoria: An Anecdotal Memoir of Her Majesty*. The following is from this source.

> For several ensuing summers, during the early childhood of the Princess, these two agreeable watering places (Ramsgate and Tunbridge Wells) were alternately chosen by the Duchess of Kent for the temporary residence of her family; and the inhabitants were equally gratified by the substantial benefits derived from these royal visits, and by the opportunity they afforded of becoming intimately acquainted with the person, manners and disposition of the heiress presumptive to the British throne, who speedily became quite the delight of both places.[17]

Included is an event that happened at William Garrow's Pegwell home.

> An anecdote was current at this period which is deserving of record here as affording an interesting proof of the remarkably amiable and affectionate disposition of the little Princess, and particularly of the strong attachment to her mother which has always formed a striking feature in her character. The royal party one day honoured Sir William Garrow with a visit at his residence at Pegwell Bay, and were conducted by the host over his house and grounds; amongst other curiosities was a fine marble bath, which the young Princess, in her eagerness to examine, approached so close that losing her balance she fell in; she of course cried loudly, but was no sooner extricated from her unpleasant situation, and found herself once more above ground, than her tears and sobs were interrupted to inquire, "Does mamma know that I am not hurt?[18]

ROBERT LOUIS STEVENSON

Forty-seven years after Garrow's death, Robert Louis Stevenson and his wife discovered the drama created by Garrow in the courts of the Old Bailey. The record of this episode in the life of the Stevensons was recorded in the prefatory note (preface) to the novel *Kidnapped* and was written by Mrs. Stevenson. While rarely reprinted in modern editions, *Kidnapped* with the prefatory note is available in many libraries. This story is best reported in the words of Mrs. Stevenson.

> While my husband and Mr. Henley were engaged in writing plays in Bournemouth they made a number of titles, hoping to use them in the future. Dramatic composition was not what my husband preferred, but the torrent of Mr. Henley's enthusiasm swept him off his feet. However, after several plays had been finished, and his health seriously impaired by his endeavours to keep up with Mr. Henley, play writing was abandoned forever, and my husband returned to his legitimate vocation. Having added one of the titles, *The Hanging Judge*, to the

16. *Treasury of Knowledge.* (1860)
17. The Education of a Royal Princess.
18. *Ibid.*

list of projected plays, now thrown aside, and emboldened by my husband's offer to give me any help needed, I concluded to try and write it myself.

As I wanted a trial scene in the Old Bailey, I chose the period of 1700 for my purpose; but being shamefully ignorant of my subject, and my husband confessing to little more knowledge than I possessed, a London bookseller was commissioned to send us everything he could procure bearing on Old Bailey trials. A great package came in response to our order, and very soon we were both absorbed, not so much in the trials as in following the brilliant career of a Mr. Garrow, who appeared as counsel in many of the cases. We sent for more books, and yet more, still intent on Mr. Garrow, whose subtle cross-examination of witnesses and masterly, if sometimes startling, methods of arriving at the truth seemed more thrilling to us than any novel.[19]

Mrs. Stevenson's play, *The Hanging Judge,* was finally published in 1922 in a collection of Stevenson plays.[20] In the play the hanging judge and central character is Mr. Justice Harlowe, a judge who is well known for his practice of issuing severe sentences. It is interesting to speculate on how much of this factious character's personality was patterned after Garrow. Perhaps more in keeping with Garrow's character would be a kindly lawyer in the play named Garroway.[21] The inspiration for each of these characters could have been, in some way, reflective of our Garrow.

However, in Robert Louis Stevenson's last and unfinished novel, *Weir of Hermiston,* there is a character Lord Justice Clerk "the hanging judge." This novel is considered by some critics to be Stevenson's best literary effort.[22] The story line is building up to a major court scene, but Stevenson's untimely death left the scene unwritten. It could be that at the very morning of this great novelist's death, Robert Louis Stevenson very much had William Garrow's courtroom dramatics on his mind.

GARROW'S LAW

As Garrow's role in the evolving history of human rights is being studied and debated, these incidental accounts of events in his life, or reactions to his life story, add a human touch to round out the public perception of this interesting historic character. In 2009, these possibilities took belated dramatic flight with the screening of the BBC1 TV prime-time mini-series "Garrow's Law", in which four separate cases he appeared in were dramatised against the historical backdrop of his times. More than 160 years after his death, Sir William Garrow finally looked set to enjoy his 'fifteen minutes of fame'.

19. R.L. Stevenson. (1993) *Kidnapped.* Ware, Hertfordshire, Wordsworth Editions Ltd.
20. R.L. Stevenson with Mrs. Stevenson.(1972) "The Hanging Judge". *Deacon Brodie or the Double Life and Other Plays.* New York and London, Charles Scribner's Sons. pp. 319-413. "The Hanging Judge" was written in 1887 and privately published at that time. It was included in this collection of plays and made available for the first time.
21. This comment was written before BBC Television decided to feature Garrow in "Garrow's Law" (see text).
22. P. Scott & R. Mortimer and others. (1994) *Robert Louis Stevenson, 1850-1894.* (an exhibit) University of South Carolina, found on the Internet at www.sc.edu/library/spcoll/britlit/rls/rls.html.

CHAPTER 17

Conclusion

The question may be asked why the long-forgotten William Garrow should be acclaimed in the twenty-first century? Indeed, why did his achievements in the late eighteenth century go unnoticed for so long? Many renowned modern academic lawyers have written in depth of the English criminal law, its procedure and leading figures, including Blackstone, Fitjames Stephen, Holdsworth, Radzinowicz and Thayer. They knew that in felony trials before the eighteenth century prisoners were not permitted to have counsel appear for them. They knew the laws of criminal evidence were rudimentary and of little protection to the accused. They were well aware that prisoners suffered lengthy confinement in a violent and disease-ridden gaol before being subjected to a terrifying trial process that many of them did not understand. That the accused enjoyed no meaningful procedural rights apart from the right to trial was evident. And not only were prisoners as cruelly treated as in medieval times but at the end of the trial they faced the possibility of death on the gallows, even for trivial offences.

Of course, these writers of jurisprudence did notice and record the striking improvements that were occurring towards the end of the eighteenth century. These were the rise of defence counsel, the lawyer-induced growth of both the doctrine of the presumption of innocence and exclusionary rules of evidence and the beginnings of adversary trial. Yet, they did not question what brought about such fundamental changes in the system.

Presumably, they were not interested in researching the 'Old Bailey Proceedings' which they may have believed to be peripheral to their work. If so, they missed the intense dramatic force of the revolution in criminal procedure and evidence that these records reveal. Only Stephen recognised there had been a transformation in procedural law, seeing it as "[t]he most remarkable change that took place in English criminal procedure." But he conceded that he was baffled as to what had brought it about.[1]

With the others there was merely silence. Langbein, who played a pioneering part in tracing the growth of adversary trial, has indicated that,

> although the importance of this transformation from lawyer-free to lawyer-dominated trial has been remarked in the historical literature, not much has been known about how and why it occurred.[2]

---

1. James Fitzjames Stephen. (1883) *A History of the Criminal Law of England.* London, Routledge Theomess Press. vol. i. p. 424.
2. J.H. Langbein. (2003) *The Origins of Adversary Criminal Trial.* Oxford, Oxford University Press. p. 253.

Only in the last two or three decades have academics like Beattie, Langbein, May, Landsman and others explored the volcanic explosion that occurred and Garrow's role in it – in the case of Langbein with distaste of Garrow as a mere "trickster". Yet, Beattie, in his earlier writing, finds the origin of adversary trial to be "obscure",[3] and Langbein considers it was initiated not by the lawyers, as was indeed the case, but by the judges.[4] Nevertheless, the research of these writers has given Garrow's name its rightful place and his work is now widely appreciated. He sparkled at the Old Bailey where he was a living legend in the dramas that unfolded in that theatre of crime. Reading his cross-examinations in the Reports gives a real sense of excitement, yet that can only be a pale reflection of hearing him in the courtroom. That is how we can picture him. But his permanent significance lies in his part, with others he inspired, in bringing about the lawyer-led triumph of adversary trial and, in the criminal law context, the defence of political liberty and the dignity of man with its precise rules of evidence. It is indicative that this occurred in an England seeking to control autocracy from where it spread to the common law countries, particularly the emerging United States of America, and is now filtering into the remainder of the non-Islamic world. Adversary trial's protection of the individual citizen against state intrusion and tyranny is an integral part of the modern theory and practice of human rights. As such, further research into its genesis and its impact on elaborate rules of evidence designed to protect the accused from oppressive questioning, which are today under attack, can only be helpful.

As we have seen, Garrow was also a law officer and a judge and had an extensive, and interesting, family whose members had an important impact upon aspects of English society and culture, including literature, as well as portraying life and revolution in Italy. His genealogy in itself is of widespread interest and casts an interesting light upon aspects of society in the eighteenth and nineteenth centuries.

From humble beginnings, Sir William Garrow won fame as a celebrity in his own day although not fully accepted by some of the self-patronising elites in society. Here is the story of a man who should be treasured in history for his vast, if unwitting, impact on criminal procedure and human rights throughout the world – an influence with far-reaching consequences for millions of human beings in many countries today.

---

3. J.M. Beattie. (1991) "Scales of Justice: Defence Counsel and the English Criminal Trial in the Eighteenth and Nineteenth Centuries". 9(2) *Law and History Review*. University of Illinois Press. p. 224.
4. Langbein. *The Origins of Adversary Criminal Trial. Op. cit.* p. 178.

Timeline of William Garrow's Life

1760	Born 13 April at The Priory at Monken Hadley
1760	Baptized 27 April Educated at father's school in The Priory
1775	Articled to Mr. Thomas Southouse, attorney at Milk Street, Cheapside, London
1778	Admitted to Lincoln's Inn on 27 November
1781	Son David William born 15 April to Sarah Dore
1783	Called to the Bar 26 November
1784	Daughter Eliza Sophia born June to Sarah Dore
1784-92	Developed extensive practice at the Old Bailey
1784	Joined the Whig Club on 26 June
1790	Purchased Pegwell Cottage near Ramsgate, Kent during July
1793	Became Bencher of Lincoln's Inn
1793	Married Sarah Dore 17 March
1793	Became King's Counsel on 17 April
1794	Crown Counsel in the treason trials
1794-97	Belonged to the London and Westminster Light Horse Volunteers
1795	At Lincoln's Inn he became:	Master of the Bench
1799		Master of the Walks
1800		Keeper of the Black Book
1801		Treasurer
1802		Master of the Library
1803		Dean of the Chapel

1803	Commissioner for Land Tax Redemption
1805	Member of Parliament for Gatton
1805-6	Solicitor-General to H.R.H. The Prince of Wales
1806-12	Attorney-General to H.R.H. The Prince of Wales 8 February
1806	Member of Parliament for Collington
1808	Vice-President of the Royal Humane Society April
1808	Wife, Sarah Dore Garrow, died 30 June
1812	Member of Parliament for Eye Solicitor-General June 1812-May 1813
1812	Knighted at Carlton House by H.R.H. The Prince of Wales 17 July
1813	Attorney-General 3 May 1813 to May 1817
1813	Left the Society of Lincoln's Inn
1814-17	Chief Justice of Chester
1817-32	Baron of the Exchequer
1827	Son David William died 11 April
1832	Retired 22 February
1832	Made Privy Councillor 22 February
1840	Died at Pegwell Cottage 14 September

Garrow Genealogical Studies: A Note

As a biography, this study is not a mainstream genealogical document in that it does not exhaustively record the types of information usually organized in such studies. While some of this information is included, the intent here is to limit genealogical data to the people directly connected to, and who were known by, Sir William Garrow. It is also to limit it to the information that supports the telling of his life story. However, for those connected to the Garrow family line, this is family story-telling, and we feel it is an honoured niche in the genre of genealogy studies.

Richard Braby approached the study of Sir William Garrow as a family story-teller. It is here that Richard tells of his experiences in the search for story material on the life of Garrow, as a descendent of this man. Now with Garrow emerging on stage as a person of historic interest, this family story takes on meaning for a much wider audience.

Richard Braby's Story

My interest in Garrow history started with stories told by my grandmother, Edith Elizabeth Hacker Snead (1879-1979). She talked of a special English ancestor, a Judge Garrow, who helped write a will that tied a sizeable sum of money to her mother, Caroline Georgina Philips Hacker. As the story went, he "tied it to her so securely that she could not touch the principal, but the interest was quite good. No one was able to touch this or take it from her." In turn my grandmother received a sizeable inheritance from that same will when she became twenty-one years old.

When my grandparents came to America from England in 1910, a family treasure they brought with them was one of Caroline Georgina's books, *A Picturesque Tour of the English Lakes*. On the back page my grandfather had drawn a picture of an English judge, and added the inscription "Edith's relation, Judge Garrow." My grandmother added the note, "Judge Garrow was related to my Mother, Signed, her daughter, Mrs. Edith Elizabeth Snead."

Clearly my grandparents wanted their posterity to know that they were related to Judge Garrow. This was an important part of the family story. However, they knew almost nothing about the man. They were even unaware of their exact relationship to him.

Grandmother recorded many things she heard and experienced in England. She did this with all the details at her command. In turn my mother became the keeper of the family story, adding her own life experiences to the narrative. Now in the next generation, I too have become interested in saving and expanding the family story.

One unfinished narrative concerned this special but essentially unknown relative, Judge Garrow. For twenty years my curiosity about this matter has led me into the musty records of Regency England, and into a study of the history of that period. It has resulted in numerous trips to England and Scotland, and a walk in the footsteps of my many English ancestors. It has helped me discover a fascinating part of my roots, and given me a sense of connection to earlier times that has enriched my life. It has also put me in touch with numerous others who are connected in one way or another to William Garrow or to this family story, people who now I consider to be close personal friends . . . and in some cases as family.

I learned that the Judge did indeed exist. He was not some distant ancestor, separated by centuries from anyone I knew. As grandmother told us, he directly influenced her life. Had circumstances been different, Judge Garrow (who we now know was Sir William Garrow) would have had an even more direct influence on grandmother, and she would have celebrated his story, for she loved to tell the family stories.

Edith was born thirty-nine years after the death of Sir William Garrow. The passing of the family story over this bridge of thirty-nine years was made ineffectual by events in the extended Garrow family. While Sir William had only two children, a son and a daughter, his children produced eleven children that lived to adulthood. However, only two of his grandchildren had children, with only three being born to that generation. It appeared the family was heading toward extinction. My grandmother, Edith Elizabeth Hacker Snead, was a child of one of these three. Sir William Garrow was her great great grandfather.

When Edith Elizabeth was born, her mother, Caroline Georgina Philips Hacker, lived only a few months and therefore did not pass on directly what she knew of her ancestry. In turn, her grandmother, Arabella Garrow Philips, died when her daughter, Caroline Georgina, was a teenager, and her daughter may not have paid much attention to her mother's family story. However it transpired, the Garrow story was lost to my grandmother, except for knowledge of the name "Judge Garrow," when my grandmother, her husband, William Howard Snead, and their two children moved from England to Independence, Missouri in 1910.

When I began this study, the scholars of the history of common law were just beginning to rediscover Garrow. In 1991 I made contact with John Beattie, who I consider to have reintroduced Garrow to those interested in legal history. He provided me with a flow of his own work and contacts with the work of others. Indeed my contacts with John Beattie over the many years has been most enjoyable and informative. Recently as I got to know John Hostettler and his interesting study on the work of Garrow, I have made another new friend, and partner in the search for more story material on my illustrious ancestor. During this time none of the American posterity of Sir William Garrow had any substantive knowledge of this ancestor.

Today there is a sizable extended family in America and England carrying genes from Sir William, and when considering his brothers and sister, it is indeed a large extended family in many countries. It is my hope that many of the children, grand-children, great grandchildren and subsequent generations of Edith Elizabeth Hacker Snead in America as well as those with Garrow genes in other countries will find this story of interest as a piece of their own family story, a narrative that helps them define who they are today. As it now happens that the scholars of common law history have rediscovered and are celebrating William Garrow as a significant historical figure, it would appear that more people will be interested in his life story. In this book, John Hostettler speaks especially to this larger community, but for me, I remain a family storyteller.

I have used material from many people in telling this story. It is here that I will give proper credit for the work of genealogists who have studied special segments of this extended family.

My good friend, Doug Monk, has been with me on almost the entire length of this journey. As a Monk, he is a direct descendent of Jane Monk, William Garrow's sister. He opened up the door to the genealogical work done by others, including Elwin Cray Pilkington in Australia, and J.D. Remnant and Herbert Hersom in England. His own careful work on the Monk family story has been of interest. Together we explored the churchyard near Darenth, Kent, and found the burial site of William Garrow's wife Sarah, and have speculated endlessly on her family back-ground. And the name Garrow lives on in his family, in that one of his newly arrived grandchildren has the given name of Garrow.

Another partner in this journey is Jan Dalton and her husband Alan. They are New Zealanders, and Jan is a direct descendant of Sarah Garrow, and the 2nd Marquis of Downshire. Sarah, as William Garrow's wife and mother of their chil-dren, connects us in a family way. It is through Jan that stories of William Garrow have come down to us through the generations within this family arriving intact to this generation. Jan is an accomplished genealogists and storyteller. She has recorded the stories of her side of the family in great detail, a tradition passed to her from earlier members of her line. My wife and I have spent interesting days with Alan and Jan in their home in New Zealand, exploring ways to find more original material on Sarah and her relationship with the Marquis, and with William Garrow, and Alan has a special gift of telling stories in an interesting way. I treasure our friendship.

And another partner on this journey is Pat Robinson of Cambridge, England. Pat is descended from Edward Garrow, William Garrow's older brother, who made his fortune in India. Pat is an accomplished genealogist and holds the genealogical records of many of those that have gone before documenting the flow of the genera-tions. She has been an indispensable partner in documenting the stories from the Edward Garrow line.

My contact in Aberlour, Scotland, the ancestral home of the Garrow family, is Grantie Garrow, a direct descendent of that ancient stock of Garrows that first inhabited the farmland north of the Spey River as described in *Chapter 1*, and indeed the line of Garrows that has inhabited it ever since. He and his wife, Aileen, guided us to walk the land of the Garrows, and they are our contact with those who continue to carry the name of Garrow in Scotland.

This book, in attempting to put Sir William Garrow into a family context, describes briefly the people he knew and for whom he cared. As previously noted, his will and trust continued to care for many members of this extended family, those that he knew, and some yet unborn. Those who made up his known family, his grandparents, parents, uncles and aunts, siblings, children, and grandchildren, are shown in the charts at the end of this appendix in the family groups and in their relationship to the larger family. It is hoped that the chart will add clarity to the reading of the main text.

In terms of my own connection with this family story, Sir William Garrow's granddaughter, Arabella, is my great great grandmother. Some of my genealogy friends have discussed the idea of including a detailed genealogical chart of the Garrow family line from the first David Garrow in the 1600s to the present. Much of this information exists privately in pieces under the custodianship of individuals within the various family lines. If assembled it would indeed be a very large pyramid of names of people who share the Garrow gene pool which today extends through approximately fourteen generations. If it were to be integrated into a single data base it would connect these people to the William Garrow story. Such a task would call for a committed genealogist. The idea was quickly rejected as being quite out of place in a biography of this kind.

While much of my work is grounded in genealogical records often collected and assembled by others, there is still work to be done in presenting this information. As a family storyteller I enjoy picking up the clues that a family story is there. Then by following the fragments of information wherever they lead me, I attempt to bring alive episodes from a person's life, especially when there is a good story that needs to be told. In terms of family story material, it doesn't get much better than discovering the events in the almost forgotten life of William Garrow.

A partner in each step of this adventure has been my wife, Carol. She has been at my side on our many research trips into the archives, research libraries and sites of genealogical records and it has usually been Carol who has located the most valuable finds. She shares with me the many new friends made along the way. As a trained journalist and dedicated genealogist her skills and perseverance have been essential in the preparation of this record. Her sister, Alice Freeman, has been very helpful in the preparation of my various manuscripts, and has shared with us the excitement of the journey.

THE SIR WILLIAM GARROW GENEALOGY 1
Significant people in Garrow's life
His Garrow ancestors and brothers and sisters

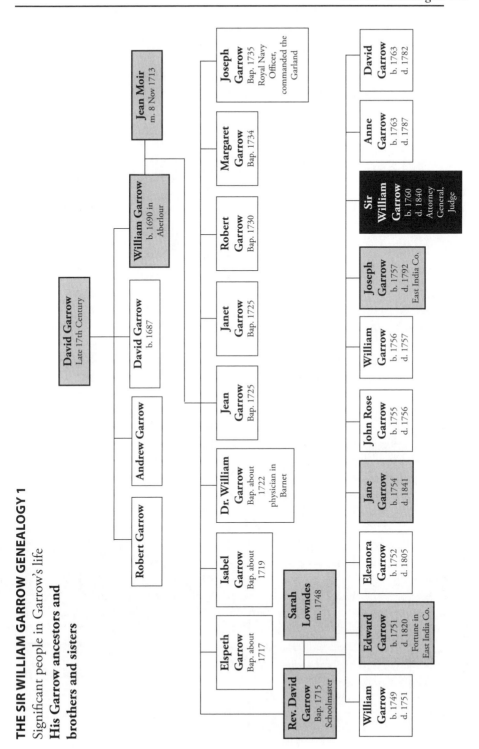

David Garrow — Late 17th Century

Jean Moir — m. 8 Nov 1713

William Garrow — b. 1690 in Aberlour

Robert Garrow

Andrew Garrow

David Garrow — b. 1687

Elspeth Garrow — Bap. about 1717

Isabel Garrow — Bap. about 1719

Dr. William Garrow — Bap. about 1722, physician in Barnet

Jean Garrow — Bap. 1725

Janet Garrow — Bap. 1725

Robert Garrow — Bap. 1730

Margaret Garrow — Bap. 1734

Joseph Garrow — Bap. 1735, Royal Navy Officer, commanded the Garland

Rev. David Garrow — Bap. 1715, Schoolmaster

Sarah Lowndes — m. 1748

William Garrow — b. 1749, d. 1751

Edward Garrow — b. 1751, d. 1820, Fortune in East India Co.

Eleanora Garrow — b. 1752, d. 1805

Jane Garrow — b. 1754, d. 1841

John Rose Garrow — b. 1755, d. 1756

William Garrow — b. 1756, d. 1757

Joseph Garrow — b. 1757, d. 1792, East India Co.

Sir William Garrow — b. 1760, d. 1840, Attorney General, Judge

Anne Garrow — b. 1763, d. 1787

David Garrow — b. 1763, d. 1782

THE SIR WILLIAM GARROW GENEALOGY 2
Significant people in Garrow's life
**His wife and their children
and grandchildren**

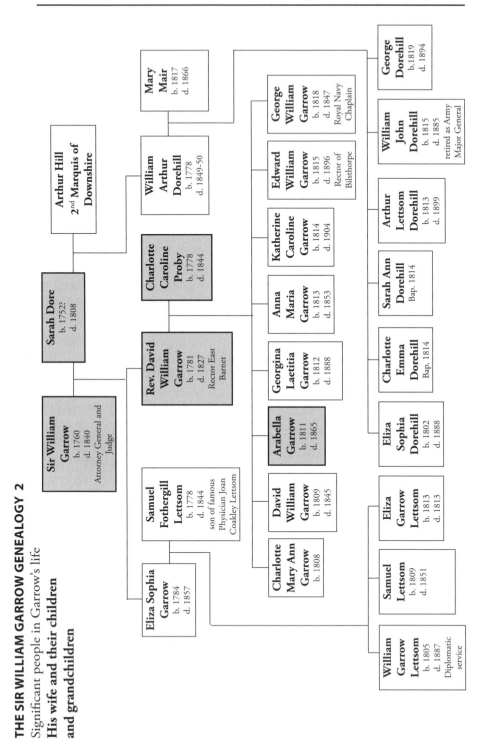

THE SIR WILLIAM GARROW GENEALOGY 3

Significant people in Garrow's life

Families of his brothers and sisters

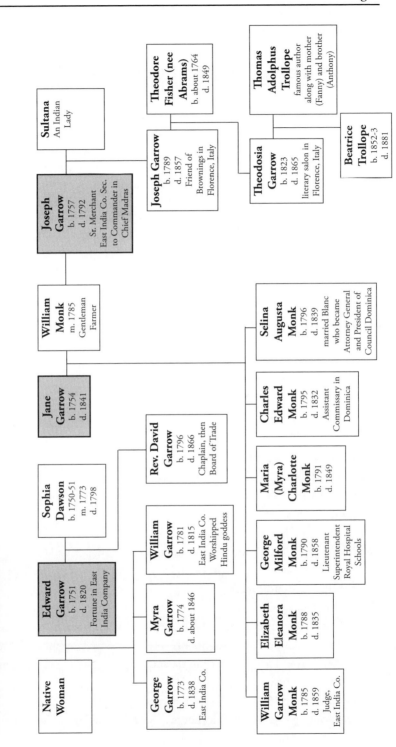

Sultana An Indian Lady	

Joseph Garrow b. 1757 d. 1792 Sr. Merchant East India Co. Sec. to Commander in Chief Madras

Theodore Fisher (nee Abrams) b. about 1764 d. 1849

Joseph Garrow b. 1789 d. 1857 Friend of Brownings in Florence, Italy

Thomas Adolphus Trollope famous author along with mother (Fanny) and brother (Anthony)

Theodosia Garrow b. 1823 d. 1865 literary salon in Florence, Italy

Beatrice Trollope b. 1852-3 d. 1881

William Monk m. 1785 Gentleman Farmer

Jane Garrow b. 1754 d. 1841

Sophia Dawson b. 1750-51 m. 1773 d. 1798

Edward Garrow b. 1751 d. 1820 Fortune in East India Company

Native Woman

George Garrow b. 1773 d. 1838 East India Co.

Myra Garrow b. 1774 d. about 1846

William Garrow b. 1781 d. 1815 East India Co. Worshipped Hindu goddess

Rev. David Garrow b. 1796 d. 1866 Chaplain, then Board of Trade

William Garrow Monk b. 1785 d. 1859 Judge, East India Co.

Elizabeth Eleanora Monk b. 1788 d. 1835

George Milford Monk b. 1790 d. 1858 Lieutenant Superintendent Royal Hospital Schools

Maria (Myra) Charlotte Monk b. 1791 d. 1849

Charles Edward Monk b. 1795 d. 1832 Assistant Commissary in Dominica

Selina Augusta Monk b. 1796 d. 1839 married Blanc who became Attorney General and President of Council Dominica

APPENDIX 2

A Snapshot of Crime and Punishment in the 1800s

For nine hundred years Lincoln Castle was used as a court and a prison with many of those found guilty of capital crimes being executed on the castle ramparts. In the past, as with Tyburn Tree in London, on execution day vast crowds would attend in the countryside around the castle to witness the ghastly scenes of terror-ridden men and women being publicly strangled in cold blood. So hungry for the gruesome spectacle was the immense assemblage that it is recorded that on one occasion at Lincoln Castle when it was announced that there would be only one execution, the pleasure-seeking throng bayed for further prisoners to be brought to the gallows despite their not having been sentenced to death. The incident portrays the brutal curiosity and ugly consequences of public executions. The following betrays the extent of the underlying barbarity of punishments in those times.

CROWN CALENDAR FOR THE LINCOLNSHIRE LENT ASSIZES.

Held at Lincoln Castle on Saturday the 7th of March 1818, before the Right Honorable Sir Vicary Gibbs and the Honorable Sir William Garrow John Chales Lucas Calcraft, Esq., Sheriff

1. William Bewley, aged 49, late of Kingston upon Hull, pensioner from the 5th Regt. of foot, committed July 29, 1817, charged on suspicion of having feloniously broken into the dwelling house of James Crowder at Barton, no person being therein, and stealing 1 bottle green coat, 1 velveteen jacket, 3 waistcoats, &c. Guilty - Death

2. John Giddy, aged 22, late of Horncastle, tailor, com. Aug. 5, 1817, charged with stealing a silver watch with a gold seal and key, from the shop of James Genistan of Horncastle. Six Months Imprisonment.

3. George Kirkhan, aged 25, and

4. John Colston Maynard, aged 19, both late of Stickney, laborers, corn. Aug. 22, 1817, charged on suspicion of feloniously entering the dwelling house of Wm. Bell of Stickney, between 9 and 10 o'ck in the morning, and stealing one £5 note and 8 £1 notes. Acquitted.

5. George Crow, aged 15, late of Frith Ville, com. Sept. 23, 1817, charged on suspicion of having entered the dwelling house of S. Holmes of Frith Ville, about 7 o'ck

in the morning, breaking open a desk, and stealing three £1 notes, 3s. 6d. in silver, and a purse. Guilty - Death.

6. Thomas Young, aged 17, late of Firsby, laborer, com. Sept. 23, 1817, charged with having, about 11 o'ck at night, entered the dwelling house of John Ashlin of Firsby, with intent to commit a robbery. Guilty - Death.

7. Robert Husker, aged 28, and

8. John Robinson, aged 28, both late of Glamford Briggs, laborers, corn. Oct. 13, 1817, charged with burglariously breaking into the dwelling house of Chas. Saunby, of South Kelsey, and stealing therefrom several goods and chattels. Guilty - Death.

9. John Marriott, aged 19, late of Osgodby, laborer, com. Oct. 18, 1817, charged with maliciously and feloniously setting fire to an oat stack, the property of Thomas Marshall of Osgodby. Guilty - Death.

10. Sarah Hudson, alias Heardson, aged 25, late of Newark, Nottinghamshire, com. Oct. 24, 1817, charged on suspicion of feloniously stealing from the cottage of James Barrell of Aisthorpe, in the day time, no person being therein, 6 silver tea-spoons and a pair of silver sugar tongs. Discharged by proclamation.

11. Elizabeth Firth, aged 14, late of Burgh cum Girsby, spinster, com. Nov. 22, 1817, charged with twice administering a quantity of vitrol or verdigrease powder, or other deadly poison, with intent to murder Susanna, the infant daughter of George Barnes of Burgh cum Girsby. No true Bill.

12. John Moody, aged 28, late of Stallingborough, laborer, com. Dec. 24, 1817, charged with having committed the odious and detestable crime and felony called sodomy. Indicted for misdemeanor. Two years imprisonment.

13. William Johnson, aged 28, late of Bardney, laborer, com. Dec. 29, 1817, charged with having burglariously entered the dwelling house of Wm. Smith, of Bardney, and wilfully and malliciously beating and wounding, with intent to murder and rob Wm. Kirmond, a lodger therein. Seven Years Transportation.

14. Richard Randall, aged 27, and

15. John Lubbs, aged 29, both late of Lutton, laborers, com. Dec. 29, 1817, charged with feloniously assaulting Wm. Rowbottom of Holbeach Marsh, between 11 and 12 o'ck in the night, in a field near the king's highway, and stealing from his person 3 promissory £10 notes, 8 or 10 shillings in silver, one silver stop and seconds watch, and various other goods and chattels. Both guilty - Death.

16. William Hayes, aged 20, late of Braceby, weaver, com. Jan. 6, 1818, charged with feloniously stealing a mare, together with a saddle and bridle, the property of Ed. Briggs of Hanby. Guilty - Death.

17. Thomas Evison, aged 24, and

18. Thomas Norris, aged 28, both late of Alnwick, laborers, com. Jan. 21, 1818, charged with feloniously setting fire to a thrashing machine and a hovel, containing a quantity of oats in the straw, the property of Thos. Faulkner, jun. of Alnwick, which were all consumed. Guilty - Death.

19. William Walker, aged 20, laborer, and

20. Elizabeth Eno, aged 19, spinster, both late of Boston, com. Jan. 28, 1818, charged with burglariously entering the dwelling house of Wm. Trentham, and stealing a sum of money in gold and silver, several country bank notes, and a red morocco pocket-book. Guilty - Death.

21. William Bell, alias John Brown, aged 30, late of Alvingham, laborer, com. Feb. 19, 1818, charged with burglariously breaking into the shop of Wm. Goy of Alvingham, and stealing 1 pair of new shoes, 1 half boot, and 1 half boot top. Guilty - Death.

22. John Hoyes, aged 48, late of Heckington, com. Feb. 24, 1818, charged with feloniously stealing 2 pigs of the value of £3, the property of John Fairchild of Wellingore. Acquitted.

APPENDIX 3

Some Primary Sources

Public Characters
4th ed. 10 v. 1799 -1809

MR. GARROW The father of this eminent barrister was a school-master at Barnet in the county of Middlesex, and, as may be conjectured from his profession, added to his numerous offspring, in circumstances much removed from affluence. A character for learning, and great respectability in the neighbourhood, had, however, procured him the patronage of most of the gentlemen of the county, and his academy became so well filled that he was enabled to educate and support a large family in a style of decent and honourable competence. His brother, who lived at the same place, was first an apothecary and surgeon, and then a physician; he had indeed united the three branches of the profession with great advantage to himself and patients, and, as he regularly possessed himself of the diploma, had nothing to apprehend from the jealousy and rivalry of his brethren. The circumstances of prescribing and mixing his own medicines, gave him a general monopoly about Barnet, and though often invited, he would never consent to remove to the metropolis. In the event he realized a fortune of thirty thousand pounds, which on his death, devolved chiefly on his nephew, the subject of our present remarks.

Mr. Garrow was born about the year 1754, and received the first elements of education in his father's school. He was early destined to the profession of the law, and to occupy a much humbler sphere than that in which he now moves. His father resolved to place him with an attorney in the city, and articled him, accordingly, at the age of sixteen; but the ambition of the young man soared above the desk, and, in his hours of leisure, he devoted himself to the study of the law as a science abounding with principles and rational truths, and not as a series of precedents to be consulted on the file. It was, indeed, formerly one of the modes of legal education to place young men with attorneys and solicitors in order to teach them the practice of the courts, but this has long given way to the present method of fixing them in the office of a special pleader, preparatory to their being called to the bar. Their employment in these offices is chiefly to copy precedents, and draw declarations and pleading; they thus relieve the gentleman, with whom they are placed, of the most burthensome part of his business, and pay him infinitely better than his clients. A hundred pounds per annum is the stipend commonly received from every pupil, and scarcely is there a special pleader of any note but who has five or six of these legal *eleves* constantly copying at his chambers. Indeed the emoluments of such gentlemen as are not dignified with a silk gown are principally derived from these academies, and, as it is a point of honour that no practicing counsel *within* the bar should receive pupils, a very lucrative branch of business is thus monopolized by the younger barristers. At this time Br. Garrow had formed to himself few presages of future greatness; the tissue of life was unfolded slowly, and with such faint promises as appeared to indicate nothing of that eminence to which he has since arrived. A circumstance, however, occurred at this time which had laid the foundation of his present fame, by throwing him, unexpectedly, into that branch of the profession to which he does so much honour. The attorney with whom he was placed in the city, retired from business with a good fortune, and Mr. Garrow's articles expired. This gentleman, who perceived and valued his talents, now advised his father to enter him of one of the inns of court, and place him for a year or two with a special pleader. The advise was followed, and Mr. Garrow now commenced a *regular training* for his profession. It is a matter of some astonishment to consider the many celebrated characters whom fortune, rather than self direction, has rendered eminent; men who had been lost in obscurity but for a happy concurrence of circumstances, which have taken them from the lumber room in which thay have been long thrown by, and, almost in despite of themselves, in contradiction at least of all prognostics, have brightened and polished up into the objects of general admiration and utility. Sir Francis Drake entered the sea service in the forty-second year of his age; Cromwell was as old when he became a soldier; and Coke, the oracle of the English law, was on the verge of forty when called to the bar. Of men who became eminent by accident, Mr. Garrow may be adduced as an example. It would be useless to inquire into his course of study, as this is a thing which modesty mostly keeps to itself, and vanity alone confesses. That he read with diligence and success may be conjectured from the progress he made, and forensic eminence, it would yet be absurd to deny that even in this line, such genius is deprived of its natural prerogative. The powers of Bacon have long since given something of elegance to the monastic structure of our English code, and the liberal taste of Blackstone has concluded what his illustrious predecessor but commenced. The splendor, the illumination, and the liberality of the *belles letters,* have been thus grafted on the rough and knotted stock of jurisprudence, and the tree may now regard its own fruit with surprise. "Miraturque novas fronds et non sua poma."

To return. In the intervals of reading Mr. Garrow thought necessary to exercise and encourage in himself a talent for which he was much noted when a boy; this talent is vulgarly called *"spouting;"* the more polite call it the art of oratory; and, to the amazement of all foreigners, there is in England no institution to teach an art of so extensive and primary and use as elocution. It is thus that our English orators are every where remarked as awkward and ungraceful in their delivery, and as fixed and attentive only to the weight and cogency of their arguments, whilst they despise all the graces and the charms of speech. Although public speaking is so essential a part of legal education, the young student disdains to practice it, and thus seldom acquires, till late in life, that promptitude and collectedness of delivery, which often-times displays inferior talents to more advantage than those which, however deep, are in want of this attractive faculty. The writer of this article well remembers an anecdote of the late Lord Mansfield, which was told him by a gentleman of great practice at the bar, who was himself the occasion of it. He went one morning to Lord Mansfield with a letter of introduction, and after some enquiries, the veteran judge asked him if he were perfect in Coke upon Littleton. He replied that he was not altogether perfect, but intended reading it over again for the *third* time. "Take a little rest, sir, take a little rest, said his Lordship, it is my advice that you should now take a turn with Enfield's Speaker." At this time London was overrun with speaking-clubs and eleemosynary orators; not an alley but had its Demosthenes and Cicero, and the alehouses were quite deserted. At the head of these institutions, we believe the origin of them all, was the celebrated Robin-Hood-Club. This was so famous in its day that men of the first literary talents, such as Colman, Garrick, and Burke, frequented and debated in it. As politics were never discussed, at least no question which immediately applied to the circumstances of the times, there was little acri-mony or warmth; and as all had a right to speak in their turns, a perfect harmony and equality prevailed. Burke was accustomed to tell of himself, that he was never so completely set down or vanquished in argument as by a master carpenter with whom he chanced to debate at the Robin-Hood; and that any one who wished to form his estimate of the powers and innate strength of mind of an English citizen in common life, could not go to a better place than this society. When it became famous it became crowded, and the speakers were so numerous and earnest to be heard, that the chair could only preserve order by fixing an hour-glass on the table, and permit-ting no man to speak longer than whilst a certain portion of sand was running out; he was then stopped, and the glass was replenished with the same quantity for another, who having consumed *his* sand, was forced to desist in his turn, though cut short in a simile, or interrupted in an argument. This method of equal allotment of time and attention continued for a long period; but the audience had at length recourse to the common practice of *"scraping,"* which was a noise made by their feet against the floor, as a hint that they were tired of their speaker. Of this club, in its decline, Mr. Garrow enrolled himself a member; and he is remembered by many when a little carrotty-headed boy, as particularly eminent in debate, and possessed of such intrepidity and collectedness, as to oppose himself, without dismay, to the most established orators. He had scarcely passed his noviciate when he ran away with the palm of eloquence from all the frequenters of the club, and is suppose to have been almost the death of a journeyman watchmaker who had long rode the *high horse* in the society, and predominated with an insuperable arrogance, by vanquishing him in cool debate, and dethroning him from his usurped eminence in fair battle. Public speaking was now, however, to be turned to more account, and Mr. Garrow, at the expiration of his terms, and at the usual time, was called to the bar. In the schools of eloquence which he frequented he had acquired some very useful qualities, and certain professional virtues of which he seems never to have lost the proper estimation. The field of litigation, therefore, in which he first adventured, was at the courts of criminal justice, and he made his *debut* at the Old Bailey bar. He was here very much admired by the attorneys and solicitors for the peculiar intrepidity, smartness, and dexterity with which he examined evidence; the good humour with which he received any retort from the badgered witness; the promptitude with which he recurred to the charge; and the perseverance with which he sifted it to the bottom, till the fact, somehow or another, from the most stubborn, practiced, and prepared witness was sure to be elicited at last. No man was, perhaps, ever so acute in cross-examination; if he is exceeded by any one, it is by his present friend Mr. Topping.

Mr. Garrow penetrates into life and character with a facility and knowledge almost intuitive; he can examine a man in his own trade, and appear as intimate with every branch of it, as though he had himself served an apprenticeship in the business; he knows every shift of roguery, every turn and colour of life; and if it were at all worth while to expose the fallacious epithet of *legal monks,* which was applied in the house of lords to the lawyers, and so gravely resented by Lord Kenyon, we need only adduce the example of Mr. Garrow, to whom almost every variety of existence is known, and whose knowledge of men and manners may fairly be presumed as more extensive than that of the loungers of Bond-street, and the members of gaming clubs, whose common-place notions of men and things are picked up in their routs and orgies, and whose station and pride alike preclude them from a general mixture with the world. Mr Garrow soon obtained the chief practice of the Old Bailey bar, and when it happened that the felons were in good circumstances, an Old Bailey brief was no bad thing. It is well known at the bar that when a crim. con. is detected, the first care of the plaintiff is to retain Mr. Erskine in the cause. It might be observed, with equal justice, that at this time, when a felon or a swindler was taken up, and cast about him for the means of safety, his eyes almost always settled on the cheering prospect of Mr. Garrow's talents. For two or three years he practiced chiefly in this court and at the quarter-sessions, without shewing his face in the King's-bench; but praise gave confidence, and he soon felt an ambition to struggle for more general and lucrative practice. There are but two ways of obtaining this at the English bar, patronage and commanding talents; what Mr. Garrow wanted in the former he made up in the latter. His talents as a lawyer were already known to possess that effect and brilliancy which command sudden admiration; he was not suffered, therefore, to remain long in obscurity, or add, without notice, another unit in the train of justice. It has often been observed that genius has been more indebted to fortune than to its own vigour for eminence. Talents, perhaps, are not so rare as is generally supposed; the flower may exist in many soils, and, if touched by the beam of a happy fortune, might more frequently emerge from its obscurity, and gladden the day with rich and unexpected luxuriance. To a fortunate concurrence of accidents the law is more beholden than any other profession; an ornament has not infrequently been derived to the bench from the sickness of a leading counsel, and to the same chance which operated in bringing a Camden into notice, the first luminaries of the present day in Westminster-hall are indebted for their rise. Mr. Garrow himself owes his eminence to this same chance, equally with the rest of his brethren. Mr. Pitt, among his many financial speculations, had resolved to lay a very heavy and unequal duty on West India or American produce, and the brunt was chiefly to be borne by the tobacco planters. An interest of such vast importance being at stake, the West India merchants having endeavoured ineffectually, by their influence in the commons and private remonstrance with the minister, to arrest the bill, petitioned to be heard before the house by their counsel. The request was granted in common course, and Mr. Garrow was charged with the management of their petition. The extensive knowledge, the commercial information, the legal acuteness which he displayed, were subject of admiration to all that heard him. His speech on the occasion was scarcely ever rivaled at the bar of the house; and although Mr. Sheridan was extremely sarcastic and witty upon the minister, on account of this offensive duty, we do not hesitate to assert that Mr. Garrow far surpassed him in every excellence of oratory and logic. The impression he made upon the house was proportionate to the importance of his subject, and the superior manner in which he treated it; in short, it first fixed his friends in an opinion that he would soon occupy a distinguished rank in Westminster-hall. Mr. Garrow's reputation was now so well established, that he was engaged in every cause of importance before the courts. The history of his life, therefore, is upon the files and records of the king's-bench; and his memoirs are best read in the Term Reports. The life of an author, it is said, is best seen in his works; that of a lawyer, it may be observed with equal justice, is to be learned best from the causes which he tries and the suits he conducts. But it is the part of the biographer to fix attention upon those more important occurrences which give a colour, and, as it were, determine the character of the subject of his enquiry. We shall observe this rule of selection in our account of Mr. Garrow, and as his eminence is chiefly shewn in his felicity of examining witnesses, we shall relate a fact which occurred in our own presence, and which is peculiarly illustrative of the importance of that talent by which he is thus distinguished. At the summer assizes in the county of Huntingdon, in 1798-1799, a cause was tried before Mr. Justice Heath respecting the legitimacy of a gentleman of the name of Day, in the same county. Mr. Serjeant Le Blanc (now one of the judges in the king's bench) led the cause, and Mr. Garrow was retained from town and his business on an opposite circuit, for the express purpose of *cross-examining* a woman who was the principal witness against his client. This woman was brought to depose that the supposititious child (alleged to be Day, whose legitimacy was questioned) had been sold by her to the pretended mother of Day at Wolverhampton, to the neighbourhood of which place she went from her husband's house, near Kimbolton, in Huntingdonshire, for the prupose of lying-in. What appeared upon the trial was, that Mrs. Day, being a Staffordshire woman, and advanced in pregnancy, left her husband's residence in Kimbolton, in Huntingdonshire, to lie in with her relations in Staffordshire; and having either miscarried or lost a child, at Kimbolton, upon whom an estate of five or six hundred pounds per annum was settled, was desirous to try the effects of a journey into Staffordshire, and was brought-to-bed of this questionable child in the January following, and returned to her husband in the beginning of March. There is no doubt but it was the intention of this woman (the mother) at all events to return to her husband, in Huntingdonshire, with *a child*, and it appeared that she had actually applied to different persons, and particularly to the workhouse at Wolverhampton, for one - which child the woman, cross-examined by Mr. Garrow, deposed that she herself had sold to Mrs. Day, and that the child whose legitimacy was questioned was the person so sold. The adroitness with which Mr. Garrow cross-examined this woman did not leave a doubt in the minds of the jury that she was perjured; but they gave their verdict in favour of the legitimacy upon that as well as other grounds. The woman said that she sold the child to Mrs. Day in the month of November; that the child was then a month old; but when Mrs. Day returned to her husband in Huntingdonshire, the child she brought with her appeared to be about five weeks old, which agreed with the time of proof of Mrs. Day's delivery at the end of January; whereas, had it been the child alleged by the witness to have been bought of her, it must have had the appearance of an infant of fifteen or sixteen weeks. The mother, (Mrs. Day) it appeared certainly had a child, as she herself suckled the child with which she returned to her husband; but it happened that, together with the mother, the persons who had attended her lying in were all deceased, so that no positive proof could be obtained of the delivery; but the [case] rested upon the conversation held by the neighbours amongst each other, and with the mother at her return, and the acknowledgment of the child by the father. In this curious and interesting case, which filled the whole country with conversation, and attracted such a crowd in the court as was seldom ever witnessed, the ingenuity of Mr. Garrow was employed to show that, even supposing the child with which Mrs. Day returned to her husband, and which he, *"good easy man,"* believed to be his own, to have been a supposititious one, yet it was not possible that it could be the same child sworn to by the woman, as that child would have been fifteen weeks old, wherens the child which was brought back by Mrs. Day, and alleged to be hers, was only five weeks old when she returned to her husband in Huntingdonshire, so that it could not possible be the witness's child. The difficulty with which Mr. Garrow established these facts, and the great art with which he extracted them from a woman who was so well trained and prepared in her story, afforded to a young barrister the finest lesson on cross-examination. No scene in any dramatic author was ever more interesting than the one, which we have now described, appeared to all that saw it. The court was in a dead silence during the examination, which lasted above three hours; Mr. Garrow's eyes were scarcely once off the witness; they seemed to penetrate into her very soul and lay open the inmost workings of her mind. She was as collected as himself for some time, but her firmness at length gave way; he broke in at last upon the truth of the story, and, finally, made her so palpable confute herself, that his victory was complete. This was the greatest triumph, in our recollection, of Mr. Garrow's talent of cross-examination; and, independent of the peculiarity of the story, we have related it in order to impress upon the gentlemen of the law the importance of cultivating an art, which, in matters not only of life and death, but where great masses of property are concerned, is able to effect so much. Mr. Garrow does not pretend to be a very deep lawyer, he chiefly shines in personal actions, and scarcely an assault, battery, or breach of the peace, is brought into court, but he is first retained as counsel. His business in the king's-bench, which is exceeded by none but Mr. Erskine's is chiefly confined to actions of this kind; and at Nisi Prius, his practice, though not so lucrative, is, perhaps, superior to that of the last-named gentleman. Mr. Garrow seldom goes further into the country, except upon a special retainer, than Guildford, and he has long monopolized the chief business on the home circuit. It must be confessed that his powers as a pleader are chiefly confined to the humorous, the ridiculous, and the light; no man better understands or better expresses these qualifications; but of the pathos he has, perhaps, less than any other gentleman at the bar. His voice, though not powerful, is clear and melodious, and, while he wisely omits all action, his countenance and expression are nicely adapted to every passion he wished to excite. No man is heard with more attention by the court, no man gains more upon a jury, or better pleases a common auditor. Yet with all these excellencies, Mr. Garrow is likely to remain stationary; he never appears solicitous for a higher station than that which he at present fills; he certainly does not look to the bench, and makes no pretensions to the great law offices of state. Mr. Garrow probably is content with the honours of Westminster-hall; he has never, we believe, had any ambition to possess a seat in parliament; indeed, he well knows that such a seat would be but a losing bargain, as it would deprive him of some very lucrative practice before election committees. We have already mentioned that he inherited a large fortune from his uncle, Dr. Garrow; and the profits of his profession have long since realized for him a considerable property of his own. But every good has its alloy, and Mr. Garrow, now possessed of affluence and a silk gown, often wants health to enjoy the means of affluence in his power. He has been at one time a martyr to the gout; at another time he has been afflicted in a manner which threatened more serious consequences. A few years ago a very delicate surgical operation was performed upon him, and his health has been improving since that period, There is no one lives more orderly and temperately; he has been a family man for some years, and is very much loved and esteemed in private life. Though not celebrated as a classical scholar, his table is liberal, elegant, and convivial, and his conversation replete with pleasantry and good humour. His chief weight is not in opinions, so much as in pleading; nevertheless his practice as a chamber counsel is very extensive, and, in the highest degree, respectable. If these strictures should fall into the hands of any student in the law, he will, perhaps, derive one benefit from them, which will compensate the want of many other professional qualities; he will learn, in the life of Mr. Garrow, the great importance of cultivating a general and extensive acquaintance with the world, and pursuing life through all its varieties and circumstances, which has chiefly, if not singly, advanced the subject of this memoir to his present eminence; he will, moreover, learn the necessity of cultivating the art of public speaking, and the talent of cross-examination; and it would be a bequest almost invaluable to the young lawyer, if Mr. Garrow, before his is summoned off the stage, would draw up a general praxis for the treatment of evidence, and canons of cross examination.

The Legal Observer[1]

Vol. III. SATURDAY, FEBRUARY 18, 1832 No. LXX.
Pages 253-256 JUDICIAL CHARACTERS.
No. V. Sir William Garrow

The resignation of Mr. Baron Garrow, which was announced in the number of last week, affords us an opportunity, consistently with our plan, of giving a short account of his professional life, and by availing ourselves of it at the earliest moment, we feel we shall consult the wishes and gratification of our readers.

William Garrow, the subject of this brief notice, was the son of the Rev. David Garrow, a clergyman of the established church, residing in the village of Hadley, near Barnet. He was born on the 13th of April, 1760, at that place, where he passed his early years; and received his education, under the superintendance of his father. At the age of fifteen he entered the office of Mr. Southouse, an eminent attorney, who carried on business in Milk Street, Cheapside. Though attentive and diligent in the performance of the technical and practical duties of the office, he soon exhibited abilities and inclinations which, to the mind of his principal, seemed to afford the fairest hopes of success in a higher sphere of action, and which led Mr. Southouse to recommend that the bar should be his ultimate destination. It was not difficult to obtain the consent of his parents to this proposal, and in consequence, after passing five years in the office of Mr. Southouse, he became a pupil of Mr. Crompton, the well-known author of the book of Practice bearing his name, and afterwards one of the most popular special pleaders, and celebrated for the number of his pupils. Two years assiduous study and attendance at the chambers of this gentleman, so far advanced Mr. Garrow's legal knowledge as to encourage him to make the attempt to

---

1. This is a well-written, and we believe authentic memoir of Mr. Baron Garrow.

commence practice, and he was called to the bar by the Society of Lincoln's-Inn, in Michaelmas Term 1783. Almost immediately after his call, Mr. Garrow attended the sessions at the Old Bailey; and here a fortunate opportunity was soon presented for a display of those abilities for which he afterwards became remarkable. Henry Aickles, one of the most adroit and accomplished sharpers upon the town, was indicted for stealing a bill of exchange, of which he had obtained possession, under pretence of getting it discounted. Being well supplied with funds to protect himself in the event of such an emergency, he had retained for his defence the leading counsel then practicing at the bar of the court, in consequence of which the conduct of the prosecution was entrusted to Mr. Garrow. The prisoner's counsel objected, that the fact did not warrant a prosecution for felony, with a degree of confidence arising as well from their belief in the validity of the objection, as from the youth and apparent inexperience of their opponent; but the readiness, power, and accuracy of the reply which he made, induced the presiding judge, Mr. Justice Heath, to leave the case to the jury; and on their convicting the prisoner, to reserve the legal point raised for the consideration of the twelve Judges, by whom the conviction was affirmed. The able manner in which this case was conducted, as well as his successful exertions on other occasions, soon secured Mr. Garrow an extensive practice at the Old Bailey. Nor was he less prosperous in other quarters. At the contested election for Bedford, in the spring of 1784, he acted as assessor for the high sheriff, in which office his conduct was so much approved as to lead to a retainer in the London Scrutiny for Mr. Sawbridge. In the same year, a few months after his call to the bar, Mr. Fox and his friends thought it advisable to secure his assistance as one of their counsel at the Westminster election. Here he so far distinguished himself, that he was appointed on the part of the electors, to appear at the bar of the House of Commons in opposition to the scrutiny; a task which he so well accomplished as to attract the notice and commendations of Lord Kenyon, then Master of the Rolls, Mr. Pitt, Lord Mulgrave, Mr. Fox, Mr. Burke, and other leading statesmen of both parties. The circuit chosen by Mr. Garrow, as being more immediately connected with London business, was the Home. Although there were many of its members of distinguished eminence as advocates, and whose names are recorded as since reflecting luster upon the judicial office, Erskine was universally admitted as the triumphant leader, subduing his more erudite antagonists by an eloquence which bore down all opposition. To this celebrated orator, then in the zenith of his fame, in the vigor of his powers, and with all that confidence which long success naturally creates, Mr. Garrow soon found himself opposed. Nor was he, in the moment of trial, found deficient in any of the qualities necessary to maintain with credit so formidable a contest. On those great occasions when public attention and curiosity were attracted, where grand efforts were requisite, and high expectations entertained, Erskine seldom failed to shine forth with unrivalled splendour; but in the ordinary run of cases, Garrow, by his acuteness and readiness; by a talent, peculiarly his own, of examining and cross-examining witnesses;

and by the ease and tact with which he adapted his eloquence to the feelings and understands of those whom he sought to persuade, often obtained the ascendancy; and thus, if success be a true test, proved himself at least equal to his accomplished and powerful opponent. In a remarkable short time, therefore, after his becoming a member of the Circuit, Mr. Garrow was found either acting as junior counsel to Erskine, or engaged against him in the conduct of causes at *nisi prius*; whilst, so far as his practice on the civil side permitted, his business in the criminal court greatly increased. From the records of the numerous state prosecutions, arising from the agitation of the times, it will be seen that Mr. Garrow very early in his professional life, was regularly retained as one of the junior counsel for the Crown. His abilities and exertions on these occasions, as well as his increasing practice, both in town and on the circuit, let to an intimation that the appointment of King's Counsel, should he be disposed to solicit it, would not be refused. The acceptance of such an advancement at so early an age, and when in the possession of so beneficial a practice as a junior counsel, to most men would have been a matter of serious anxiety, since it is well known not at all times to have advanced the real interest of those, who actuated by an honourable ambition, have hastily accepted this promotion. But to Mr. Garrow no such danger was presented, as he had already been often tried in those situations, which as leading counsel, he would by this step be almost invariably called upon to fill. In less than ten years, therefore, from the date of his commencing practice at the bar, he was appointed by his Majesty one of his Counsel. The ability which Mr. Garrow, from the time of the Westminster Scrutiny, had frequently displayed professionally in the discussion of public and political questions at the bar of both Houses of Parliament, made his accession, as a member of the House of Commons, a desirable object to the leading political parties. It has been seen, that early in life he had been professionally connected with Mr. Fox and his friends; but his political sentiments according with those of Mr. Pitt, he did not hesitate to accept an offer made by that minister, of a seat for the borough of Gatton, for which place he was returned to Parliament. In 1806, His Royal Highness the Prince of Wales was pleased to nominate Mr. Garrow his Attorney-General, which office he held until the year 1812, when he was advanced to the rank of Solicitor-General to the King; on which occasion, as is usual, he received the honour of knighthood: and on the promotion of Sir Thomas Plomer, to the Vice-Chancellorship, he succeeded him in the office of Attorney-General. The manner in which Sir William Garrow acquitted himself in discharging the general duties of these high state offices, when candidly examined, cannot fairly be considered as open to exception; whilst it must be universally admitted that one of the most unpopular and responsible, the directing and conducting of state prosecutions, was carried into execution during the time that he was Attorney-General, with singular forbearance and propriety. Convinced, by long experience and observation, of the dangerous effects of failure in proceeding of this nature, caution and deliberation seem to have characterized his resolutions, and to have dictated the advice he was called upon to offer to the government upon such subjects. Hence it may be seen that, although during his official responsibility the number of state prosecutions were few in comparison with those instituted by some of his predecessors, rarely can there be found an instance in which an acquittal added to the evil intended to be suppressed, and, by bringing the law itself into odium and contempt, encouraged a repetition of the offence. Well may it therefore, without any invidious disposition, be remarked, that in this respect at least, Sir William Garrow's discreet and vigilant exercise of the powers entrusted to him as a public law officer, entitles him to no mean commendation.

On the promotion of Sir Richard Richards to the office of Lord Chief Baron, the office of Chief Justice of Chester was offered to and accepted by the Attorney-General. The discontinuance of circuit practice, (consequent upon his promotion to the Solicitor Generalship,) enabled him to perform the duties of a Judge, without inconvenience or interruption to his other professional engagements; and accordingly he continued to hold this office, and to enjoy a most extensive practice both in his public capacity, and as one of the most successful and popular advocates at the bar in private causes, until the spring of the year 1817. Of course, however, he met with his reverses, and a victory over him was one of the earliest triumphs of the present Lord Chancellor. A vacancy on the Exchequer Bench then occurring, and the Attorney-General signifying his wish to obtain the appointment, in Easter Term he took his seat as a Puisne Baron in that Court; in which station he has continued to the date of his recent retirement. He was considered by his friends as not having done justice to himself, in not waiting for some higher judicial office. It must be obvious, that any detailed observations or criticisms upon the merits and talents of this celebrated advocate and respected Judge, would, at present, be unbecoming and improper; but it may be allowable to say, that with him has retired one of the last of that race of men who, by a rare and splendid genius, have exalted in public estimation, no less their own character than that of the profession they adorned. The early and rapid success of Garrow, and a long career of uninterrupted prosperity, against rivals of extraordinary merit, sufficiently attest to possession of abilities of the highest order; as an advocate gifted, indeed, with natural talents such as fall to the lot of few, which had been improved and cultivated with care and diligence, the opportunities presented by fortune were not suffered to escape, but became immediately the foundation of fame and prosperity in his hazardous and uncertain profession. Of his skill in the art of cross-examination, many remarkable instances might be mentioned; but the attempt would be vain, by description, to convey any idea of the extent of his powers when called forth by such occasions as demanded their full exercise. Of the style and force of his eloquence there remain records in the State Trials, and in other publications of legal proceedings of interest, in which he was engaged. It would be difficult perhaps, on a deliberate exercise of the judgment, to direct attention to the recorded speeches most worthy of notice; but we may merely, from memory, as affording specimens of varied and superior abilities, advert to the defence of Dr. Symonds, the prosecutions against Picton, against Bligh, against Codling, Reid and others; the case of Doherty v. Wyatt; and to a very short, but powerful and conclusive address to the jury, for the defendant, in the King v. Faulder.

The nature of the duties of a barrister in great practice must necessarily sometimes engender feelings of private dislike and hostility; whilst the mortification of defeat, and the sense of inferiority, it is to be feared, too frequently raise an unfavourable disposition in professional rivals. From such misfortunes it cannot be expected that one so celebrated should be altogether free; but his courteous demeanour, and a genuine and unostentatious kindness, both as a barrister and a judge, were well calculated to remove any unjust or unfavourable impressions. The recollection of this must serve to mitigate the regret which cannot but be felt by him, on retiring from a scene where for nearly fifty years he has performed so prominent and so honourable a part; and the knowledge, that though absent from view in our Courts, there are many there whose regard, respect, and gratitude, must ever cherish his memory, cannot fail to gladden the hours of repose and retirement, and to shed a pleasing luster upon the evening of his days. As a mere lawyer, his character as a Judge was not conspicuous; but his powers at *nisi prius* and in the Criminal Courts were very considerable. His health has, however, of late declined; but the fault of remaining on the bench after the judicial faculty had departed, cannot justly be imputed to him.

The Times

Saturday, November 7, 1840
Memoir of Sir William Garrow
(From the *Monthly Law Magazine*)

Sir William Garrow, as the public has already been amply and frequently informed, was the son of the Rev. Dr. Garrow, as schoolmaster at Monken Hadley, in Middlesex. He was born in 1760, and received his education entirely under the paternal roof. As there was nothing in the circumstances or alliances of his family, which opened the prospect of brilliant fortune or superior station, he received and profited by the portion of instruction usually given in his time to those who were destined to the profession of an attorney. He knew the English language well; had a moderate acquaintance with the Latin, and, as an accomplishment, added a considerable proficiency in French. At a proper age, he was placed in the office of an eminent attorney, and pursued his profession with assiduity and perseverance. Soon it was discovered that he had talents which qualified him to shine in a higher department of the law, and his contemporaries, his master, and many professional men consorted with the house, exhorted him to bend his faculties toward that direction. He took their advice, and placed himself under the tuition of a special pleader.

In those days, the meetings called debating societies were the places in which alone a young orator could make an advantageous effort to display and perfect his power of public speaking. He had to meet, not a prepared party of friends or fellow-students, who would fondly consider his success as conferring honour on a body to which they all belonged, but a band of competitors gifted with various portions of ability and equally with himself candidates for approbation from the numerous, and generally well-informed, audiences which the hope of enjoying, at a very moderate price, the pleasure of witnessing a good display of intellectual struggle, never failed to collect. From the caricatures of Foote and other writers of farces and novels, or from the degenerate conditions into which, at a later period, these assemblages were reduced, when they were made the lecture rooms of sedition and sometimes of impiety, no correct notion can be formed of their state at the time when Burke had recently breathed out the inspirations of his mighty genius; when Erskine, to perfect his style and facilitate his elocution, had been among their frequent speakers; when Stephen charmed the understanding by his talents, and won the heart by his engaging modesty; and when Dallas illuminated the debates with the copiousness of his knowledge, and adorned them with his suavity and politeness. In these places, a young man who aspired to be a public speaker could advantageously exercise himself. He would find that, without intending to be harsh, everyone of his auditors would consider himself a competent critic, and unceremoniously castigate him for his faults; he would be inured to bear severe and unmeasured animadversions; some-times purposed misrepresentations; and occasionally (for the vigilance of a president could not be unremitting) interruptions and derision which far over-stepped the bounds of liberality and decorum; but this was only the rough exercise by which the hunter was prepared for the chase, or the charger for the field; powerful qualities and ardent spirit would enable him to turn these obstacles to profit, and to display in their full effect his courage and his vigour.

To one of these societies, which met at Coachmaker's hall, in Foster-lane, Cheapside, young Garrow went, accompanied by a few friends; and, such was his timidity, they found it necessary to force him from his seat, and to bold him by main strength while he delivered his maiden essay, lest he should shrink back from the task he had undertaken. To those who superficially observed him in after life, this want of self-confidence will appear surprising, at least, if not incredible; but they who had opportunities of viewing him more closely will know that it was perfectly in keeping with a reserved and retiring disposition, by which, until lengthened acquaintance had smoothed the path of intercourse, or the call of professional duty had cleared off the mist of diffidence, he was always distinguished.

His success in his early essays was amply sufficient to dispel the alarms which chilled his bosom, and to animate the hopes of his friends. He was soon recognized as the first of the debating orators. When he appeared, the audience congratulated themselves on the certainty of an interesting discussion; and when Mrs. Cornelys, planning a new species of entertainment at Carlisle house, in Soho-square, devised a debate as a portion of the evening's amusement, her first care was to secure the assistance of Mr. Garrow.

In 1783 he was called to the bar by the Honourable Society of Lincoln's-inn. To enter on that profession at that time was an arduous and anxious undertaking. The voice of Dunning still seemed to sound in the public ear; the sun of Bearcroft, although past its meridian, shone with heat and splendour; that of Erskine shed unrivalled radiance; and Mingay, with a host of brilliant stars, always illumined, and sometimes ruled the legal hemisphere. Garrow had not, by practice as a special pleader, collected around him a host of attornies, accustomed to shape their proceedings by his advice; he had not advertised himself by editing, with notes, some old legal author, or by launching an essay on any popular and interesting topic; he had no powerful family connexion to sustain his interest; no school or college associations to advance his pretensions; nor had he made himself a member of any of the political clubs or societies formed to promote peculiar notions in religion or politics; he was known to the public only as a powerful and favourite speaker at the debating societies.

His first success was not in Westminster-hall, but in the Criminal Court at the Old Bailey, where, at that time, great intellectual vigour was required to insure success. There, in course, the judges presided in rotation, and, in their absence, the Recorder, Mr. Sergeant Adair, who, by learning and experience, was equally qualified with any member of the Bench to sustain the due administration of the law. To practice before him, as before them, with success, flippant fluency or audacious invective was not sufficient; the advocate was required to possess a learned insight into the criminal law; a discerning tact in the practice of evidence; the acquisitions of a scholar, and the manners of a gentleman. Very soon, indeed, was Garrow distinguished in this court. His acuteness in examining witnesses, and his dexterity and judgment in seizing and discussing points of law, raised for him a distinguished character and most favourable public opinion. At an early period of his progress, in January 1784, a case occurred, that of Aickles, in which, opposed to two of the most experienced and able practitioners of the day, Mr. (afterwards Sir) John Sylvester and Mr. Fielding, he made an argument, so able, cogent, and luminous, as to establish at once a new, or, at least, doubtful point of criminal law, and his own fame as an acute, sensible, and judicious lawyer. In the margin of his own copy of Leash's Crown-law Cases, where this discussion is recorded, he wrote a note, declaring that he attributed to this argument the notice which chiefly occasioned his success in life; and many years afterwards, when he had attained the rank of Attorney-General, he reiterated, in a supplementary note, his more early assertion.

And how, it may be asked, did this particular case so powerfully aid him! The answer is this; on the dissolution of Parliament in 1784, he was at the

Hertford election, as an assessor to the returning officer, when Alderman Plomer, a warm and active adherent of Mr. Fox and his party, said to him, "Pray, Sir, shall you have any objection to be engaged for Mr. Fox at the approaching election for Westminster!" Garrow answered, that he should consider it a high honour. "Then, Sir," said the alderman, "you may consider this conversation as a retainer" To the natural inquiry, what had occasioned this favourable notice, the alderman answered, that he had read his argument in "The King and Aickles," which convinced him that the man who could produce that was equal to any task in his profession. He added, that as Mr. Phillips (a gentleman who had written a book on election law) had long been consulted by Mr. Fox's committee, and was retained by the present contest, he must, from his standing, be considered as the leading counsel; but the chief, or indeed only reliance would be on Mr. Garrow.

How worthy he was of this confidence, he evinced during a protracted and contentious poll of forty days. The high bailiff delayed the return and granted a scrutiny, which lasted two sessions of Parliament, when it was stopped by a vote of the House, and Mr. Fox obtained his seat. In this contest Mr. Garrow distinguished himself by great firmness, activity, and ingenuity. During this whole period, he was daily assailed with abuse and ridicule by two morning papers on the adverse side; among other topics, the easy pun which his name presented was not forgotten, the [words] "garrulous" and "garrulity" adorned the daily paragraphs. An ordinary or a doubtful talent would have shrunk before those attacks; the gangrene of contempt would have seized and destroyed it; but Garrow acquired only new strength, and flourished in increasing favour from the scurrility of his opponents. Among the most malignant of these was a certain Mr. Jackson, who is delineated by Sheridan under the name of Snake in the *School for Scandal*, and who, many years afterwards, fell down dead, self-poisoned, in the dock of a criminal court in Ireland, where he stood charged with high treason.

But it was not on the hustings, nor in the scrutiny-room alone, that Mr. Garrow obtained high renown from this extraordinary and important contest. An incident occurred, which may be related, not exactly perhaps in his own words, but strictly according to narration; "I was one evening at a consultation with Mr. Lee," (Honest Jack Lee, he used to be called, the Attorney-General of the Coalition Administration,) "and when the business under discussion was disposed of, Well, said he, what do you think of the conduct of our honourable house in the question of the Westminster election![?] I answered, that I thought the honourable house was acting in a most dishonourable manner. Well, said he, you must go to their bar to-morrow and tell them so. That, I said, is impossible; the business we have been consulting upon will then be on, and that will be sufficient to engage all my attention. I tell you, said he, you must go, and there is no avoiding it. No attorney waited on me, nor was any message sent; so I thought no more of the matter, but on the following morning, when I was in court at Old Bailey, I was told that a gentleman wished to speak with me; I went into the Lord Mayor's parlour (a room to which in those days counsel used to retire to consult, to refresh themselves, or to see their friends or clients) and there I found Mr. Fox. Oh, Mr. Garrow, he said, my petition is to be heard at 4 o'clock, and I shall depend on your assistance to support it. I said I could not do it; I had no time for preparation, nor any instructions. Instructions! pooh pooh! Said Mr. Fox, you know the business better than anybody; and if instructions were required, we should look to you to give, not to receive them. We shall expect you – I won't detain you from your other business - good morning - good morning! and so he bowed himself out of the room. I went to the house, and Mr. Douglas (Lord Glenbervie) was first heard on the petition. I made my speech, determined to suppress no portion of my opinion, unless compelled by authority."

Of this speech no trace or record remains. Unfortunately, and by some unaccountable means, the notes of the short-hand writer were lost or purloined, and no copy preserved; but of the effort of the speech a truly remarkable evidence may be given. Sir Lloyd Kenyon (then Master of the Rolls) had shown himself, during the election and after its close, a strenuous partisan of the interest opposed to Mr. Fox. When Mr. Garrow had concluded, he rushed to the bar, and seizing him by both hands, exclaimed - "Young man! I congratulate you! You have made your fortune, young man! I never heard a finer speech in all my life." Such was the high and honourable professional impulse of this great lawyer, which could control and surmount every political and party prejudice.

During this period, the reputation of Garrow became perfectly established, his emoluments vary considerable, and his assistance was sought for in every case in the criminal courts. At that time there was an established etiquette at the Old Bailey, that counsel of a certain standing, possessed of a certain portion of business, would not hold briefs, unless marked with a fee of a certain amount; and this not from arrogance or imputing any peculiar value on their own exertions, but out of generous consideration for the juniors - just as gentlemen in silk gowns at Westminster have always referred half-guinea motions and opening briefs. When first Garrow was called, he proposed to place himself in the higher rank, and to refuse minor fees; but Mr. Fielding, whose advice he sought, and whose example probably influenced him, repressed the inclination. "When I came to the bar" he said, "I adopted this rule, lest it should be supposed that I relied for business on such solicitors or clients as my uncle (Sir John Fielding) could recommend; but there is no reason why you should make yourself singular, or even conspicuous." The young advocate acquiesced; but such was the rapidity of his advance that in two or three sessions found himself not only entitled but called upon to follow the original impulse of his mind.

The Home Circuit, which was selected by Mr. Garrow, was soon deprived, by succession, of the brilliant talents of Erskine and Mingay; the leading business was then in the hands of Mr. (Sir Arthur) Piggott and Serjeant Bond, and with these and some others less known to fame he had to compete. In gaining, as he soon did, an ascendancy over them, his main struggle was with Mr. Piggott, and it was conducted, on both sides, with no small asperity. In time, an unfortunate dispute with a whole body of attornies induced Mr. Piggott to quit the circuit, and ultimately to practice entirely in the Court of Chancery and the Houses of Parliament. Far from regarding with unmanly exultation this triumph over so distinguished and honorable an opponent, Mr. Garrow, at an advanced period of his professional life, used to acknowledge that in many of these conflicts he found reason to blame himself; and he boasted that, among all his friends, he could not name one more warm and true, than Sir Arthur Piggett. As proof of the sincerity of this sentiment, when he became Attorney-General, and the course of business called on them to consult together, he always went to Sir Arthur's chambers; for he would not permit a person so eminent and honourable, so much his senior, to come to his chambers on a consultation.

In less than seven years, Mr. Garrow had the entire lead in the Crown courts, and a very superior portion of civil business. The time arrived, and the extent of his practice required that he should apply for rank; but still his native diffidence and distrust of himself made him doubtful. He consulted his friend, Mr. Mainwaring, the Chairman of the Middlesex sessions and member for the county, who had observed his progress with friendly interest; and having received from that worthy and honourable magistrate every encouragement, he waited on Lord Kenyon, then Chief Justice of the King's Bench. On his name being announced, his lordship came into the room, and anticipating his business, exclaimed, "So, Mr. Garrow, you want a silk gown, I suppose; I have been expecting your application these two years." A recommendation went immediately to the Lord Chancellor, and, without further solicitation or delay, he obtained that elevation which has been so often withheld or delayed, when applied for by gentlemen of much longer standing that himself, and of undisputed learning and ability.

In his subsequent life he was always eminent, and highly esteemed. On circuit he maintained the foremost rank, jointly with Sarjeants Shepherd and Best, and amidst competitors of the greatest talent and learning; and in Westminster and London he was always amply employed and highly favoured, although in constant comparison and competition with the greatest men of his day, such as Erskine, Mingay, Law, Gibbs, Park, Topping, Brougham, Scarlett, and Denman. He was successively, Solicitor and Attorney-General to His Royal Highness the Prince of Wales, and to the Crown, and was finally appointed a Baron of Exchequer.

As a judge, he displayed the great and useful qualities which had distinguished him at the bar. He neither possessed nor affected profound reading, or recondite research; but in all that experience and readiness of judgment, a prompt and accurate insight into the affairs and feelings of men could supply, he was pre-eminent. He could unravel a subtle statement, detect an artful evasion, or latent ambiguity, discern the difficulties of a case, and compel the advocate to surmount or succumb to them, with unfailing tact and effect. At length, after a service of fourteen years in this station, he retired to that leisure which his health required and to which he so was so well entitled by the labours of almost 50 years.

Of the estimation in which he was held as an advocate enough has already been said. His eloquence, formed at an period when that art was carried to an unequal height, both in Parliament and at the bar, partook of the characteristics of the time. It was fervid or persuasive, commanding awe or winning assent, as the occasion required. If it could not be deemed of the same quality as that of Erskine in his highest displays, it exhibited, in a merely approaching degree, the power of warming the feelings, fixing the attention, gaining the favour, and convincing the reason of those whom he addressed. If a difficulty was started, he could always afford a specious if not satisfactory solution, and possessed unrivalled readiness in availing himself of every intimation which fell from the bench, and turning it most advantageously to account. His speeches were often adorned with wit, and, if he was not equal in this particular to Erskine and Jekyll, still his flashes of merriment, his felicitous allusions, and his pointed sarcasms always produced great effect; and in that which is properly termed humour he had few equals. Above all, he could command an uninterrupted, continuous flow of choice, apt, and impressive words, so well chosen and skillfully combined as to defy any efforts of critical animadversion. Mr. Fox, indeed, expressed an opinion that Mr. Garrow would become a useful and an influential debater in Parliament; his estimate proved incorrect; experienced showed, that Mr. Garrow, like many other eminent lawyers, made a complete failure in the senate; the cause is not inscrutable, but not at present necessary for discussion.

But the faculty for which, above all others, Mr. Garrow was celebrated and admired, was the examination of witnesses. In that he had neither model, rival, nor successor. To the casual or superficial observer, cross-examination presents the greatest and most frequent topic of admiration; but they who understand the arcana of the profession know that examinations in chief requires much greater skill, ability, and circumspection, especially when the advocate is watched by such judges as Lord Kenyon and Lord Ellenborough, from whose experience and penetration nothing could escape, and encountered by such opponents as Gibbs and Scarlett, who were sure to detect and arrest the slightest deviation from those strict rules which justice has established for the protection of right and the advancement of truth. With consummate ability and address, Garrow could simplify an entangled or difficult statement into a series of direct, intelligible, apt, and perspicuous questions; and without trespassing on forbidden ground, by leading his witness, would extract the facts he wanted to prove by indicating them in a manner which afforded to his opponents no ground of objection. His re-examination never failed to strip from the evidence all the collateral circumstances which might tend to perplex and mislead the jury, leaving most prominently before them the true and real points, and nothing else. In cross-examination severity and sternness were sometimes necessary, and in them he was not deficient; but his greatness was shown in suggesting facts, in a manner which would entangle a dishonest witness, or put one whose conscience was a little more tender in such good humour with himself, that he let escape the truth he had been desirous to conceal.

With all the zeal which he was ever ready to display in causes confided to him, with all the desire of wealth and honour which could inflame a youthful mind, Garrow was never ready to undertake a case which would oblige him to profess, in a public manner, opinions which were repugnant to his principles. Thus, at an early period of his life, when the question concerning the manner in which Negroes were obtained, and conveyed from Africa to the West Indies, was in agitation, he had formed a most decided judgment on the facts and on the traffic. One day Mr. Fuller (Jack Fuller, of rose-hill, as he called himself), a great West India Proprietor, meeting him in the street, said, "Well, Mr. Garrow, here is plenty of business, and plenty of money for you; the committee have determined to retain you, an give you the management of all their business in Parliament and elsewhere." He answered, "Sir, if your committee would give me their whole incomes, and all their estates, I would not be seen as the advocate of practices which I abhor, and a system which I detest."

At a much later period, when the Committee of the Stock Exchange determined on the prosecution of Lord Cochrane and some other persons for a conspiracy, a retainer was offered to Sir William Garrow; but as the noble defendant was strenuously opposed to the Government in which he was Attorney-General, he apprehended that any earnestness which he might display would possible be attributed to a political feeling, and declined to act. The prosecutors selected Mr. Gurney as his substitute; and it is a memorable fact, that his skill, judgment, and eloquence, left them nothing to regret in their choice. He obtained a verdict against all the parties, although they were defended by the combined talents (naming them according to the order in which they appear in the printed report of the trial), of Mr. Park, Mr. Richardson, Mr. Serjeant Best, Mr. Scarlett, Mr. Topping, Mr. Brougham, Mr. Serjeant Pell, Mr. D.F. Williams, Mr. Denman, and Mr. Alley.

In this effort Mr. Gurney was cheered and supported by the warm good wishes of his firm friend, Sir William Garrow; and it was with no small satisfaction, when retiring from the Court of Exchequer, that he saw his seat on the bench occupied by the same highly-valued individual.

If the friendships of Garrow were not indiscriminate or even numerous, they were strong and sincere. Besides Sir Arthur Piggott and Mr. Baron Gurney already named, he maintained with Sir Vicary Gibbs an intercourse of brotherly regard, which rivalship in their arduous profession could never interrupt or abate. To these may be added Mr. Sarjeant Shepherd, Sir William Adam, Sir John Leach, Mr. Baron Bollard, Mr. Nolan, and several other eminent men, besides many less distinguished, who were largely indebted to him for patronage, countenance, and support. Indeed, it was his characteristic never to thwart or interrupt the progress of any promising junior, unless, in a presumptuous manner, he showed an inclination to overwhelm or degrade him.

A career like that of this great and successful advocate could not be passed without some enmities. The knaves whom he detected, the fools whom he exposed, would not fail to scream, to hoot, and to clamour in return; but it is worthy of observation that busy malice could never impute to him a disgraceful or dishonourable act. The host of daily libelers, and their leader, Mr. Jackson, have already been mentioned; there was besides, an unhappy crack-brained foreigner, Baron Hompesch; and pamphlets against him were written by an angry apothecary, named Russell John (commonly called Jew) King, and Mr. (usually styled Tom) Hague. Of these three the first was hardly an accountable agent, and the other two were they stamped their names on the coinage of their brains, pronounced, most authentically, it utter worthlessness.

It is not intended to enter into the private affairs of this distinguished man; to detail how he educated and endowed his children; to state what property he possessed at his death; how it happened that he was so rich, or why he was not more wealthy. It may suffice to say, that he never increased his store by an unjust, a harsh, or an oppressive act - he prevented the diminution of his means by any act which denoted meanness, penuriousness, or want of humanity and benevolence.

This sketch may serve as an encouragement to those who, inspired by genius, and gifted with talent, would desire to tread the honourable path of the legal profession, and aspire to the attainment of its dignities, but it should also administer a wholesome caution to avoid mistaking the impulse of self-love, or the promptings of fancy for the dictates of true genius - that distinguishing quality which unites the confidence necessary in all lofty undertakings, the indefatigable industry which results from a feeling that all which has already been performed may be excelled - which resists alike the pressure of lauditude, the blandishment of pleasure, the allurement of indolence and the enervating suggestions of mollified vanity.

Law Review (1844-5)

ART. IV. – MR. BARON GARROW
(Attributed to Brougham)

Neminem ex iis quidem qui in aliquo numero (jurisconsultorum) fuerunt cognovi, in omni genere homestarum atrium tam indoctum, tam rudem. Nullum ille poetam noverat; nullum legerat oratorem; nullam memoriam antiquitatis collegerat; non publiecum jus, non privatum et eivile cognoverat. - Cicero, Brut. 59.

Mr. Garrow was, in a certain line of the legal profession, without an equal, certainly - in a portion of that line, without a rival. He had early in life devoted himself to the practice of the criminal law, and he arrived in a short time at considerable eminence. By attending almost exclusively to this branch of business, and exercising upon it his great powers of steady attention, extraordinary quickness in apprehension, and a singular circumspection, he soon reached the lead of the Old Bailey practice, and domineered without a competitor at the bar, and with little control from the bench. He had the good fortune to acquire the friendship of the late learned Mr. Shelton, then clerk of the arraigns in that court, and perhaps the most accomplished criminal lawyer of his day. This gentleman, it was well known, freely unfolded to him his vast stores of knowledge, and where any complicated case arose, filled his mind both with principles and authorities. Such was the great experience of Mr. Shelton, and such the confidence reposed in him by the judges, that his opinion was solicited even by the most learned of their body in cases of much difficulty.

In consequence of some opening upon the Home Circuit, which Mr. Garrow travelled, and which is easily combined with the Old Bailey, (then only held eight times a year, but now twelve times, ever since the establishment of the great Central Court,) he gradually became a candidate for civil business, and attended regularly in Westminster Hall. His success here was far more rapid than any one expected the *"Old Bailey Solicitor"* could attain. His talents were found to be perfectly well suited to the Nisi Prius business in general, and he before long had so large a share of it, that, having given up the Old Bailey some time before, he was soon raised to the rank of King's Counsel.

There have probably been few more ignorant men in the profession than this celebrated leader. To law, or anything like law, he made no pretence. What little he could have known was rather mechanical than scientific. He began as Assessor at the great Bedford County election in 1784, under the patronage of the Whigs, to whose party he appertained, without probably knowing very distinctly the meaning of the term, and with certainly no notion of the division in principle which distinguished the Whig from the Tory. The knowledge of a few statutory provisions being all that an assessor has to regard, he could go through the routine of that election safely enough, if not very respectably. Then the little criminal law required at the Old Bailey he could pick up by a few months attendance there, and for any out-of-the-way point, he must trust to the suggestion, or rather the prompting of the moment from his junior or his client.

The practice of evidence, that is, of examination of witnesses, he soon acquired, without rule or the notion of principle, by use and observation, till he knew by sure and unerring instinct what questions might and what might not be put; and when a rare matter presented itself, he must here again be primed or prompted for the nonce. Then with so slender a provision of law, his ignorance of all beside, of all that constitutes science, or learning, or indeed general information, nay even ordinary information, was perfect; and yet one important branch of knowledge had became familiar to him - his intercourse with prisoners, with juries, above all with witnesses, had given him extensive knowledge of human nature – though not certainly in its higher, more refined, or even more respectable forms.

With all these great deficiencies, with this confessedly slender stock in trade, Mr. Garrow was a great, a very great advocate. To describe him as merely quick, clear-seeing, wary, prompt, nimble, bold, in every sense of the large word, skilful, would be too general, though it would be quite correct if each of these phrases were extended to the superlative degree. But more is wanting to pourtray distinctly his extraordinary merits. The giddy and superficial vulgar - meaning by this the vulgar of the legal order – would admire without stint his cross-examination. It was, no doubt of the matter, very brilliant; in every sense, striking. He seemed every now and then to destroy, almost to annihilate, an adverse witness; and often he would, without effort and unperceived, be winding about him, throwing a net around, gradually contracting it into a noose, or drawing after him or towards him the witness, his appointed but unconscious prey, all else already seeing the fate that awaited him, and then would on a sudden pounce forth upon him, and tear him to pieces. But, generally speaking, his cross-examination had this great defect, that he trusted to attacking the witness hostilely, and made war upon him far too soon. Now, be a counsel ever so expert, there is one limit necessarily appointed to the success of such a hostile operation. If the witness is calm, or confident, or well trained, above all, if, without being honest, he is cool and self-possessed, he may bid defiance to any cross-examination. But in most cases a great deal may be obtained by gentle treatment - by calmly throwing him off his guard – by kindly treating him - by presenting things to his mind without the warning which a hostile attack always gives an acute witness; and of this Mr. Garrow far too seldom availed himself. Men said his Old Bailey practice, by making him familiar with the lower and more tutored kind of witnesses, had spoilt him in other particulars. It is more likely that he could not resist the temptation of making a great impression on the jury and on the bystanders. Those bystanders - and the professionals, we again must observe, are not to be excepted from the number - never failed to commit the mistake of supposing a loud and angry examination to be a successful one; and they constantly supposed that the credit of a witness had been demolished when his person had only been scolded.

And here as to the uses of cross-examination, we may make an extract from Mr. Butler's "Reminiscences."[2] "Cross-examination," says that gentleman, "is sometimes abused, but it is certainly the surest method of eliciting truth that has been devised. When the affair of the necklace of the late Queen of France was in agitation, a person observed to Lord Thurlow that the repeated examinations of the parties in France had cleared up nothing. 'True,' said his Lordship, 'but Buller, Garrow, and a Middlesex jury would, if such a matter had been brought before them, have made it all in half an hour as clear as day-light.'"

But Mr. Garrow's real forte was in truth his examination in chief, which was unri-valled, and which is, indeed, a far more important and not a less difficult attribute

---

2. vol.ii. p. 50.

than the cross-examination which so captivates the ignorant. It requires the most perfect knowledge of the facts, and the most skilful leading of the witness through them, so as to make him tell the story clearly, connectedly, and strikingly, and to avoid the parts of the case, which, being tender, it would be perilous to let him come too near. But it also demands the most vigilant attention to every word, tone, look, gesture of the witness, because from this close and wakeful survey it will frequently appear how far the instructions may be relied on, how far the same things are likely to be told upon oath and in public, which were before related by the witness privately and unsworn to the client. No description can give the reader an adequate idea of this eminent practitioner's powers in thus dealing with his witnesses. They who had lying before them the instructions on which his examination proceeded, saw a case brought out which they scarcely seemed to have read before. How different the mechanical examinations of ordinary barristers, yawning over their briefs, pursuing the order of the written statement line by line, and only turning into a question, not seldom a leading or irregular question, the short sentences which the attorney has given as what *"this witness will say!"* Then, when the fire of cross-examination had shaken the credit of the evidence, how admirable did the great tactician, in re-examination, restore, comfort, set it up! These were things which the *connoisseur's* understanding could relish; they were to the vulgar audience as "a stumbling block, or perhaps foolishness."

It may easily be supposed that his statement, his narrative, was of a high order. No man more clearly, more continuously presented a picture of his case to those he was addressing. His language was plain, but it was well strung together. He reasoned little, he jested less; he not rarely declaimed, and he had sufficient force to produce his effect. He was worst when he tried to tell some long story of his feelings for his learned friend on the other side, or when he ventured to indulge in the pathetic. But his voice was powerful, and it was pleasing when raised; his action was good and moderate; his countenance, though not very refined, was expressive enough when he was roused; his whole manner was successful. His discretion, his perfect judgment and entire self-command, exceeded that of most men. Among the other singular anecdotes of his professional life we used to be told, that going on a special retainer to defend a gentleman charged with a capital offence (it was murder indeed), he sat in court during the whole trial, and of course watched each word, look, and gesture of each witness, as well as of the prosecuting counsel, and the judge, and the jury, with the eyes of an eagle, and never once uttered a word from the beginning to the end of the proceeding.

Mr. Garrow's ignorance of law, except the most ordinary matters which are of hourly occurrence at Nise Prius, has been often mentioned with astonishment. But the real wonder was this, that he could suddenly take up a point from his learned coadjutors, and state his objection or answer his antagonists, as clearly, tersely, and accurately as the best special pleader or mercantile lawyer of the day. You generally found him quite to seek, if the same point arose a few weeks, possible days, after. It seemed as if he had no niches in which to store, no pegs on which to hang the shreds and scraps of law which he was constantly obtaining, as the pressure of the moment made him turn around to his junior, and stoop down to pick them up. Indeed, it was perhaps better that he should not keep them at all; had he retained them, having no means of understanding and arranging them, a kind of patchwork would have been formed of no use for any future emergency, and the poor *chiffonnier*[3] must have again exercised his humble trade as before.

He was sufficiently aware of his own deficiencies to shun the occasions which might display them. Accordingly, he avoided, when in high office, appearing to argue legal questions before the House of Lords; and on one occasion Lord Eldon, then presiding there, had the cruelty to insist upon his attendance, when some peerage question was in the House. Being told that Mr. Attorney was engaged in the Court of King's Bench, he asked "if it was in a horse case," and if he could not leave it to attend his duties in that House. The case was postponed to let him come another day.[4] He had gotten an argument prepared for him, which he read word for word at the bar; and, unable to give the citations which were made by Mr. Nolan (the writer of the paper) in the most abbreviated form, he read them as written, to the great amusement of the malicious Chancellor, who did not soon forget the legal authorities he had that day been introduced to, such as *one Lev.* and *Cro. Jac.* Nor did Lord Eldon confine his jocularity on this subject to the House of Lords. "Two days afterwards, (says Sir Samuel Romilly, in his Diary,) in the Court of Chancery, on a question whether a manager of a theatre could discharge the duties of his office without personal attendance, I, who had to argue that he could not, said that it would be as difficult as for a counsel to do his duty in that court by writing arguments and sending them to some person to read for him. The Lord Chancellor interrupted me by saying, 'In this court, or in any other?' and, after the court rose, he said to me, 'You know, I suppose, what I alluded to? It was Garrow's written argument in the House of Lords.' So little respect has his Lordship for an Attorney-General whom he himself appointed because he was agreeable to the Prince." It must, indeed, be confessed that all others had better right to laugh on this occasion than Lord Eldon. He it was who had promoted to the head of the profession a person plainly ignorant of its most common and best-known learning, and he had placed him in a position which gave him an irresistible claim to a seat on the Bench wholly incompetent to fill it. It was Lord Eldon's duty, however, to resist that claim, and prefer offending Sir William Garrow to outraging justice by

---

3. The rag-gatherer in Paris, who rakes among the dust for his small fragments of cloth, or silk, or trinkets.
4. The question arose on a claim to the earldom of Airlie; and the point to be decided was whether a Scottish entailed title of honour was forfeited by its devolving on an attainted person, subsequent to his attainder; or whether it was merely suspended during his life, and, on his death, came to the next heir of entail. The same question was again raised and argued before the House of Lords in 1831 on the Lovat Peerage, and has never yet been decided.

so unfit an appointment. We were accordingly fated to hear the unlearned Baron, in an Equity suit, commend Lord Eldon as the parent of the doctrine of Trusts in Equity. When told of this numerous progeny so unexpectedly put upon him, as it were dropt at his door, his Lordship thought it quite sufficient to join heartily in the laugh, as he had formerly done upon the presentation to him of *Cro. Jac.*

His ignorance was, as we have already said, not confined to his own profession; he seemed as a man without education, probably because he had not been educated; he seemed as a man who never read, probably because books formed no portion of his reading. He now and then saw a play, or went to church; and he heard the Erskines, the Laws, the Dallas', the Gibbs' expatiate on various points of learning. From thence he might pick up a few phrases and fewer ideas; but he was most cautious in their application, for fear of awkward mishaps; he was far from adventurous out of his own line, within which his boldness was as remarkable as his prudence was consummate; he hardly ever soared from the ground he loved, dreading a quick fall. Instances are recorded, no doubt, of his yielding to the temptation of visiting higher regions; as when he would discourse on the connection between the mind and the body, on some will-clause which raised the question of sanity. The topic was not judiciously chosen, for it was among the more obscure and indeed inscrutable points of metaphysical science. Nor will future inquirers derive much aid from his effort, in promoting these psychological researches. "You see, Gentlemen, the mind and the body have a close, an intimate, I may say, an inseparable connection. Gentlemen, they chum together." Probably he speedily perceived some hint in the judge's face - as when he asked Mr. Gaselee, indulging in a similar barn-door flight - if "we weren't getting into the high sentimental latitudes?" - for the metaphysician came quickly down to the matter before him, and went on with his luminous and plain statement of the case he should prove by witnesses - there being none, we should imagine, to the point of the commorancy and joint occupancy of the two tenants above mentioned.

On the Bench, and especially in the Criminal Court, where he found himself at home, he occasionally ventured on these very perilous oratorical experiments. A flight of his on the Oxford circuit, when passing sentence of death on an unhappy sheep-stealer, will not be soon forgotten. At Stafford, after expatiating at great length and with much solemnity on the heinousness of the offence, he assured the offender that all hope of mitigation was illusory. "I have however (added he), on precious conclusion – this is not the final trial which awaits you – you will ere long appear before another and all-merciful Judge, who will hear with patience all you have to say, and *should he feel a doubt, will give it in your favour.*" It is, perhaps, right to add, that he afterwards recommended a mitigation of the sentence, as indeed was his custom where he felt at liberty to indulge the natural humanity of his disposition. It was, however, by no means unusual with him, perhaps by way of admonition to the by-standers, to excite apprehension which he never intended to realize.

The success of so consummate an advocate, when he had once made up his mind to quit the Old Bailey and dwell in Westminster Hall, was rapid, and though he never was popular with his contemporaries, like Erskine, the darling as the pride of the gown, yet did they not at all grudge his progress, so plainly were his extraordinary merits perceived, and so willingly admitted. It may be questioned if either Erskine or Gibbs ever had such hold as Garrow of the common business of the Court. It is certain that he retained it far longer than either of them; for he must have been nearly thirty years in the lead both at Westminster and Guildhall, and his business, like Mr. Scarlett's, abode by him to the last. Those who have witnessed it cannot easily forget the struggles between him and Gibbs, after he had fairly driven out of the field, Mingay, an artist of a very inferior description. He was often, indeed, on ordinary cases, an overmatch for Erskine himself; but Erskine could afford to sustain this defeat, or this overreaching, and his temper was sweet as his nature was noble. Not such the temper of Sir Vicary. When Garrow would "run around him," get verdicts from him, beat down his damages by course clamour, or horse-laughing, even make points against him, or take them from him (*filch* them, as he was wont to phrase it); the bystander saw such bitterness manifested in the defeated face, that he could not have wondered as seeing him cry from mere vexation. The business, however, especially at Guildhall, was admirably managed by these three great leaders, to whom Mr. Park and Mr. Topping may be added. They conducted it, too, so as to greatly save the public time. They would confer previously, or as the cause was trying. Abandoning on either side and at once, the untenable points, they would bring the others at once forward, so as to obtain the opinion of the judge on the law, or of the jury on the fact, and a new cause was called. It was thus, and it was in such times as these when leaders were strong and briefs were concentrated in a few hands, that Lord Ellenbouough was enabled to meet a cause list of six hundred at one sitting, Lord Mansfield having complained of his entry once reaching sixty. But of this dispatch much also depended on the presiding and animating vigour of the judge. After being away, towards the end of his life, for a few weeks, and having his place supplied by a puisne judge, Lord Ellenborough came back and disposed of eighteen defended causes in a day. We are, however, very far from holding up such examples as worthy of all imitation. Causes were more fully if not so brilliantly tried before Lord Tenterden, especially during his last seven or eight years. In his great predecessor's time the saying was, in describing the two sides of the Hall, or rather the passage which then led into it, and on one side of which Lord Ellenborough judged, while on the other Lord Eldon sat - that the one was the Court of *oyer sans terminer,* and the other of *termjiner sans oyer.*

The placing of Sir W. Garrow upon the Bench has been adverted to. He was far, indeed, from a brilliant judge, except at Nisi Prius, and there not clearly a very good one. Perhaps he was seen to most advantage when presiding in the Criminal Court, with the routine of which he had been so long familiar. Even at Nisi Prius there was a perpetual *fidgetiness* observable, arising, no doubt, from a consciousness that some legal point might at any moment occur, calling for a decision to which he felt himself inadequate. But no such apprehension disturbed his self-complacency when he had the dock before him. After the counsel on both sides had exhausted their questions, it was his custom to luxuriate in an examination of his own, and here he often evinced his perfection in the art of which he was an admitted master. Nor did he shrink at times from, as it seemed, lowering his dignity, by the most lavish display of that peculiar knowledge which can only be acquired at the school in which he had studied. There was no mystery in the profession of the *"appropriators,"* in which he was not an adept. There was no term of art in the vocabulary of crime with which he was not familiar. At times the effect produced by him was most amusing. None who were present will forget the impression thus made upon an unhappy coiner, tried before him on the Oxford circuit. This man conducted his own defence, and did so with much skill and more effrontery. The judge seemed quite absorbed in admiration of the prisoner's ingenuity, and contrived to fill him with the delusion that he was so - a delusion from which there was soon to be a fearful waking. "My Lord," he vociferated, "there were only two bad half-crowns found upon me. If I was making a trade of it, it stands to reason I'd have had more;" and he looked up to the bench quite confident of its sympathy. Garrow's white eyes glared upon the culprit, and in a tone which assured him all their secrets were in common, playfully replied, "Perhaps, sir, the WALLOP was exhausted." The word, and the tone of its enuncia-tion, at once unnerved the prisoner - he felt he had before him a professor of his craft, whom it was quite useless to attempt to mystify, and he resigned himself to his fate. "Gentlemen, (said Garrow blandly to the jury, who shared in the ignorance of all around them,) a WALLOP is a term of free-masonry amongst coiners. It means the hidden heap of counterfeits to which they resort for a supply when the exigen-cies of the profession may require one." The Court of Exchequer, then composed of Chief Baron Richards, and Barons Graham, Wood and Garrow, used to be thus rather more wittily than correctly described, as consisting of one who was a lawyer and no gentleman; another a gentleman and no lawyer; a third, both the one and the other; and fourth neither. The truth of the description is here sacrificed, as usual, to the point of the epigram.

In Parliament, it needs scarce be observed, this very celebrated advocate had little or no success. Indeed he cordially hated the place, and was with difficulty induced to enter it, or having entered, to address it. Speak, however, he did, and he began to say that he had made, on entering Parliament, a covenant with himself not to speak, against which he was now compelled to act. His speech was a very bad one, and Mr. Windham, inheriting from Mr. Burke his dislike of lawyers, began his comment on this expression, as in a declaration; he "complained of covenants broken." "Many parties," he observed, "had a right to complain of the breach which had been committed - the House - the subject - himself - but the party most entitled to complain," he added, "was the *covenantee,* he with whom the covenant had been made." Unlike the epigrammatgic description which had been quoted above, the truth of this remark was fully as manifest as the wit.

In private life Mr. Garrow was not only blameless, but in every way to be commended. In all its relations he was unimpeachable; and beside the kindly nature of his social intercourse, he was to be admired for extraordinary generosity to all that wanted his aid. He gave and he lent large sums of his hard-earned gains to assist those who were in embarrassment or in distress. It is singular, that, probably from never having frequented good society, or, indeed, almost any society at all, he was in private one of the most shy and bashful of men, though very, very far otherwise in public.

Select bibliography

Primary sources

Black Books of the Honourable Society of Lincoln's Inn. vol. iv.

Blackstone, Sir W. (1830) *Commentaries on the Law of England*. vol. vi. London, ThomasTegg.

Bonner, A.W. (1831) *The Picturesque Pocket Companion to Margate, Ramsgate & Broadstairs with Places Adjacent.*

Bridgman, R.W. (1804) *Reflections on the Study of the Law*. London, Brooke & Clarke.

Brougham, H. (1836) *Review of a Popular and Practical Introduction to Law Studies* by Samuel Warren. Edinburgh, 64 *Edinburgh Review*. Longman, Ross & Others.
(1838) *Speeches*. Edinburgh.
(1844-5) "Mr. Baron Garrow". *The Law Review and Quarterly Journal of the British and Foreign Jurisprudence*. vol.i.

Campbell, Lord John. (1847) *Lives of the Lord Chancellors*. London, John Murray.

Convention for the Protection of Human Rights and Fundamental Freedoms. (1950) (www.hri.org/docsECHR50. html).

"Crim. Con!! Damages Fifteen Thousand Pounds, Trial between Lord Roseberry and Sir Henry Mildmay for Criminal Coversation with the Plaintiff's Wife. " (1814) London, John Fairburn.

Crook, J.M. (1992) "Metropolitan Improvements: John Nash and the Picturesque". *London – World City 1800-1840*. New Haven, Yale University Press.

Euer, Sampson. (1677) *Doctrina Placitandi: Ou L'Art & Science De Bon Pleading*. (2 vols) London, R. & E. Atkins.

Farington, Joseph. *Diary*. (1796). New Haven, Yale University Press.

Forsyth, W. (1849) *Hortensius: The Advocate*. London.

Fairburn, John (1814) *Trial Between Lord Rosebery and Sir Henry Mildmay for Criminal Conversation with the Plaintiff's Wife*. London.

Garrow, D.W. (1818) *The History and Antiquities of Croydon*. Croydon, W. Annan.
1820) *Sermons Comprising Various Matters of Doctrine and Practice*.London, F.C. & J. Rivington.

Gronow, R.H. (1862) *The Reminiscences and Recollections of Captain Gronow, at the Close of the Last War with France*, London, Smith Elder.

Hague, T. (1812?) *A Letter to William Garrow, Esquire, in which the Conduct of Counsel (especially W. Garrow) in the cross-examination of Witnesses, and commenting on their testimonay, is fully discussed and the licentiousness of the bar exposed*. London, J. Parsons.

Hardcastle, M.S. (1881) *Life of John, Lord Campbell*. London, John Murray.

Hawles, Sir John. (1689) *A Reply to a Sheet of Paper, entitled, The Magistry and Government of England Vindicated.* London.

Letter. (1818*)* *To Sir William Garrow from Jasmes Hamilton, M.D. Fellow of the Royal College of Physicians of Edinburgh and Professor in Midwifery in the University of Edinburgh.* 2nd edn. London.

Letter. (1840) William Arthur Dorehill to Lord Downshire.

Locke, John. (1689) *The Letter for Toleration.* London.
(1690) *Two Treatises of Government.* London, Awnsham Churchill.

Noel, Amelia. (1797) *Twenty-four Picturesque Views.* London, 189 Piccadilly.

Old Bailey Proceedings. (www.oldbaileyonline.org)

*Parliamentary Debates. (*1794), (1809), (1810)

Percy, R. (1868) *The Percy Anecdotes.* vol. i. Anecdotes of the Bar. *Learned Apothecary.* London, Fredrick Warne & Co.

Phillips, Arabella. (1830). *Last Will and Testament.* London, Public Record Office.

Public Characters. 4th edn. (1799-1809) (10 vols.) London.

Richardson, C.T. (1885) "Memoranda of the Cliffs". *Fragments of History.*

Romilly, Sir S. (1840) *Memoirs of the Life of Samuel Romilly, Written by Himself.* London, John Murray.

State Trials. (1816), (1822) London, Thomas Howell.

Trollope, Frances Milton. (1832) *Domestic Manners of the Americans.* New York, Whittacker, Treacher & Co.

Trollope, Theodosia. (1861) *Social Aspects of the Italian Revolution, in a Series of Letters from Florence.* London, Chapman & Hall.

Wilson, J. *A Biographical Index to the Present House of Commons to April, 1807.*

Year Books. 30 and 31, Edw. I (Rolls Series).

Journals and newspapers

Atlantic Monthly (1864)

East European Constitutional Review (2002)

History Today (1991)

Journal of Legal History (2005)

Law and History Review (1991), (1993)

Law Magazine (1812)

Law Quarterly Review (1899)

London Review of Books (2003)

*Modern Law Review (*2003)

Norfolk Chronicle (1830), (1831)

Ohio State Law Journal (1983)

Parliamentary Debates [6] (1806), [7] (1806), [24] (1813), [25] (1813), [27] (1814)

The Gentleman's Magazine and Historical Chronicle (1805)

Time Magazine (1966)

The Times (1786), (1789), (1790), (1800). (1840)

The Times Literary Supplement (1920)

UCLA Pacific Basin Law Journal (2000)

Wayne Law Review (1990)

Windsor & Eton Express (1827)

Books and articles

Abraham, J.J. (1933) *Lettsom, His Life, Times, Friends and Descendants.* London, William, Heinemann Medical Books Ltd.

Aspinall, A. (1963 edn) *The Correspondence of George, Prince of Wales: 1770-1812.* London, Cassell.

Baker, Sir John. (2007) *Legal Education in London 1250-1850.* London, Selden Society.

Baldwin, O. & Wilson, T. (2004) "Tom Trollops's Mother-in-Law". *Trollopiana.* Journal of the Trollop Society.

Barker, G.F.R. (1975) *Dictionary of National Biography.* Oxford, Oxford University Press.

Beattie, J.M. (1986) *Crime and Courts in England 1660-1800.* Oxford, Clarendon Press.
    (1991) "Garrow for the Defence". *History Today.* History Today Ltd.
    (1991) "Scales of Justice: Defence Counsel and the English Criminal Trial in the Eigtheenth and Nineteenth Centuries". 9(2) *Law and History Review.* University of Illinois Press.
    (2007) "Garrow and the Detectives: Lawyers and Policemen at the Old Bailey in the Late Eighteenth Century." 11(2) *Crime, History and Societies.* Geneva, Switzerland.

Cairns, D.J.A. (1998) *Advocacy and the Making of the Adversary Criminal Trial 1800-1865.* Oxford, The Clarendon Press.

Cass, F.C. (1880) *The Parish of Monken Hadley.* Westminster, Nichols & Sons.
    (1882) *The Parish of East Barnet.* Westminster, Nichols & Sons.

Churchill, Winston. (1957) *A History of the English-Speaking Peoples.* vol. iii. London, Cassell & Co.

Cornish, W.R. (1968) *The Jury*. London, Allen Lane. The Penguin Press.

Cox, M.H. & Norman, P. (1926) *Survey of London*, vol. x. *The Parish of St.Margaret, Westminster – part I*. London, B.T. Batsford, Ltd.

Cranston, M. (1962) *Human Rights Today*. London, Ampersand Books.

Dalton, Jan. *Unpublished Correspondence*.

Dictionary of National Biography

Dwyer, D. (2003) Review of Langbein's *The Origins of Adversary Criminal Trial*. 66 *Modern Law Review*. Oxford, Blackwell Publishing.

Ferguson, W. (1968) *Scotland 1689 to the Present*. Edinburgh, Oliver & Boyd.

Ferri, Enrico. (1884) *Criminal Sociology*. London, T.F. Fisher Unwin.

Fisher, G. (1997) "The Jury's Rise as Lie Detector". New Haven, 107 *Yale Law Journal*.

Foss, E. (1864) *The Judges of England; with Sketches of their Lives and Miscellaneous Notices Connected with the Courts at Westminster from the Time of the Conquest*. (vol.9) London, John Murray.

Garafalo, R. (1885) *Criminology*. Montclair, Patterson Smith.

Green, J.R. (1874) *A Short History of the English People*. London, The Folio Society.

Handler, P. (2005) Review of May's *The Bar and the Old Bailey 1750-1850*. London, 26 *The Journal of Legal History*.

Hobsbawm, E.J. (1962) *The Age of Revolution: Europe 1789-1848*. London, Weidenfeld & Nicolson.

Holdsworth, Sir William. (1966) *A History of English Law*. (vol. v) London, Methuen & Co. and Sweet & Maxwell.

Hostettler, John. (1992) *The Politics of Criminal Law: Reform in the Nineteenth Century*. Chichester, Barry Rose Law Publishers.
  (1993) *Thomas Wakley: An Improbable Radical*. Chichester, Barry Rose Law Publishers.
  (1996) *Thomas Erskine and Trial by Jury*. Chichester, Barry Rose Law Publishers.
  (2004) *The Criminal Jury Old and New: Jury Power from Early Times to the Present Day*. Winchester, Waterside Press.
  (2006) *Fighting for Justice: The History and Origins of Adversary Trial*. Winchester, Waterside Press.

King, Peter. (2000) *Crime, Justice, and Discretion in England, 1740-1820*. Oxford, Oxford, University Press.

Landsman, S. (1983) "A Brief Survey of the Development of the Adversary System. 44(1) *Ohio State Law Journal*.
  (1990) "The Rise of the Contentious Spirit: Adversary Procedure in Eighteenth Century England." New York, 75 *Cornell Law Review*.
  (1990) "From Gilbert to Bentham: The Reconceptualization of Evidence Theory". 36 *Wayne Law Review*. Univeristy of Oregon School of Law.

Langbein, John H (1983) "Shaping the Eighteenth Century Criminal Trial: A View from the Ryder Sources." Chicago, University of Chicago Law Review.
  (2003) *The Origins of Adversary Criminal Trial*. Oxford, Oxford University Press.

Lemmings, David. (2002) *Professors of the Law: Barristers and English Legal Culture in the Eighteenth Century.* Oxford, Oxford University Press.

Longford, E. (1972) *Wellington, The Years of the Sword.* London, Weidenfeld & Nicolson.

Mander, N.(1998) *Varnished Leaves: A Biography of the Mander Family of Wolverhampton.*

May, Allyson. (2003) *The Bar and the Old Bailey, 1750-1850.* Chapel Hill, The University of North Carolina Press.

Meyer, L. (1993) *Masters of English Landscape.* Paris, Pierre Terrail.

Milsom, S.C.F. (1981) *Historical Foundations of the Common Law.* London, Butterworths.

Neville-Sington, P. (1997) *Fanny Trollope, The Life and Adventures of a Clever Woman.* New York, Viking.

Parkes, W.T. *Musical Memories. An Account of the General State of Music in England 1784-1830.*

Pilkington, E.C. (1995) *A History of the Elwin Family in Australia.* (Unpublished)

Radzinowicz, Sir L. (1948) *A History of English Criminal Law and its Administration from 1750: The Movement for Reform.* vol. i. London, Stevens & Sons Ltd.

Remnant, J.D. *The Garrow Family.* (Unpublished)

Rogers, S. (1899) "The Etihics of Advocacy". 15 *Law Quarterly Review.* London, Stevens & Sons Limited.

Shapiro, A.H. (1993) "Political Theory and the Growth of Defensive Safeguards in Criminal Procedure: The Origin of the Tresaon Trials Act of 1696". Illinois, 11(2) *Law and History Review.* American Society of Legal History.

Simmons, J.C. (2000) *Star-Spangled Eden.* New York, James C. Simmons.

Solomon, P.H. (2002) "Putin's Judicial Reform: Making Judges Accountable As Well As Independent." 11 (1-2) *East European Constituional Review.*

Steiner & Alston. (1996) *International Human Rights in Context: Law, Politics, Morals.* Oxford, The Clarendon Press.

Stephen, James Fitzjames. (1883) *A History of the Criminal Law of England.* London, Routledge/Thoemess.

Stephenson, M.C. (2000) "A Trojan Horse Behind Chinese Walls? Problems and Prospects of US-Sponsored 'Rule of Law' Reform Projects in the People's Republic of China". 18 *UCLA Pacific Basin Law Journal.*

Stevenson, R.L. (1993 edn) *Kidnapped.* Ware, Hertfordshire. Wordsworth Editions Ltd. & Mrs Stevenson. (1922) "The Hanging Judge" in *Deacon Brodie or the Double Life and Other Plays.* New York, Charles Scribner's Sons.

Stewart, R. (1986) *Henry Brougham 1778-1868: His Public Career.* London, The Bodley Head.

Thorne, R.G. (1986) *The History of Parliament: The House of Commons 1790-1820.* London, Secker & Warburg.

Venn, J.A. (1940-54) "Garrow, Joseph", *Alumni Cantabrigiensis, Part 2.*

Vogler, Richard. (2005) *A World View of Criminal Justice.* Aldershot, Ashgate Publishing Company.

Werkmeister, L. (1967) *A Newspaper History of England 1792-1793*. Lincoln, University of Nebraska Press.

Wharam, Alan. (1992) *The Treason Trials 1794*. Leicester, Leicester University Press.

Wigmore, J.H. (1974 edn) *Evidence in Trials at Common Law*. Chadbourne.

Index

Putting justice into words

Also by John Hostettler

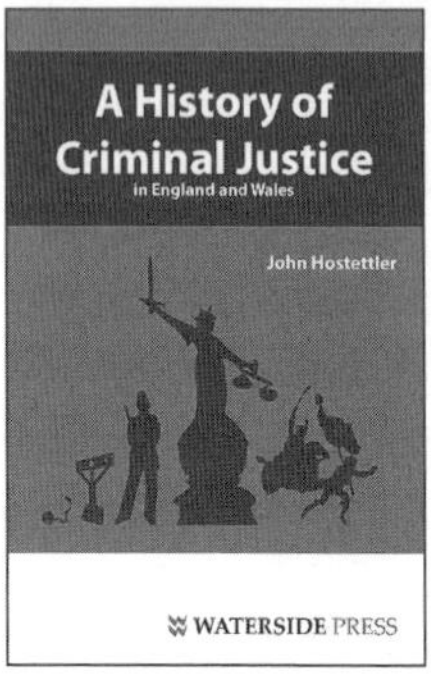

A History of Criminal Justice in England and Wales

An ideal introduction, charting all the main developments of criminal justice, from Anglo-Saxon dooms to the Common Law, struggles for political, legislative and judicial ascendency and the formation of the modern-day Criminal Justice System.

Jan 2009 | 352 pages | Paperback | ISBN 9781904380511

Fighting for Justice

The History and Origins of Adversary Trial

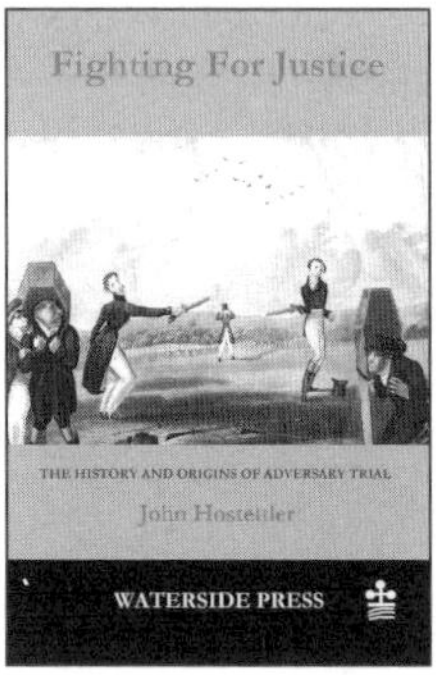

This book shows how adversary trial evolved in England only in the 18th century. Its origins and significance have tended to go unrecognised by judges, lawyers, jurists and researchers until relatively modern times when conflict has become a key social issue.

2006 | 140 pages | Paperback | ISBN 9781904380290

Also from Waterside Press

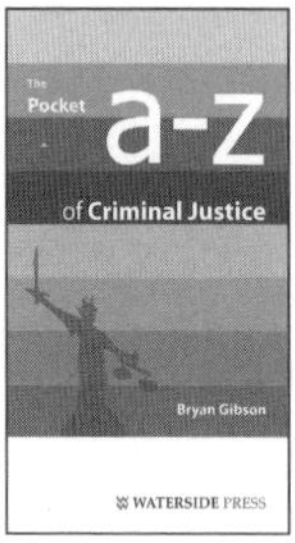

The Pocket A-Z of Criminal Justice

by Bryan Gibson

A quickly absorbed jargon-busting introduction to the language of criminal justice and its unique and fascinating usages.

May 2009 | 240 pages | Paperback | ISBN 9781904380504

More details at WatersidePress.co.uk

WATERSIDE PRESS